The
ST. LOUIS
CARDINALS

■ The notorious St. Louis heat
and humidity apparently got to
our friend **Harry Schulman**, the
San Francisco Chronicle's baseball writer. After Sunday afternoon's Giants-Cardinals game at
Busch Stadium, Schulman wrote:

"If you are ever given a choice
of going to hell or St. Louis in
July, think long and hard before
you answer. It was so hot and
humid at Busch Stadium yester-
day the fans cheered a cloud that
brought shade in the fourth inning." *July 9, 2000*

The

ST. LOUIS
CARDINALS

The
100th Anniversary
History

◆

ROB RAINS

ST. MARTIN'S PRESS   NEW YORK

Library of Congress Cataloging-in-Publication Data

Rains, Rob.
    The St. Louis Cardinals: the 100th anniversary history / Rob Rains; foreword by Jack Buck.
        p. cm.
    ISBN 0-312-07089-6
    1. St. Louis Cardinals (Baseball team)—History. I. Title.
II. Title: Saint Louis Cardinals.
GV875.S3R35 1992
796.357'64'0977866—dc20   91-35870
                                                                          CIP

First Edition: May 1992

10 9 8 7 6 5 4 3 2 1

This book is dedicated to Sally, Bobby, and Mike,
for their patience, their support,
their understanding, and their love—
100 years worth of each.

Contents

◆

Acknowledgments

◆

This book would not have been possible without the help and support of a number of people, starting with the St. Louis Cardinals and Fred Kuhlmann, the team's chief executive officer.

The author also wishes to thank Jeff Wehling, Brian Bartow, and Marty Hendin of the Cardinals front office, and all the team's past and present managers, coaches, and players, especially Joe Torre, Ted Simmons, Stan Musial, Terry Moore, Red Schoendienst, Bing Devine, Al Hrabosky, and Whitey Herzog.

All the past and present reporters in St. Louis had a hand in the production of this book in the fine coverage they gave the Cardinals over the years, especially Bob Burnes, Bob Broeg, and Rick Hummel.

Jack Buck was kind enough to write the foreword, and Mike Shannon provided numerous insights. Robert Hyland and the staff of KMOX Radio must be thanked for their cooperation.

This book also would not have been possible without the support of Paul White, Tim McQuay, and the staff of *Baseball Weekly* as well as the contributions of Charles Brown of the St. Louis Mercantile Library and Steve Gietschier, the archivist at the *Sporting News.* Jack Tippett was a valuable aid in researching items for the book, as was Sally Rains.

Bob Costas offered his assistance. Help in the photos from Art Phillips.

The biggest thank yous are reserved for George Witte of St. Martin's Press, who edited the project, and Tim Hays, an agent who understands what writing and publishing is all about.

Any material not otherwise credited came from either a personal interview or from clips from the *St. Louis Globe-Democrat*, the *St. Louis Post-Dispatch*, the *St. Louis Star-Times*, or the *Sporting News*. The sources for statistics were *The Baseball Encyclopedia*, *The Sports Encyclopedia: Baseball*, and various issues of the St. Louis Cardinals media guide.

Foreword

BY JACK BUCK

◆

There always was a star.

I think you could make the case that through the 100 years of Cardinals history, the team always has had a star. Thirty-three players have appeared in a Cardinals uniform and gone on to the Hall of Fame. The tradition and history of the Cardinals is one of the great strengths of the organization.

I did my first broadcast of a Cardinals game as they played the New York Giants in 1953 at the Polo Grounds. It was an on-air audition for a regular job in 1954, and that one game should have given me some indication of what the future was going to be like. In what still ranks as the greatest comeback in history, the Cardinals fell behind the Giants 11–0 and rallied to win 14–12.

When I joined Harry Caray in the broadcast booth in 1954, I didn't know I was starting a career with the Cardinals. I thought I would eventually end up going to some other city, but I was content to be number two to him and with him. We had fun.

We didn't have the opportunity to watch Rogers Hornsby or Frankie Frisch or Dizzy Dean or some of the other early greats of the Cardinals, but in the 37 years from 1954 to 1991, there were many other great performers who wore the birds-on-the-bat logo into their place in history.

The first was Stan Musial. When you first hear about him, you say it can't be true that any man is that perfect. When you see him, you think maybe it's an act. When you know him, you realize he's just one in a million, who combines all the attributes he has. He is one of the greatest players, he's nice to everybody, and he's consistent.

One of Musial's lifelong best friends has been Red Schoendienst, his roommate through many years with the Cardinals. Red is the same way. The word *consistent* goes for him, too. I think they learned from each other. Basically, they are just nice people.

In the 1960s, there were Bob Gibson, Ken Boyer, and Lou Brock. Gibson was without a doubt the toughest athlete I ever saw. He was the most focused, the most determined. You hate to try to beat him in anything. There was a fight in a game against Cincinnati one time and he threw three guys in the dugout. He knocked one guy, Tommy Helms, down twice. I'm sure whatever sport he had gone into, he would have gone to that sport's Hall of Fame.

The best words that describe Brock are *tough* and *happy*. A lot of people are able to do things that no one else can do but for some reason don't enjoy it. It's so much work for them they can't enjoy it. Brock did it all with a smile on his face.

Boyer also was happy, and he was talented. He played like a cloud in whatever he did, whether it was fielding, running, or hitting. He was so fluid. I was so happy he got to be manager of the Cardinals before he died. He was a Cardinal through and through. It didn't turn out too well for him, but at that time it didn't really matter who the manager was.

Through all my Cardinals years there was Gussie Busch, who bought the team for Anheuser-Busch in 1953 at a time when it was about to be sold and moved out of town. He prevailed during the transformation of the game from a fun game in which the owners made the money and the players didn't to a business. He used to have parties for the players at Grant's Farm and give gifts and make down payments for homes and give loans while making money. The strike meant that he, like every other owner, had to get out of the realm of running a baseball team as a hobby and a civic endeavor, which it was originally for him, and get into heavy business. He enjoyed the game and the Cardinals very much.

Gussie's enjoyment was increased after he brought in Whitey Herzog as manager in 1980. I always thought it was a shame that Whitey couldn't remain the field manager and the general manager at the same time, but that's an impossible job. Whoever could do that wouldn't last too long—it's just too much work. But of all the people who made it work for a period of time, he was the best.

It's tough to take something that's in place like a baseball team and come in and have the impact as an individual that he had. He was so brilliant. He's not smart or intelligent, he's brilliant. And he got results. It's an amazing thing to have such an impact. I said that if Whitey had not come along when he did and picked up the spirit of the team and the town, I might have quit. It was embarrassing to be with the club at that low period. Broadcasting is far from fun when you know your club is not going to win, that it doesn't have a chance to win, and the characters on the stage are not admirable.

We really had a roller-coaster ride in the years I've been with the Cardinals. From the Eddie Stanky days when we finished third, through a whole stream of managers, for better and for worse, and front-office people. Then winning as they did with Johnny Keane and Red in the 1960s, then back down again in the 1970s before Whitey came along.

The big player on the great teams in the 1980s was Ozzie Smith. Even though I'm friends with a lot of players on other teams, he was the first guy who, when he played in San Diego, always made it a point to go out of his way and run across the field and say, "Hi Mr. Buck, how are you feeling today?" I've never had a player really care how I felt. Baseball is, and I think necessarily so, a self-centered game for those performers. They have to perform. They have to take care of themselves—the sport demands it.

Ozzie is the greatest shortstop I've ever seen. He's a hard worker and a forward thinker. I don't think they would have won any pennants in the 1980s if Herzog or Ozzie hadn't come to St. Louis. And look at what Ozzie and Whitey did for the attendance. It was revolutionary to go to three million from where they were. Even when they lost, they were a fun team to watch. They adapted the ball club, not strictly by accident, to the ball park. Whitey made excellent use of the bullpen.

What I consider one of the best games I ever saw was at New York in the 1985 pennant race, when Cesar Cedeno hit a home run in the 10th inning to win 1–0. Whitey had been considering putting him in the starting lineup, but then said no, he might need him as a pinch hitter. It was like watching a rerun. It doesn't always have to be a winning effort to enjoy the ball game. That same month, Darryl Strawberry hit a homer off the clock on the scoreboard in the 11th inning to win a game for the Mets. Back in Sportsman's Park one time, Duke Snider of the Brooklyn Dodgers hit a home run that hit the Longines sign and knocked out the "ines" so it just read "Long."

I guess I must have broadcast 6,500 or so games, but a lot of them stand out. There was the twenty-five-inning game in New York, all the clinchers, Brock's 104th and 105th stolen bases, Gibson's no-hitter, Musial's five homers, Boyer's grand slam in the 1964 Series, Ozzie's and Jack Clark's homers in the 1985 playoffs. Some broadcasters are with teams for a long time and never have those thrills. I remember missing one game in 1985 I wish I had seen. When Tommy Herr hit a home run in the ninth inning to beat Montreal in a critical September game, I was in Washington, D.C., doing a football game and was talking on the telephone with Mike Shannon. He was giving me the play-by-play as he was getting ready to do the Star of the Game show, and all of a sudden he said, "I've got to go, Herr just hit a home run." I knew then the Cardinals were going to win the division. I missed not being there. With every game, you always know that something else is going to present itself and become a part of the lore. You're certain of it.

I'm also reminded every time I go to a prison or a hospital, or see people who come to one game a year, how much listening to the broadcasts of the games means to them. It makes you aware of the impact you have. When I was a kid growing up in Cleveland, I used to listen to Jack Graney. After he retired, he moved to Bowling Green, Missouri, and every once in a while I'd hear from him, every once in a while I'd say hello to him. After he died, his daughter wrote me a letter. It was quite a twist. I grew up listening to him, and he faded out listening to me.

All my years with the Cardinals could not have been any better. The things I will remember most are the people and the pennants. There have been just enough lowlights and bad years to give you perspective and enough thrills to last forever, however long forever may be.

1

The Early Years

1892–1919

◆

Chris Von der Ahe was excited on the morning of April 12, 1892. It was the dawn of a new baseball season, and it also was the beginning of a new era for Von der Ahe and his beloved team, the St. Louis Browns.

Von der Ahe's team, which he had helped establish in 1881 as a means to draw more customers to his saloon and beer garden, had been one of the most successful franchises in the American Association in the 1880s. The Browns won four consecutive pennants from 1885 to 1888 and even defeated the Chicago White Stockings in the 1886 World Series, the only time an American Association club defeated a team from the rival National League.

But the American Association had run into insurmountable problems trying to keep itself afloat. In December 1891, owners of the two leagues voted to merge. It was hoped this would put an end to all the player snatching and name-calling that had been going on for years.

The National League agreed to purchase the Association clubs in Chicago, Boston, Columbus, Milwaukee, and Washington, D.C., for a total of $135,000. The Washington franchise was shifted to Philadelphia, and the Association clubs in St. Louis, Baltimore, and Louisville were admitted to the 12-team National League.

So it was on a chilly Tuesday afternoon that the franchise that would in 1899 become the Cardinals played its first game, battling the Chicago White Stockings, a team that would later become the Cubs and turn into the Cardinals' biggest rival.

Von der Ahe, Der Boss President (as he liked to be called), wasn't the only person excited about the game, even though the advance publicity consisted of a one-paragraph mention near the bottom of the page in that morning's *Globe-Democrat*, informing readers that the game would be preceded by a parade featuring both teams riding to the field in carriages.

A crowd estimated at between 8,000 and 10,000 turned out for the game, including notables Lillian Russell and boxer John L. Sullivan. They saw the Browns lose to Chicago, 14–10. More important to Von der Ahe was that when he backed up his grocery wagon to Sportsman's Park to collect the day's profits and take them to the bank—as was his custom—he had come away with a sizable profit.

Von der Ahe's biggest interest in baseball had always been in how much money he could make off the game, and the switch from the American Association to the National League did not change that desire. The Association had been quicker to adopt Sunday baseball and the sale of beer at the ball parks, and Von der Ahe had been successful in the merger in getting the National League to allow both practices to continue.

Von der Ahe was born in Hille, Germany in 1851. At the age of 18, in 1870, he came to the United States and migrated to St. Louis. He opened a saloon and boardinghouse at the corner of Grand and St. Louis avenues. The land that would later become Sportsman's Park was a nearby vacant lot on which boys and young men played baseball for recreation.

Von der Ahe saw how his business improved because of the attendance at those games, and that got him interested in investing in a professional team when it was established a few years later. By that time, Von der Ahe's business had expanded to include a grocery store and beer garden, and when a game was played, his waiters had to bring in extra kegs of beer to make sure everyone had all they wanted to drink. Their actions were noted in a brief history of the Cardinals written by J. Roy Stockton of the *St. Louis Post-Dispatch* for *Sport* magazine in January 1951:

> As they laughed and shouted and cheered or berated the ballplayers, the spectators developed lovely thirsts. The sun beat down on players and spectators alike. Supporters of the teams that gained victories celebrated by ordering many rounds; the followers of the vanquished teams, while less hilarious, had sorrows to bury. They buried them deep in Chris's beer.

Von der Ahe could not help but become a baseball fan, especially during the Browns' glory days of the 1880s. He would run up a golden ball over his Golden Lion Saloon if there was a game that day, or if there wasn't a game, a flag so informing his patrons. Beer and baseball had built Von der Ahe a nice life.

What Von der Ahe didn't know on that Tuesday morning was that the move to the National League would be a disaster for the Browns and for him personally. While the team had been successful in the American Association, which was considered at the time to be a major league, the Browns struggled once they switched to the National League. As quickly as he had made money in the previous decade, Von der Ahe would lose money in the 1890s. Eventually he would lose his team as well.

Because he did not have a good background in or knowledge of baseball, Von der Ahe relied on other people to tell him what to do, and he often followed the actions of others. When he saw other teams sell players to other clubs for sizable amounts of cash, he began to do the same—especially when a few rainy days had produced a drop in the receipts.

Von der Ahe was a good-hearted, generous, loyal character

who took good care of his players, but, probably partially because of those attributes, he became his own worst enemy. It was estimated by the *Sporting News* that Von der Ahe earned more than half a million dollars through baseball in the first eight years he owned the Browns, but he ended up losing it all.

He became a laughingstock and an embarrassment to the game, and the *Sporting News* took to calling him "Von der Ha! Ha!" in print and frequently made him the target of derogatory cartoons. His personal-life problems were well documented and were front-page news—his divorce; his attempt to evict his mother-in-law because she hadn't paid sixty dollars' rent; his being kidnapped and taken in handcuffs to Pittsburgh after he had had the Pittsburgh owner arrested a few years earlier in St. Louis. All those actions convinced the other owners and most baseball people that the team would be better off in the hands of another owner.

"Von der Ha! Ha's ideas of business are 'get every dollar in sight without any regard for the future.' This is evidenced by his many sales of star players. He has not the acumen to see that he loses more momey in attendance by weakening his team when he sells a great and popular player than he receives from the trade. His losses in this way foot up thousands of dollars and the bad effects are felt for years," the *Sporting News* wrote.

Von der Ahe's problem in selling off his best players was that he didn't have adequate players ready to replace them. As a result, the Browns, who had been so successful in the 1880s, became a doormat in the 1890s, finishing 12th (last) twice, 11th three times, 10th once and ninth once in a seven-year span (from 1892 to 1898). Von der Ahe tried to put the blame on his manager at the time or whomever else he could think of except himself. He went through six managers in 1895 alone.

When Von der Ahe saw that his baseball fortunes were dropping, he tried to come up with a new way to bring people to his ball park and to keep the money coming in. He conceived the idea to make Sportsman's Park the Coney Island of the West. Fred Foster, a local horse-racing entrepreneur, persuaded Von der Ahe to build a racetrack within the limited enclosure of the baseball field. It was part of Von der Ahe's grand scheme that included building a shoot-the-chutes ride in center field; boating; an all-girl coronet band; a Wild West show; and boxing.

The park and all its added attractions was in business for two years, 1896 and 1897, and like everything else Von der Ahe tried in the 1890s, it was a total failure. What Von der Ahe thought was a great deal, renting the horse-racing track to Foster, turned out to net him just $600 a month. Von der Ahe was also in charge of the books that took the gamblers' bets, and a smart man would have grown rich under that plan. Von der Ahe lost money because his workers were claiming winning bets that were actually made after the races had been run.

The team that Von der Ahe put on the field in 1897 was one of the worst in baseball history. It lost 45 of its first 56 games and won just 8 of its final 50, finishing with a record of 29–102, a .221 winning percentage, and a whopping 63½ games out of first place.

At one point when his team was playing so badly, a delegation of fans called on Von der Ahe and complained about the way the team was being run. "If this ball club doesn't improve, we are not coming out here any more," the spokesman for the group said.

Von der Ahe was ready for them. "What's the matter anyhow with you fellers, ain't you got any patriotism about you?" Von der Ahe asked in his thick German accent. "Why do you always mention dose Browns? Can't you come out and see the other teams play? Some of dose visiting ball clubs are not so bad."

But Von der Ahe—who was living above his office at the ball park to try to save money—was not pleased by the performance of his team, and he could see that he had to do something if he was going to salvage his baseball fortunes. So before the 1898 season started, he removed himself from direct supervision of the team and installed B. Stuart Muckenfuss as the team president. Muckenfuss's first major decision was to have the team concentrate on baseball. He had all the racing facilities and amusement park rides removed. The season began, and for the first time in three years, expectations were great that the Browns would field a competitive team.

Those dreams lasted for one day. During the second inning of the second game of the season, on April 16, 1898, with about 4,000 people in the park, a fire broke out under the grandstand, which was made of wood. The fire spread quickly and in 30 minutes had destroyed the grandstand, the left-field bleachers, the club's offices, and Von der Ahe's saloon. Ticket sellers could get out only about half the day's receipts before they were forced away by the flames, and most of Von der Ahe's personal effects, including the Browns' championship trophies from the 1880s, were destroyed. While nobody was killed in the fire, hundreds were injured or burned trying to get out of the stands.

The manager of the visiting Chicago team, Cap Anson, wanted the next day's game shifted to Chicago, but the Cardinals manager, Tim Hurst, refused. Hurst ordered his players to help 150 carpenters clear away debris and make the stadium suitable for Sunday's game. Many players were working past midnight, and by the next morning, 4,000 circus seats were in place for fans and the field had been cleared of all the debris. But wearied by their hard night of work, the Browns were no match for the White Stockings and lost 14–1.

The fire ruined whatever last hopes Von der Ahe had for salvaging his baseball life. Several thousand dollars had already been spent on improvements at the park, and the club now had to spend its money rebuilding the facility and didn't have enough money left to pay its bills. Von der Ahe was faced also with hundreds of lawsuits from people who had been injured in the fire. It was the fifth major fire at the park in the 1890s, including one in which Von der Ahe's pet greyhound dog, Fly, was trapped in the clubhouse and killed.

Von der Ahe was distraught after the final fire, and his team continued to play poorly on the field. Out of money and out of hope, Von der Ahe's beloved Browns were forced into receivership on August 10, 1898. In March 1899 the team was finally sold by court order on the steps of the St. Louis courthouse for $33,000 to G. A. Gruner. Gruner quickly sold the club for a $7,000 profit to St. Louis attorney Edward C. Becker, who was acting for brothers Frank DeHaas Robison and Matthew Stanley Robison of Cleveland, who also owned the Cleveland Spiders of the National League.

For all his faults, Von der Ahe had established a good rapport with his players. One of his favorites was Charles Comiskey, who would later become the owner and president of the Chicago White Sox.

"He was the grandest figure baseball has ever known," Comiskey said in the *Sporting News* after Von der Ahe's death. "All I am in the baseball world I owe to him. He was one of the truest friends any man could have. For the 10 years I was with him in St. Louis I never had dealings of a business nature with a squarer or more liberal owner or manager.

"Never did an owner have the goodwill and cooperation of his players better than he. They all recognized him for what he was—the best and most liberal-hearted friend they could have. He was never penurious with his club, and with his friends he was just as liberal."

Von der Ahe's teams did have some good players in those days, even if their collective performance as a team was poor. Two of the players would go on to be inducted into the Hall of Fame—pitcher Pud Galvin and first baseman Roger Connor. Some of the other good players on those teams included pitchers Ted Breitenstein and Kid Gleason—who would later go on to fame as the ill-fated manager of the "Black Sox" of 1919—and catcher Heinie Peitz.

Gleason and Von der Ahe had a stormy two-year relationship, with Von der Ahe frequently levying fines totaling $500 against Gleason. When Gleason refused to pay, he quit the team. Von der Ahe sold him to Baltimore for $2,400, but Gleason refused to report. Finally, when Von der Ahe could see the money slipping through his fingers, he agreed to drop the fines if Gleason would report to Baltimore. He did.

Breitenstein, on the other hand, was never fined by Von der Ahe. He did come close on one occasion, however. Breitenstein had pitched two games of a three-game series against Pittsburgh, including the Saturday game. On Sunday, there was a German picnic scheduled with lots of beer. Breitenstein figured he had earned the day off and went to the picnic. On Monday, he was advised to report to Von der Ahe's office, where the team's board of directors was meeting.

"You are fined feefty dollars," Von der Ahe told Breitenstein. But two of the directors spoke up challenging the fine, and when one offered to pay it for him, the fine was dropped.

Breitenstein, a native of St. Louis, had stood up to challenges before. Once, when he was pitching in the minor leagues, he was approached by gamblers who wanted him to throw a playoff game that would decide the league championship. When Breitenstein refused, the gamblers warned him that his Green Bay team would not win its game against Appleton. On the first play of the game, a brick came sailing past the Green Bay first baseman's head. The Green Bay players decided on the spot to pull out of the game and left the field armed with bats and a police escort.

Breitenstein never had things quite so rough in St. Louis, where he formed half of the famous "pretzel battery" with Peitz. Peitz recalled how the duo earned the nickname in an interview with the *Sporting News:*

"We got that name in the old Golden Lion Saloon in St. Louis," Peitz said. "The saloon was operated by a man whose name escapes me, but who was a partner of Chris Von der Ahe in the ownership of the Browns. After the game it was the habit of the St. Louis players who liked a glass or two of beer to go to that saloon to get it.

"After a game on a hot day, Breitenstein, Perry Werden, and I were in the back room cooling off with some beer. On the table in front of us was a bowl of pretzels. A fan looked in, saw us, and shouted to those in the front of the saloon, 'Here's that pretzel battery of Breitenstein and Peitz back here.' And for the rest of our baseball days that's how we were known."

After Von der Ahe was stripped of his baseball team, he returned to the saloon business full-time. He also struggled in that, however, and tried moving to several locations without success. He was bankrupt a few years later, in 1908, when the Cardinals and the new American League Browns played a benefit exhibition game arranged by his old friends. After deducting expenses, Von der Ahe received a check for $4,294. Comiskey and several other out-of-town baseball officials sent in cash contributions even though they hadn't attended the game. Comiskey donated $500. Von der Ahe died five years later, in 1913, completely broke.

A lot had happened to Von der Ahe's old team by then, starting with a change in the team's name shortly after the Robison brothers purchased the club.

The Robisons, who had made their money operating streetcar companies in Fort Wayne, Indiana, and Cleveland, had not found a great deal of success running their team, the Cleveland Spiders, either. Sensing that St. Louis would become a better home for their team than Cleveland and with Cleveland having better players, the owners basically switched the entire two teams before the 1899 season—sending the old Browns team to Cleveland, where they would establish the worst record in baseball history—20–134.

Virtually the entire Cleveland team, including future Hall of Famers Cy Young, Jesse Burkett, and Bobby Wallace, was transferred to St. Louis. A crowd estimated as high as 18,000 showed up, despite a streetcar strike, for opening day to see Young stop the former Browns, now playing for Cleveland, 10–1.

The Robison brothers had changed most of the players, but they knew they needed to make other changes as well to further distance themselves from the disappointing Von der Ahe teams. They outfitted their team in new bright red-trimmed uniforms, including red socks. The club was still being called the Browns by the St. Louis press, but legend has it that the switch of the team name to Cardinals came about after a female fan saw the uniforms and said, "Oh, what a lovely shade of cardinal." William McHale, a baseball writer for the *St. Louis Republic*, is credited with being the first to call in print for the change of the team name to Cardinals, an idea that met with the approval of the Robison brothers. The owners also changed the name of the team's ball park to League Park in another break from the Von der Ahe teams and years.

The eastern press and the *Sporting News*, however, were slow to be convinced of the change in the team's name, calling the team the *Perfectos* all through the 1899 season before finally referring to them as the Cardinals the following year.

Except for one player who was out of baseball, the entire Cleveland starting lineup in 1898 was playing for the Cardinals in 1899, and the result was a much more competitive team—finishing fifth with an 81–68 record.

At the turn of the century came a restructured National League, now slimmed down to eight clubs, with the sad Cleveland team being one of the four dropped from the league.

One of the new players on the Cardinals in 1900 was John McGraw, who would go on to fame and success as manager of the New York Giants. McGraw didn't really want to be in St. Louis, but he didn't have much choice. He had been on the Baltimore club that folded, and his contract and that of catcher Wilbert Robinson was sold to St. Louis. After a holdout in which the Cardinals finally met his demand of a $100 salary per game and the exemption of the reserve clause in his contract—therefore making McGraw a free agent at a time when players were totally controlled by their teams—McGraw signed and joined the Cardinals.

McGraw told Robison he would be in St. Louis for only one year, knowing that Ban Johnson was planning on expanding the fledgling American League in 1901 and putting a team back in Baltimore. McGraw played just 94 games for the Cardinals and even though he hit .344, he reportedly had himself tossed out of several games so he could go to the horse track across the street.

Despite high hopes, the Cardinals slipped to seventh place in August and Robison decided to change managers, firing Patsy Tebeau. He wanted McGraw to replace him, but McGraw refused, knowing he would be leaving St. Louis at the end of the season. Instead, Robison named Louie Heilbronner, the chief of concessions, manager for the rest of the season. Heilbronner stood barely over five feet tall and he had nothing in common with the players, who quickly tried to show him up and get the best of him.

In those days, the players sat on benches placed out on the field instead of in the current-day dugouts. While Heilbronner went through the motions of managing the club, the Cardinals gradually edged up the bench until Heilbronner was dumped off the end onto the ground. Pitcher Jack Powell once threatened to lock Heilbronner up in the team safe, and outfielder Mike Donlin once picked him up by his feet and dunked him headfirst into a rain barrel. Despite Heilbronner's managing, the team had enough talent that it moved up to fifth place when the season ended. McGraw, true to his word, left St. Louis immediately after the last game and ceremoniously dumped his Cardinals uniform in the Mississippi River as the train chugged out of town.

Robison was not pleased with the finish of his club, however. Four players—McGraw, Robinson, Patsy Donovan, and Young—received their final paycheck for the year but Robison withheld payment to his other players. They were notified by

Robison that their services for the year were not satisfactory. Robison wrote to the players that "in your contract for the past playing season of 1900, said contract called for ———— per month for playing and producing first class baseball for the American Baseball and Athletic Exhibition Co. of St. Louis, Missouri. This you have not done."

Robison, who had the opulent habit of withdrawing $100 cash each day from the bank and vowing to spend it before the sun rose the next morning, was in for more challenges in the coming seasons as the upstart American League, including the in-town rival St. Louis Browns, raided his and other National League teams, signing away its best players.

Of the team's eight starters and three top pitchers in 1900, only one—Donovan—was still with the Cardinals in 1902. And Donovan by then was the manager. McGraw went back to Baltimore. Young went to Boston. The new Browns signed Burkett, Wallace, John Heidrick, Powell, Jack Harper, Willie Sudhoff, and Dick Padden. Dan McGann joined McGraw in Baltimore.

Robison and the Cardinals were particularly upset at the defection of Wallace, who jumped to the Browns for a five-year, $32,500 contract that included a $6,500 signing bonus and made him the highest paid player in the game. The Browns even included a no-trade clause in the agreement, and when Wallace offered the Cardinals a chance to match the contract, Robison called the pact absurd. After he signed, the Cardinals went to court in an attempt to keep Wallace from playing for the Browns but lost the case.

Despite a peace agreement that ended the player raids, Robison gradually began to lose interest in his team and the sport. After a last-place finish in 1903, the team made one of its worst trades in history, sending pitcher Mordecai "Three Finger" Brown to Chicago, where he would help the Cubs to league championships in 1906, 1907, and 1908. In exchange the Cardinals received pitcher Jack Taylor, who would win 43 games for St. Louis over the next two and a half years but couldn't help the Cardinals finish any higher than fifth.

After losing 96 games in 1905 and 98 games in 1906, Robison turned over the Cardinals to his brother Stanley in 1906 and moved back to Cleveland, where he died two years later, still heartbroken by the defection of his star players.

Stanley Robison had finished the 1905 season as manager, after Kid Nichols, another eventual Hall of Famer, was fired in midseason. Nichols's firing came after he had a dispute with Robison over one of his duties. It was the custom then for visiting clubs to assign a pitcher not working that day to watch the gates and count the tickets, making sure the visitors received the correct share of the receipts. Nichols was familiar with the job and, after counting 30,000 tickets one day at the Polo Grounds when he was pitching for Boston, remarked that it was "tougher than pitching nine innings."

On this day in Cincinnati, however, Nichols refused when asked to work the gates. He instead went to the Latonia racetrack and was fired.

Perhaps Nichols was ready for his dismissal after trying to put up with players such as Larry McLean, a good catcher and hard hitter who was just a little eccentric. One of McLean's habits was to dive into the goldfish pool in front of the old Buckingham Hotel in his street clothes.

The first baseman on those clubs was Jake Beckley, another player who was headed for the Hall of Fame because of his hitting ability but who displayed a terrible throwing arm. One play stands out from Beckley's career with the Cardinals: In a game at Pittsburgh, he fielded a bunt by Tommy Leach and threw the ball 10 feet over the pitcher's head as he attempted to cover first. Beckley chased the ball down himself while Leach took off around the bases, and when he recovered the ball, Leach was almost to third.

Beckley, knowing he had no chance to throw Leach out, took off running with the ball toward home and the two staged a footrace from opposite ends of the field. Beckley won, diving into the sliding runner at the plate and tagging him out and also breaking two of Leach's ribs in the collision. Beckley was not hurt.

Stanley Robison didn't have much more success running the Cardinals than did his brother. Finances were so low that for two winters, Robison slept in an office over the clubhouse, returning to a custom of former owner Chris Von der Ahe's. After consecutive last-place finishes in 1907 and 1908 in which the Cardinals lost 101 and 105 games, respectively, Robison was desperate. He issued an appeal for help to the National League. He had to find a new manager.

Among the people who heard Robison's appeal was one of his former players, John McGraw, who then was the manager of the New York Giants. McGraw knew that his catcher, Roger Bresnahan, wanted to be a manager, and McGraw also had not forgotten that Robison treated him well his one season in St. Louis.

On the Giants' last trip to St. Louis in September of 1907, McGraw arranged for Bresnahan and Robison to meet—in a cloak-and-dagger sequence that calls to mind a modern spy novel. A St. Louis newspaper reporter, Hal Lanigan, was used as the go-between for Robison, McGraw, and Bresnahan. On the day of a rained out game, Robison was instructed to take a room at the Marquette Hotel using the fake name John Doakes. He also was told by McGraw to leave the door unlocked. The plan then called for Bresnahan to check with the front desk for Doakes's room number, then he was to come up and enter the door without knocking.

The plot may have actually been written by Bresnahan, who spent the off-season working as a hotel detective in his hometown of Toledo, Ohio. When he arrived at the hotel, just to further confuse anybody who might have been watching, Bresnahan took the elevator to the fourth floor, then walked down the stairs and into Robison's room on the third floor.

It didn't take long for Robison and Bresnahan to work out a deal—Bresnahan would get a $10,000 salary, a free reign, and promises of new players. But what stalled the deal was the agreement with McGraw and the Giants on which players the Cardinals would give up for Bresnahan.

In the end, the Cardinals gave up outfielder Red Jack Murray and pitcher Bugs Raymond, then traded pitchers Art Fromme and Eddie Karger to Cincinnati for catcher Admiral George Schlei, who also went to New York in the deal. The three pitchers had been the best on the Cardinals staff in 1908 and even though the club was happy to have landed a manager in Bresnahan, it didn't make his job any easier that the heart of the pitching staff had been stripped away.

But Bresnahan's arrival gave St. Louis fans a shot in the arm. Attendance increased by 94,000 in 1909, even though the team's performance on the field wasn't much better, losing 89 games and climbing only to seventh place.

Bresnahan was smart and shrewd and a natural baseball leader. But he also found himself getting into many run-ins with umpires, which resulted in several suspensions. Robison didn't lose faith in his manager, however, and before the 1910 season, Robison delivered on his promise to bring in new players, swinging a five-player deal that brought second baseman Miller Huggins to St. Louis.

Despite the addition of Huggins, the Cardinals finished seventh again in 1910 and Bresnahan continued to battle the umpires. In one game, he stationed all his players out of position to protest a decision that had gone against the Cardinals.

Part of Bresnahan's anger also was in doubt from frustration he experienced in trying to deal with some of his own players. He had one pitcher, Slim Sallee, who stayed up all night so he could ride around with the milkmen on their predawn rides. And he had an outfielder, Steve Evans, who one day tried to play right field carrying a paper parasol to shield him from the hot St. Louis summer sun.

Attendance was up again, however, and the team's finances were improving. Robison was able to move back into a luxurious suite at a St. Louis hotel and pay off all his club's bills. He envisioned the team making a run at the pennant in 1911.

But Robison never got to see the 1911 season. He died on March 24 of that year, leaving the ball club to his niece, Frank Robison's daughter, Mrs. Helene Hathaway Robison Britton, major league baseball's first female executive.

The Cardinals did in fact make a run for the pennant in 1911 but had their hopes dashed in July when the team was involved in a train wreck in Bridgeport, Connecticut. Other than a few skinned knees and elbows suffered when they were thrown to the floor, none of the players were injured, but the team was never the same after the July accident and slid to fifth.

Still, it was the best finish by a Cardinals team since 1904 and the first time since 1901 they had finished above .500. The Cardinals enjoyed the best financial year in their history and had a profit of $165,000. Mrs. Britton was so impressed with Bresnahan and his performance that she awarded him a five-year contract for $10,000 a year—plus a civil agreement that called for him to receive 10 percent of the club's net earnings.

It didn't take Mrs. Britton long to find out she had made a serious mistake. She had several disagreements with Bresnahan during the 1912 season; Bresnahan also had to fight off a charge by the president of the Philadelphia Phillies, Horace Fogel, that Bresnahan had intentionally benched his best players against the Giants in an attempt to help his old team win the pennant. Bresnahan demanded that his name be cleared, and when he was found innocent, Fogel was banished from baseball.

But Bresnahan's biggest problem with Mrs. Britton was his habit of using crude, vulgar language in her presence. After a final blowup in her living room following the team's sixth-place finish, Mrs. Britton decided she had to make a change.

She called James Jones, the team's attorney and president, and told him to fire Bresnahan. Jones, well aware that Bresnahan's contract had four more years to go, argued against the move but could not convince Mrs. Britton to change her mind.

"I do not care if we have to buy up his contract, if we have to pay him in full for four years," Mrs. Britton said. "I do not want him running my club any longer."

The firing, as Jones had suspected, wasn't easy. Four clubs—the Cubs, the Phillies, the Pirates, and the Dodgers—refused to grant waivers on Bresnahan. Bresnahan also hired an attorney to try to force the Cardinals to honor the profit-sharing aspect of his contract as well.

Finally, in a special National League meeting in June 1913, the dispute was resolved. Bresnahan agreed to a $20,000 settlement with the Cardinals, and the Cubs assumed his contract, purchasing him from the Cardinals.

Mrs. Britton, who earned the nickname "Lady Bee" from the St. Louis writers, had moved from Cleveland to take over the club. She was a good fan and was active in running the ball club and representing the Cardinals at league meetings. Mrs. Britton knew whom she wanted to take over managing the Cardinals—Miller Huggins. She had quickly become a fan of the scrappy second baseman since he had joined the Cardinals, and she knew he was much more of a proper gentleman than Bresnahan.

Partially because of his close relationship with Mrs. Britton, Huggins's job was not in jeopardy even after a last-place finish in 1913—a year that also saw the American League St. Louis Browns finish last, the *only time* both local teams finished in the cellar.

Huggins took advantage of his position with Mrs. Britton to offer his advice on trades and other player moves. He pulled off a big deal with the Pirates before the 1914 season—sending Ed Konetchy, Mike Mowrey, and Bob Harmon to Pittsburgh for five players—Dots Miller, Owen Wilson, Art Butler, Hank Robinson and Cozy Dolan. The immediate reaction to the trade wasn't positive, but Huggins had the correct attitude, noting that he had finished last the year before, had to make changes, and could go in only one direction.

The fans' view of the deal improved as the 1914 season went on and the Cardinals climbed into the race. In one game late in the season, Huggins, coaching third, pulled a move that managers still warn their pitchers about today. Playing against the Dodgers, with the score tied in the seventh inning, the Cardinals had a runner on third with two outs. Huggins, without warning, yelled at the young Brooklyn pitcher to let him see the ball. The Dodger pitcher, caught off guard by the request, complied and flipped the ball toward Huggins. Huggins, however, knowing time had not been called, stepped out of the way and let the ball roll away into foul territory while the runner headed home with the eventual winning run.

While it might not have been pure sportsmanship, it did mean a win for the Cardinals in the pennant race, and that was more important to Huggins.

Even though he stood less than five feet six inches tall, Huggins had a commanding presence on the baseball field. He had broken into professional baseball using a fake name, Proctor, out of respect for his father, a devout Methodist who never would have permitted Huggins to play baseball on Sunday. By using a fake name, Huggins was also able to preserve his amateur status as he attended and graduated from law school at the University of Cincinnati. Huggins never practiced law, however, and never held a single position outside baseball.

Despite Huggins's managing, the Cardinals faded down the stretch and finished third in 1914. The club slipped back into the second division in 1915, winding up sixth, but did discover a new player who would in time become the team's first major star.

On September 10, 1915, the name Hornsby first appeared in a major league box score. His appearance did not create any excitement, however, and a St. Louis newspaper merely noted his arrival in the major leagues with one line: "A 19-year-old Texas kid, Rogers Hornsby, dug up by Bob Connery in the Class D Western Association, finished the game for the Cardinals at shortstop."

In 18 games the rest of the season, Hornsby—who had signed for a $500 bonus—hit .246. When he asked Huggins about his performance, he was told he likely would need some time on the farm.

Hornsby, whose father owned a farm, didn't realize that Huggins was talking about a minor-league club. When Hornsby left St. Louis that fall to return to his father's Texas farm, he weighed 155 pounds. When he showed up for spring training in 1916, he had built himself up to 180 pounds. He started the season as a reserve infielder but moved into the lineup later that year and was there to stay.

By 1916, however, Mrs. Britton had decided she had had enough of baseball and wanted out. She called Huggins and her legal adviser, James Jones, to her home for a meeting. She told them she wanted to sell the club and if either of them was interested, she would prefer to sell it to them.

Huggins was interested. Together with Bob Connery, his friend and scout, they went to Huggins's hometown of Cincinnati to try to obtain the financial backing necessary to buy the club. Huggins found the support he needed from Julius Fleischmann of the Fleischmann yeast family. But before he could get back to St. Louis and present his offer to Mrs. Britton, Huggins read in the newspaper that the team had been sold to a group organized by Jones.

It was bitter news for Huggins. Jones had put together a group of most of St. Louis's leading businessmen to buy stock in his new ownership group, which paid $350,000 for the team and Robison Field, the ball park Mrs. Britton had renamed in honor of her father and uncle.

Early in the 1917 season, Jones arranged a meeting of seven of St. Louis's baseball writers and sports editors in his office. He wanted some advice on whom he should hire to be the club president. He asked each to write a recommendation on a piece of paper and drop it into a hat. When Jones took out the slips of paper, the same name was on each of the seven slips—Branch Rickey, then the business manager of the rival St. Louis Browns. Jones offered Rickey the presidency of the Cardinals, and he accepted.

The same year, 1917, also was the year the Knot Hole Gang was established. The idea of one of the Cardinals' stockholders, St. Louis insurance man W. E. Bilheimer, the plan called for one youth to receive a free season ticket for every twenty-five-dollar stock purchased in the club. A section of the stands was reserved for the youngsters.

The Cardinals finished third in 1917, but Huggins was looking for a change. In another clandestine move, similar to when the Cardinals hired Bresnahan, a scheme was unveiled that would wind up with Huggins being named the manager of the New York Yankees.

Ban Johnson, the president of the American League, was still smarting from the Cardinals' snatching of Rickey away from the Browns. At dinner one night in St. Louis, Johnson proposed that J. G. Taylor Spink, the publisher of the *Sporting News* and a friend of Huggins's, suggest to Huggins the idea of managing the Yankees; if Huggins was interested, Spink would advise him to call Colonel Jacob Ruppert, a co-owner of the Yankees.

Huggins was interested. When the Cardinals arrived in New York for a series against Brooklyn, Huggins met with Ruppert. The two agreed to meet again after the season, when Huggins would be free from his Cardinals contract.

After the last game of the city series against the Browns, Huggins boarded a train for New York to attend the World Series between the Giants and the White Sox. When he went up to the observation platform after dinner, he bumped into someone he had not counted on seeing—Rickey, who also was en route to New York. Neither knew the other was going to be on the train.

Huggins was careful not to reveal the real reason for his trip. "Rickey's surprise, in fact, bordered on amazement, when he learned Huggins was making the trip at his own expense to see the World Series," Spink would write later in the *Sporting News*. "Rickey was well aware the thrifty little manager was not accustomed to lavish outlays on his own personal entertainment—particularly to see a ball game. But he received no further enlightenment from the taciturn Miller."

When he arrived in New York, Huggins went to the Hermitage Hotel, where he registered under an assumed name. He also put on a cap and pulled it down over his eyes, further trying to obscure his identity. He then telephoned Johnson, who arranged a meeting for Huggins with Ruppert the following morning.

The meeting did not go well. Ruppert was cold to Huggins, who left very discouraged. Huggins, instead of going to the second game of the World Series the next day, departed for his home in Cincinnati.

When the World Series shifted to Chicago, Johnson again got into the negotiations. He said Huggins was insisting on scout Bob Connery going with him to the Yankees. A deal was arranged with Connery, and it appeared everything was set for Huggins to be named manager of the Yankees.

Still, Ruppert delayed. Finally, in January he offered him the job, and Huggins signed his contract.

"What caused Colonel Ruppert's long hesitancy about signing Huggins? Oddly enough, it was a trivial circumstance that almost kept Hug from the job—and the Yankees from the start on the victory highway," Spink wrote.

"When Miller visited Colonel Ruppert during the 1917 World Series, he was wearing a cap. Coupled with his gnome-like appearance, the cap accentuated his midget stature and made Huggins look like an unemployed jockey. And Colonel Ruppert, himself an immaculate dresser, instinctively shied away from a cap-wearing job applicant."

The Cardinals again finished last in 1918—the eighth time in their first 27 years in the National League that the Cardinals had finished in the basement. The team had lost 14 players to the World War I effort. Rickey also served in the war and when he returned in 1919, he took on the additional duties of manager. Rickey would prove to be a better front-office man than a manager, however, as his 1919 club finished seventh.

The Cardinals' history up until 1920 had been interesting, but it had not been very good. That was about to change.

2
Taste of Success
THE 1920s

◆

Through his first three years of running the Cardinals, Rickey tried desperately to keep the team afloat despite having virtually no money with which to operate the club. In 1919 he kept the team in St. Louis for spring training—at Washington University—because there wasn't enough money in the team's bank accounts to afford to pay any expenses. The uniforms from the previous season were sewn back together to save the team from having to buy new ones. At various times, Rickey even went without a salary when the money was needed by the club to pay other bills. On one occasion, while his wife was away from home, he borrowed a rug and some chairs from his house to make his office look more impressive for an important visitor.

Rickey knew this was no way to operate a ball club. Every time his chief scout, Charley Barrett, found a player whom he liked in the minor leagues, some other team—usually the Giants—would top the Cardinals' meager bid and purchase the player. Rickey understood the only way the club could earn more money was to bring in more fans, and to do that they had to have a better team. And to have a better team he had to field better players, which he didn't have the money to buy.

One of the stockholders watching Rickey try to keep the

Cardinals afloat was Sam Breadon, a St. Louis automobile dealer who had bought into the team only as a favor to a friend.

Breadon had invested $200 in the club when Jones organized his group of investors and later increased his holdings to $2,000 after he was impressed by Hornsby and some of the other players at a dinner put together for the owners.

Breadon could see his investment failing. The team called an emergency meeting of the 26 directors, but just a few showed up. Breadon loaned the club more money, a total of $18,000.

Breadon's loans convinced Jones that he was serious about baseball as an investment, and he offered him the job of running the Cardinals as its president. Breadon agreed, but only if the number of directors was shrunk from 26 to five. They finally compromised on seven, and in 1920, Breadon took over as president of the Cardinals. Rickey remained as the manager and vice-president of the club.

Rickey and Breadon were an unlikely pair; they could not have been more different in their personalities or life-styles. J. Roy Stockton compared the two in his *Sport* magazine history of the Cardinals in 1951.

"Breadon loved lively parties, and after a few highballs, would break into song," Stockton wrote. "Rickey, a teetotaler, moved in an entirely different social circle. But they grew to have great respect for each other. Breadon sifted Rickey's ideas and discarded those that were not practical. He knew the good ones, too, and would back them to the limit of his resources."

One of those good ideas had been churning around in Rickey's mind for some time, waiting for the money to put it to work: the idea of developing his own players instead of buying them from other teams.

Rickey had already proved to be an excellent judge of young baseball talent, and that ability was quickly noted by minor-league club owners. Whenever Rickey or his top assistant, Barrett, would visit a minor-league team to watch a particular player, that owner knew the player must be good. But the owner also knew the Cardinals didn't have much money. Rickey would ask the team to set a price for the young player, but instead of selling him to the Cardinals, the owner would wire the richer clubs, explain that Rickey liked a certain player and had offered so much money, and asked the club what they would offer.

"Sometimes, without even looking at the player, the rival major-league club came through with a [higher] offer, and right under Branch's nose his discovery was sold to the wealthier club," Fred Lieb wrote in his history of the Cardinals.

Rickey, in essence, was scouting players for other clubs, and nothing infuriated him more. After he was able to borrow $10,000 and buy pitcher Jesse Haines from the Kansas City club in 1919, Rickey decided enough was enough. Haines became the last player purchased by the Cardinals for more than 25 years.

Breadon was all for the idea of developing players, and he had enough faith in Rickey's ability to find talent that he knew it would work.

"I'll find the players somewhere," Rickey told Breadon. "I don't know where, but I have a lot of friends all around the country who know their baseball. I'll get them to look around their corner lots, their college diamonds, their semipro parks, and we'll eventually develop a farm system in our own business. We'll send those kids to our minor-league ball club, and we'll grow and grow, until we get even with [John] McGraw and the Giants and the rest of them."

A lot of baseball people would have scoffed at Rickey's idea, and many later did. But not Breadon. Rickey and the Cardinals overcame considerable opposition to their plan, including that from Commissioner Judge Kenesaw Mountain Landis, who thought it threatened the success of the minor-league clubs. The invention of the farm system also led Rickey to the idea of holding tryout camps; another way he was able to find players.

Rickey's first move was to purchase shares in the Houston Buffaloes minor-league club. The Cardinals also were able to buy into the teams in Fort Smith, Arkansas, and Syracuse, New York. The legendary Cardinals farm system was on its way.

The Cardinals had found the money to start the farm system because of Breadon's insistence that the team move back into Sportsman's Park, as tenants of the Browns. Robison Field was the last wooden structure in the major leagues and was hopelessly outdated.

Breadon, through persistence, was able to convince Browns owner Phil Ball to lease him Sportsman's Park for $35,000 and half the annual cleanup costs. While on a road trip in June 1920, the leases were signed, and on July 1 the Cardinals moved back into Sportsman's Park, which was to be their home for the next 46 years. They played Pittsburgh in the annual benefit game for the St. Louis Tuberculosis Society and lost 6–2 to the Pirates in 10 innings.

In turn, Breadon and the Cardinals sold the land where the old Robison Field had stood to the St. Louis school board and to a transit company for $275,000. The school board built Beaumont High School on the site, and the transit company set up a streetcar loop.

The influx of money allowed the Cardinals to get out of debt, start the farm system, and build a much more respectable team.

With money to operate and the means to bring his young players along, Rickey was on his way to making the Cardinals a winner. But the team still wasn't ready yet, even though Hornsby won his first of six consecutive batting titles in 1920.

Rickey's ideas about how to run a ball club had been established a long time before, during his early upbringing on an Ohio farm, through his days as a teacher, in law school, as a college coach, and as a player for the Browns. Rickey was extremely religious; even though he was the Cardinals manager, he wouldn't attend Sunday games, having one of his coaches, Burt Shotton, fill in for him as the designated Sunday manager. Many people thought that stance was requested by his devout Methodist parents, but Rickey said that was not the case.

"I might as well admit that it pleased my mother and father too to know that I took such a position," Rickey once said. "But neither demanded it, nor would have demanded it of me. It was my own doing and I am glad to say that it has always given me one day a week to be with my family." True to his upbringing, Rickey never swore, and his strongest expression, when he was really upset, was "Judas Priest." He was an incessant cigar smoker who earned the nickname the 'Mahatma.'"

Perhaps because of his teaching and law school background, Rickey took more of an educational slant in his role as manager than did others in the same position. He originated blackboard talks during locker-room meetings, diagraming plays and explaining what he wanted his players to do in certain situations.

There was no doubt Rickey knew what he was talking about, but making the players understand and execute his ideas properly was another matter. The Cardinals, despite the hitting of Hornsby, were still struggling on the field.

Except for a brief stay in first place in 1922—when the St. Louis Browns also found themselves in first place in the American League—the Cardinals failed to contend for the pennant. Their best finishes were in 1921, when they won 87 games and placed third, and in 1922, when they won 85 games and tied for third.

Just as Rickey had learned baseball through a long apprenticeship, Sam Breadon's evolution as the successful president of the ball club was a direct result of the lessons he had learned growing up, first on the streets of New York and then in St. Louis.

As a youngster in New York, Breadon belonged to the 20th Street gang, a neighborhood clique. One day, all the gangs had a picnic, but Breadon missed the boat carrying his friends. He went instead with the 19th Street group and committed the sin of dancing with the gang overlord's girl. When the boat docked, Breadon knew he would be in trouble, as related by John Carmichael in the *Chicago Daily News:*

"Not only the 19th Street bully, but his brother, an amateur fighter weighing around 150, faced Sam. It was the brother who broke the news. 'Whatcha mean dancin' wid me brudder's girl?' he snarled. 'I'll pound you soft.' In his own mind, Sam agreed with the youngster. He was more afraid of little brother than the big guy.

"'I always thought the older brother was yellow,'" Breadon said. "'But I was afraid of the kid. So I turned on the younger and said: 'Who are you? It isn't your girl, is it? Keep out of this.' Then I said to the older one: 'If you don't like it, come on, I'll beat your ears off.'

"'Well, damn if I didn't get away with it. The gang wouldn't let the young punk fight his brother's battle and the big guy was what I thought . . . scared. But when I was 50 yards away from 'em I ran like hell. He might-a changed his mind.'"

Already street smart, Breadon quit school when he was 15 to go to work. He got a job at a bank and eventually worked his way up to being a clerk, earning $125 a month. But he wasn't happy.

Breadon knew two brothers who had moved to St. Louis to enter the fledgling automobile business, and Breadon kept writing them about a job. Probably as much to stop him from bothering them as anything else, the brothers—Gus and Oscar Halsey—offered Breadon a job working as a grease monkey for $75 a month. In 1902, over his mother's wishes and tears, Breadon packed up and moved to St. Louis.

"I didn't know a thing about automobiles," Breadon later confessed. "But most all of the others were in the same boat. The automobile was a new contraption. However, the customers who came to the Halseys looked upon me as the expert from New York. Nor did I open my mouth to set them right. I just went about my job."

Part of what Breadon considered his job was refusing tips. He was sending home $40 a month to his mother and living in a one-dollar-a-week room, but he didn't accept tips because he didn't want people thinking he had done anything extra for them. But he was also planning for the future. He didn't intend to work in a garage forever.

When the Halseys got word that Breadon had been talking about going into the automobile sales end of the business, they fired him. That plunged him into one of the lowest points of his life. On a borrowed $300, Breadon was living on a budget of 15 cents a day. He didn't tell his mother he had lost his job and continued to send home the same forty dollars a month. His clothes were almost worn out, and he ate whatever food he could find and afford.

Breadon's luck finally turned around. The World's Fair dedication parade was coming to town, and Breadon talked the Plow Candy Company into consigning him cases of Honey Boy popcorn on credit. He received permission from two sisters to store the popcorn beneath the reviewing stand they had set up for the parade and recruited about 20 boys to sell the popcorn along the parade route. All the boys returned with their empty cases, and when the receipts were totaled, Breadon had netted a profit of $35.

After buying a few steak dinners and a new suit, Breadon called on businessman Marion Lambert—one of his early customers from whom he had refused a $10 tip—and received a guaranteed backing of $10,000 in his new car dealership.

In his first week at the Western Automobile Company, Breadon made $300. During the World's Fair year of 1904, the company cleared $20,000. Breadon was so devoted to the business that for more than a year, he slept in a little room off the garage office.

His prosperity in the auto business brought him into contact with the Cardinals. Just as Breadon had proved to be a shrewd businessman, he was just as effective running a baseball team.

After taking over the presidency of the team, Breadon

bought up as much of the Cardinals' stock as he could. Within three years, he owned two-thirds of the team's stock and later increased his holdings to 78 percent.

Breadon knew the Cardinals' two biggest assets at the time were Rickey and Hornsby. So it wasn't hard for him to sit in a hotel room with William Wrigley, the wealthy owner of the Cubs, and turn down his attempt to buy Hornsby in 1923.

"I came down here for one reason," Wrigley said in that meeting. "To buy Rogers Hornsby."

Breadon was unmoved, stating that Charley Stoneham, the owner of the Giants, already had offered $250,000 for Hornsby.

Wrigley nodded and said, "That's a lot of money." Breadon replied. "And twice $250,000 is $500,000. That's a lot more money. But Hornsby is not for sale, at any price."

To some, that might have been just the beginning of long and detailed negotiations. But Wrigley took one long look in Breadon's face and knew the Cardinals president meant what he said. He got up, left the room, and never mentioned the idea to Breadon again.

The directness with which he dealt with Wrigley was the way he approached all the business decisions of the Cardinals, whether it was approving Rickey's idea to start the farm system, selling Robison Field and negotiating the lease at Sportsman's Park, or finally telling Rickey he was through as the Cardinals manager.

Breadon, while he shunned publicity for himself, knew that the way to attract more fans to the games was to have a winning team and also to get more information about the games to the fans. He first suggested the creation of the National League Service Bureau, for the dissemination of information, in 1923. He also proposed the establishment of the Most Valuable Player award in 1924, and later, in 1932, he was the first owner to propose that major-league teams play games at night.

He was an extremely loyal owner who remembered the people who were nice to him. But when he had made up his mind, the decision usually didn't change. At least twice, Breadon made exceptions, both times involving veteran scouts. Once, one of the Cardinals scouts had failed to renew the liability insurance on his car. During a trip, he had a wreck, and as a result, the Cardinals were faced with a big bill for damages. Breadon was incensed that neglect was the only reason the insurance had not been renewed, and he ordered the scout fired.

The scout was heartbroken. Not having anything else to do, every morning he sat down on the doorstep of a building opposite the Cardinals office and stared at Breadon's office window. Breadon couldn't stand it. Every time he looked out the window, he saw the scout sitting there staring at him. After several days, he finally ordered the scout put back on the payroll to "get him off that doorstep."

Another occasion when Breadon reversed a decision was when the scouting department was being cut back in an economic move. Breadon informed Rickey that scout Jack Ryan had to be let go, and even though Rickey opposed the idea, he accepted it if Breadon would break the news to Ryan.

The day after Breadon told Ryan he was fired, Ryan was sitting on a bench in a small reception area outside Breadon's office when the owner came to work. They exchanged nods, but no words were spoken. When Ryan was there again the next day, Breadon stopped and asked Ryan if he had understood what he had been told.

"Yes I did, Mr. Breadon," Ryan replied.

"And that, well, you're off the payroll?" Breadon said.

"I understood you, Mr. Breadon," Ryan said. "But when I came here, I was hired by Branch Rickey and I worked for Branch Rickey. And until he fires me, I'm still working for Branch Rickey whether you pay me or not."

Ryan started getting paid again.

One decision in which Breadon did not reverse himself was when he finally decided Branch Rickey should not continue as the Cardinals manager. For some time he had felt that the

Cardinals were not responding as well as they should to Rickey's leadership and decided before the 1925 season that he wanted to move Rickey into a full-time front-office role.

"For a long time, Breadon had a growing idea that Branch was a little over-the-head of the rank and file of ballplayers," Stockton wrote. "His ideas were good, but frequently they were too complex. . . . An erudite and articulate man, he spoke to his ballplayers as a professor would talk to a graduate class in psychology or metaphysics. The laws of average and probability, the graphs he presented, were too much for many of the players. They were bored and frequently amused. Polite at the meetings, they would ridicule the Rickey theories and high-sounding phrases behind the master's back."

Breadon also knew, however, how proud Rickey was to be the Cardinals manager and how much it would hurt him to be fired. So, during spring training in Stockton, California, he told Rickey he wanted to make a change. But he also told Rickey, who bitterly protested the move, that Rickey could make the announcement on his own that he was moving into the front office so it would appear to be his decision.

Stockton picks up the story:

"But Rickey wouldn't go through with the abdication. Breadon waited and waited in his Los Angeles hotel room, watching the newspapers for the announcement that Rickey had named a new manager. Finally, Sam became weary of staying in his $20-a-day room and went to the Cardinals camp at Stockton.

"Rickey explained that he had changed his mind and pleaded for another chance at handling the reins. Breadon finally agreed to let him start the season as manager."

That reprieve was short-lived, however. With the team struggling in last place, Memorial Day was approaching. The Cardinals were to play a doubleheader in Pittsburgh on May 30, a Saturday, and then return home to play Cincinnati on Sunday the 31st. A few days prior to the game, Breadon called up the ticket office to get a report on the advance sales for the game.

When he was informed that only a few tickets had been sold, Breadon exploded. He wouldn't wait another day to change managers. He boarded an overnight train to Pittsburgh, called Rickey into his hotel room, and told him he was making the change.

Perhaps to prove to Rickey that he wished he had made the switch when he wanted to in spring training, he also refused to pick Burt Shotton as Rickey's replacement. He no doubt hoped that his decision would spur some ticket sales for Sunday's games, especially when fans found out that the new manager was also the team's star player—Rogers Hornsby.

Hornsby was indeed a superb player and is still generally considered the greatest right-handed hitter in the history of the game. In 1925 he was at the peak of his game.

He was en route to his sixth consecutive batting title and his third .400-plus season. He also was headed toward his second Triple Crown in four seasons, leading the league in average, home runs, and RBIs. He would win the NL Most Valuable Player award, an honor most people thought he had deserved in 1924, when he led the league with a .424 average.

Hornsby didn't win back-to-back MVP honors because a writer in Cincinnati, Jack Ryder, deliberately left Hornsby off the 10-man ballot, arguing that he didn't see how valuable a player could be—no matter what type of season he'd had—if his team finished in sixth place, as the Cardinals had done.

When Breadon learned that Brooklyn pitcher Dazzy Vance, who compiled a 28–6 record, had beaten Hornsby out for the award and the accompanying $1,000 bag of gold coins by three votes, he telephoned writer Fred Lieb, the head of the MVP committee, at the *New York Evening Telegram*.

Lieb described the call:

"While the voice came from St. Louis, for a moment the accent had me confused. It didn't sound like Middle America, but much nearer at hand, as in Brooklyn. 'Who is this calling?' I asked.

"'It's Sam Breadon, president of the Cardinals, that is who

is calling. I want to know what you and your committee are trying to do to one of our players. Didn't you fellers ever hear of Rogers Hornsby?

"'All that I gotta say [is] it was a helluva way to treat a .424 hitter,' snapped Breadon as he hung up."

Even though Hornsby was a great player, he had an abrasive personality that rubbed many people the wrong way. He was dedicated totally to baseball, avoiding reading the newspapers and going to movies for fear they would hurt his batting eye.

Hornsby, while he respected Rickey's knowledge of baseball and his ability to evaluate players, was not a big fan of Rickey's managing ability. One of his first actions as manager was to throw Rickey's blackboard out the window.

"He was too smart, I believe, for the ballplayers," Hornsby would say later about Rickey. "He talked over their heads. He was one of the greatest percentage players in baseball, one of the first to utilize each individual's special skill. But his language in the clubhouse was not the language of the ballplayers. They were a little confused by it all, a little tight trying to think of all the things he outlined to them in speeches and in blackboard sessions."

Rickey and Hornsby had clashed openly on occasion, the most notable time coming at the end of a game against the Giants at the Polo Grounds late in the 1923 season. What started as a vocal argument on the bench erupted into a fistfight in the clubhouse that had to be broken up by Shotton and other players.

Later the same year, the two feuded again when Rickey fined Hornsby $500 and suspended him for the rest of the year because Hornsby said he was too ill to play, while team physician Dr. Robert F. Hyland had cleared him for action. Hornsby was suffering from a skin irritation, but Rickey said Hornsby's problem was "more a state of mind" than anything else.

And while Hornsby was not popular with Rickey, he also had few friends among his teammates, even though they all had tremendous respect for his ability. Jack Sher, in a biography of Hornsby for *Sport* magazine in 1949, said:

> As Hornsby's fame as a slam-bang hitter grew, he became less popular with the Cardinals players. Few of them disliked him, but none were really friendly. The harder he hit, the more of a 'loner' he became. He was sufficient unto himself. The only time his own teammates really loved him, felt close to him, was when he was out there on the field in uniform, giving everything he had for his team, going all out to win a ball game.

Hornsby did have the respect of umpires, whom he rarely criticized. On one occasion, at a game in Brooklyn, pitcher Jumbo Jim Elliott had a 2–2 count on Hornsby and threw a fastball that he thought was a certain strike.

But umpire Cy Pfirman called it a ball, evoking loud complaints from both Elliott and catcher Hank DeBerry. Elliott then threw another fastball, and Hornsby promptly slammed it over the wall. Umpire Pfirman brought a new ball to the mound and told the pitcher, "You see, Mr. Elliott, Mr. Hornsby will tell you when a pitch is a strike."

Hornsby, when he became the Cardinals manager, also became a part owner when Rickey, mad at Breadon and the organization, said he wanted to sell his stock. Hornsby, through the financial help of Breadon, bought it.

As Breadon had expected, the switch in managers provided some new life for the Cardinals, who in 1925 climbed back into the first division with a fourth-place finish, one game above .500.

Only once that season did Hornsby's anger get the best of him. Hornsby objected to a Philadelphia pitcher leaving the field to get a dry uniform, and when it appeared Phillies manager Art Fletcher was winning the ensuing argument with the umpires, Hornsby reached out and punched Fletcher in the jaw. Fletcher went down, and the fight was over. "Apparently, the umpires were lenient in those days or thought Hornsby had grounds for retaliation," the *Sporting News* wrote years later. "No punishment was meted out for the one-punch fight."

Hornsby's explanation: "I couldn't make any headway against him talking."

Hornsby did have better results with his players, and when the club reported to spring training in San Antonio, Texas, before the 1926 season, Hornsby and Breadon thought they had put together a club capable of winning the pennant.

Hornsby told the club that it was going to win. "Don't go around telling everybody we're going to win, but we are," he said. "And if there's anybody here who doesn't believe we're going to win, there's a train leaving for the North tonight."

When the season started, there didn't appear to be any great difference between this Cardinals team and those of the past few seasons. For the first seven weeks, the club limped along in the second division. But in June the club's fortunes changed, thanks in large part to the help of two of their rivals—the Giants and the Cubs.

On June 14, just before the trading deadline, Giants manager John McGraw approached the Cardinals and said he would like to acquire outfielder Heinie Mueller and would give up outfielder Billy Southworth. Breadon and Rickey agreed.

Eight days later, the Cubs gave up on aging ace pitcher Grover Cleveland Alexander and placed him on waivers. Alexander had gotten into constant trouble with the new Chicago manager, Joe McCarthy, and finally, McCarthy had no choice but to release him.

Breadon was in the Cardinals' offices when the waiver notice crossed the wire. Rickey was out of town, visiting one of the farm clubs, so Breadon sent a wire to Hornsby to find out if he was interested in putting in the $4,000 waiver claim for Alexander.

The Cardinal pitching coach that season was Bill Killefer, and he told Hornsby he thought Alexander could help the

Cardinals win the pennant. Hornsby knew all about Alexander's reported alcoholism, but he also knew Killefer would be able to handle him. The Cardinals put in the claim for Alexander and were awarded his rights.

"I'm no Sunday School teacher," Hornsby was quoted as saying at the time. "I don't care what Alexander does off the field. He always looked like a great pitcher to me. At $4,000 he's the greatest bargain I ever saw."

Even if he had never won more that one game for the Cardinals, Alexander earned back the price of the waiver claim the first time he pitched for the team, on June 27 against his former Cub teammates. Phil Ball, the owner of the Browns, had double-decked the grandstand at Sportsman's Park before the season started, increasing the seating capacity from 18,000 to 33,000, thinking his team had a good chance to win in 1926.

But it was the Cardinals who benefited from Ball's move. The crowd for Alexander's first game was 37,718—the first time in the team's history it had drawn more than 25,000 at home. Alexander won, beating the Cubs 3–2 in 10 innings.

The Cardinals moved into the pennant race but still were trailing Pittsburgh when the Pirates came to St. Louis for a six-game series in late August. The Cardinals won four of the games, including sweeping a doubleheader on August 31 that moved the team into first place. It was the first time in history a Cardinals team had entered September leading the league.

The pennant still hadn't been won, however, and through an odd quirk in the schedule, the game against the Pirates on September 1 was the Cardinals' final home game of the season. They had to play their final 25 games on the road—playing a series at each of the other seven cities in the league.

Halfway through the trip and the month, the Cardinals found themselves in second place, a game behind the Reds. But the club then traveled to Philadelphia for a six-game series and won the first five—moving back into first place to stay, on September 17. After visiting Brooklyn, where they split two games, the Cardinals clinched their first pennant on

September 24 against the Giants at the Polo Grounds, winning 6–4. Southworth's homer provided the winning margin. The Cardinals finished their 25-game road trip with a record of 14–11 and a final two-game margin over the Reds.

The news of the pennant-clinching victory touched off a raucous celebration on the downtown streets of St. Louis when it came over the wires and radio. Parades lasted well into the night, and the only celebration that came close to matching the party had been the festive day years earlier when the news came that World War I had ended.

Despite Hornsby's claims in spring training that the Cardinals would win, it's doubtful they would have pulled it off without the acquisition of the 39-year-old Alexander, who went 9–7 after he joined the Cardinals. Southworth also proved to be a worthy pickup, hitting .317 after joining the Cardinals, with 11 homers and 69 RBI.

Just as important to the Cardinals' success, however, were the homegrown players—the first products of Rickey's farm system that had produced their first successful season. Less than seven years after Rickey signed his first minor-league players, the Cardinals had reached the World Series with 13 players who had come up through their system.

The Cardinals also had their second straight MVP winner, this time catcher Bob O'Farrell, who won the award even though he ranked seventh among the Cardinals starters in average and fifth in RBIs. He won on the strength of his superior defense and throwing ability, which cut down many opposing base runners.

While Hornsby was still basking in the glory of winning the pennant, he returned to the team hotel in New York, where a telegram was waiting for him. His mother had died that afternoon in Texas. Hornsby thought back to the last time he had seen his mother, in the spring. She was already seriously ill, but she told him, "Your team is going to win the pennant this year, Rogers. I'll live until you win it."

Calling home after he received the telegram, Hornsby found

out his mother had indeed lived until the Cardinals had clinched the pennant. She also had left a final message for him—go on and win the World Series, and "I know he will able to do it."

Hornsby's other relatives agreed to delay the funeral for 10 days until after the World Series ended, and hours after the final out, Hornsby boarded a train for Texas to help bury his mother.

It was with his mother's death hanging over him that Hornsby led the Cardinals into Yankee Stadium to open the World Series against the favored Yankees, managed by the former Cardinals manager, Miller Huggins.

The Yankees won the opening game 2–1, as Herb Pennock stopped the Cardinals on just three hits. The Cardinals tied the Series at one win each in the second game, winning 6–2 behind the pitching of Alexander and home runs from Southworth and shortstop Tommy Thevenow. Thevenow's homer was an inside-the-park homer, coming when Babe Ruth couldn't find his line drive that got lost in a section of the right-field fence. Alexander, making his first World Series appearance since 1915, allowed just four hits and struck out 10.

The clubs then took a day off to travel, but that just created another controversy for Hornsby. Commissioner Landis had declared the New York Central the "official" railroad for the World Series for the travel of both teams, umpires, and other officials. Hornsby had already arranged for the Cardinals to travel on the Pennsylvania Railroad. Landis called Hornsby to his hotel suite and asked him if that was true, and Hornsby confirmed it.

Hornsby told Landis he didn't care about the commissioner's official designation. "Your job is to run the World Series and not to tell the ballplayers how to travel," he said. "If the Yankees want to take the New York Central, it's all right with me. We're taking the Pennsylvania."

Landis probably could have forced Hornsby and the Cardinals to switch trains or fined him, but he backed off, and the Series shifted to St. Louis without incident.

The city was totally enthralled with the first ever postseason game played in St. Louis since the Cardinals joined the National League. The *St. Louis Globe-Democrat* devoted its entire front page to the upcoming game beneath banner headlines: GREATEST DEMONSTRATION IN CITY'S BASEBALL HISTORY STAGED AS FRENZIED MULTITUDES LIONIZE BASEBALL HEROES AMID BEDLAM OF NOISE AND JOYOUS ENTHUSIASM.

A crowd of 37,708 jammed the park to watch Jesse Haines pitch and hit the Cardinals to a 4–0 victory, putting them ahead in the Series two games to one. Haines hurled a five-hitter for the shutout and also smacked a two-run homer.

The lead was short-lived. In the fourth game, Ruth put on a one-man hitting display never before seen in World Series play, blasting three homers, including one that flew out of the park, across Grand Avenue, and broke a window at the Wells Chevrolet Company. The Yankees' 10–5 victory evened the Series at two wins each.

The Yankees moved back in command of the Series in the fifth game, as Pennock again outdueled Wee Willie Sherdel, 3–2, in a rematch of the game-one starters, winning on Tony Lazzeri's 10th-inning sacrifice fly.

The Series then shifted back to New York, and all the Yankees had to do was win one of the two remaining games at home to win the world championship. But Hornsby inspired his team to 10–2 rout behind Alexander to force the deciding seventh game.

What happened in the seventh game is still remembered as one of the classic contests in World Series history. The Cardinals grabbed a 3–1 lead by scoring three times in the fourth, and the Yankees cut the lead to 3–2 in the sixth.

In the seventh, the Yankees loaded the bases against Haines, whose knuckles had started bleeding from all the knuckleballs he had thrown. Hornsby had to go to the bullpen, and he selected Alexander, even though he had pitched a complete game the day before.

Many stories have been written suggesting that Alexander

was drunk or hung over when he came in to face Lazzeri with two outs and the bases loaded. Alexander would later say he wasn't. Hornsby met him in short left field as he came into the game.

"Alex, we're in a tough spot," Hornsby said. "There's no place to put Lazzeri."

"I'll be damned if you're not right," Alexander said. "There's no place to put the batter. I reckon I'd better strike him out."

On his third pitch, with the count 1–1, Lazzeri hit a tremendous line drive that crashed into the left-field seats, just foul. Then Alexander came back with a low outside curve, Lazzeri swung and missed, and the Cardinals were out of the jam.

The Yankees still had two more chances, however, but Alexander was up to the task. He retired the Yankees in order in the eighth and got the first two outs in the ninth before walking Ruth on a 3–2 pitch.

Alexander walked toward the plate after umpire George Hildebrand called it ball four and asked about the location of the pitch.

When Hildebrand replied that it was just outside by a matter of inches, Alexander said, "If it was that close, I think you might have given it to an old guy."

Alexander didn't need the break, however. With Bob Meusel up and Lou Gehrig on deck, Ruth unexpectedly took off in an attempt to steal second base. O'Farrell's throw to Hornsby was in time, and Ruth was tagged out, giving the Cardinals the world championship.

Even though the game had been played in New York, the news of the Cardinals' victory touched off another wild celebration that didn't end until well after the victory train returned from New York.

Even though it might not have been the best team he ever played for or managed, Hornsby later praised the 1926 Cardinals as his favorite club.

"I like to think that the Cardinals team of 1926 was the

pluckiest outfit I ever managed," Hornsby said. "Get me now, I don't say the best team I ever played on, but the gamest and hardest to lick that I ever handled.

"It was a team that went along—everybody fighting for just one thing—to win. There were no second-guesers on that club and nobody was better than the other guy."

That included Alexander, even though he was now the star of the moment. A couple of days after the World Series victory, Breadon called Alexander on the phone to try to get him to speak at an important banquet honoring the Cardinals. Alexander's wife, Aimee, found him at the governor's mansion, replaying the Series to Governor Reid.

"The governor got real mad when I wanted to take Alex away," Aimee said. "You see, everybody loved him, all sorts of people."

Earlier in the season, one of Alexander's fellow pitchers accompanied Alexander on a drinking spree the night before Alexander was scheduled to pitch. When called on the next morning by Rickey to tell what happened, he offered the following explanation:

"I asked him point-blank why he had imbibed too freely the previous night and I braced myself for the answer," Rickey said. "He said, 'I did it for the good of the team.' That one even took me aback.

"'It's this way, Mr. Rickey,' he continued. 'Pete Alexander and I had a bottle of whiskey last night and I suddenly realized that it was Alex's turn to pitch the next day. And I also realized that he wouldn't be at his best if he drank too much.' This, I knew, was going to be rich. I edged forward in my chair.

"'And so, Mr. Rickey,' he resumed with a perfectly straight face, 'I decided to sacrifice myself for the good of the team. The more whiskey I drank the less Alex would have to drink. So I just consumed twice as much as he did. But it was for the good of the team, Mr. Rickey. That's the real reason.'"

It also was for what Breadon thought was the good of the

team that prompted him to make one of the most controversial decisions in Cardinals history, just three months after winning the World Series.

While Hornsby was the toast of the town, Breadon could not forget an incident that had happened late in the season in Pittsburgh. For most of the season, Hornsby had been feuding with Breadon about having to play exhibition games. Hornsby wanted to have the days off for his team instead, and he was afraid that some of his key players would be injured.

When the Cardinals found themselves in the pennant race in September, Hornsby wanted Breadon to cancel a scheduled exhibition game in New Haven, Connecticut. Breadon reluctantly agreed with Hornsby and sent a telegram to George Weiss, the organizer of the game, telling him of the Cardinals' desire to cancel the game.

Weiss responded that he had already spent $500 advertising the game and would not cancel it, even though the Cardinals offered to pay back the $500. When Breadon got the news, he went into the clubhouse to tell Hornsby. Unfortunately, the moment he picked to tell him was minutes after a tough defeat.

Hornsby exploded. He called Breadon every imaginable name, and the owner was embarrassed in front of his team. He made a mental note to remember the incident, deciding on the spot that no employee of his could get away with talking to him like that.

Hornsby later admitted that both he and Breadon likely erred in the incident—Breadon for picking the wrong time to bring him the news and him for popping off to his boss.

"It might have been different if Breadon had waited until we all cooled off," Hornsby said. "I suppose I spoke more bluntly than usual. I told him what I thought of exhibition games and people who would book them to take away the days of rest that ballplayers needed. He was flushed and angry when he left the clubhouse. I believe he made up his mind then and there that, come pennant or last place, Hornsby wouldn't be with the Cardinals the next season."

Breadon did attempt to sign Hornsby to a contract to manage and play for the Cardinals in 1927, offering him a one-year deal worth $50,000 that he secretly hoped Hornsby would reject. And Hornsby did, saying he wanted a three-year deal.

The two held a final negotiating meeting on December 20 in Breadon's office, but it lasted just 15 minutes. Hornsby, whose feud with Rickey also had never really cooled, reportedly demanded that either Rickey went or he went. Breadon left the office in a hurry and went home, where he called Charley Stoneham, the owner of the Giants.

When he finally reached Stoneham several hours later, Breadon told him that the tentative deal the two teams had arranged earlier in the month was on—the Cardinals would trade Hornsby to the Giants for second baseman Frankie Frisch and pitcher Jimmy Ring.

News of the deal exploded across St. Louis, the reaction rivaling that of the Cardinals' victory over the Yankees three months earlier. This time, the fans were outraged, not ecstatic.

Breadon had to take his telephone off the hook. Fans hung crepe paper on Breadon's house and his automobile dealership, and as he drove to work the next morning they peppered his car with wads of paper. Thousands of letters poured into the Cardinals office. Breadon was hanged in effigy.

The Chamber of Commerce passed a resolution condemning the deal. The *St. Louis Post-Dispatch* ran a large cartoon showing the St. Louis Cardinals' stocking empty, the Giants' stocking bulging. The sports editor of one of the St. Louis newspapers vowed that he would never again attend a Cardinals game. Petitions were started by fans who wanted to join in that boycott. Members of the team's board of directors, who weren't notified in advance of the deal, threatened to resign in protest.

"I knew that would be the answer from the fans," Breadon said. "I realized I would be in for a tough winter."

The deal didn't look good the first time Frisch wore a Cardinals uniform in St. Louis, for the annual preseason city series against the Browns in 1927.

In that first game, Frisch made two errors. The crowd again went berserk, chanting about wanting Hornsby back. It was the last occasion they had to boo Frisch. In the eighth inning, Frisch came back and homered to give the Cardinals the victory.

Frisch went on to have a spectacular season. He hit .337 with 52 extra-base hits, drove in 78 runs, and stole 48 bases to lead the league. He lost the MVP award by one vote.

While Frisch didn't make Cardinals fans forget Hornsby that year, his performance did teach Breadon a valuable lesson he would always remember.

"He saved my life, that's why," Breadon said. "If he hadn't come through the way he did—and there wasn't another guy in baseball who could have come through like that—I'd have been finished. Cooked. I'd have had to leave town."

Frisch's performance helped the Cardinals' attendance increase from 681,575 to 763,615—and convinced Breadon that he should never worry about what the fan reaction would be when he traded a player.

"After the season of 1927, I never again was afraid to dispose of a player, regardless of his ability or popularity," Breadon said. "I knew after that year that what the fans want is a winner, and that a popular player is quickly forgotten by one who is equally popular."

Before Breadon could be free from Hornsby completely, however, Hornsby's stock in the Cardinals had to be sold, since he couldn't be playing for the Giants while owning stock in the Cardinals at the same time.

Hornsby set a high price for the stock, and it finally took all the National League owners kicking in $5,000 apiece to meet the difference between what Breadon had offered Hornsby and how much he wanted, before the deal could go through.

Partially to help stem the public's outburst over the Hornsby deal, Breadon moved quickly to name O'Farrell, the league MVP, as the manager for the 1927 season. He had first offered the job to coach Bill Killefer, but he turned it down saying he was too close to Hornsby to accept the post. Frisch was named the team captain, but a doubting public still had to be convinced that Breadon knew what he was doing.

Even though the Cardinals did not win in 1927, finishing one and a half games behind Pittsburgh, they actually had a better season than they had had the year before, winning three more games. Many observers felt the team could have repeated as champion if shortstop Tommy Thevenow had not suffered a broken leg after only 53 games and O'Farrell had not been limited to just 61 games because of a sore arm.

Even if the Cardinals had won, they might not have been able to play the World Series in their own ball park. On the last weekend of the season, while the Cardinals were playing in Cincinnati, a tornado almost blew down Sportsman's Park. It ripped the roof off the pavilion in right field and blew debris from nearby houses that were destroyed into the ball park.

Even though the Cardinals had come so close to winning, Breadon was not impressed with O'Farrell's managerial ability. So when the 1928 season began, the team had its third manager in as many years—Bill McKechnie, who had won a World Series with Pittsburgh in 1925 and had been a coach for O'Farrell. To show he wasn't really mad at O'Farrell, Breadon gave him a $5,000 raise over his 1927 salary, just to play.

The Cardinals were in the 1928 race all season, and two deals Rickey made in the middle of the year a day apart helped push St. Louis over the top. In May, he traded O'Farrell to the Giants for outfielder George Harper and the following day sent catcher Virgil "Spud" Davis and outfielder Homer Peel to Philadelphia for catcher Jimmie Wilson.

The club also inserted veteran Rabbit Maranville at shortstop in place of Thevenow, who never really recovered from the broken leg he suffered the previous year.

Led by first baseman Sunny Jim Bottomley—one of the first and best products of Rickey's farm system—the Cardinals finally clinched the pennant on the next-to-last day of the season and wound up two games in front of the Giants. Bottomley won the MVP award by hitting .325, scoring 123 runs, and driving in 136.

Bottomley had been playing semipro ball when a St. Louis policeman saw him hit two home runs and three triples and recommended him to scout Charley Barrett. Barrett brought him to St. Louis, where he worked out for a few days. The young prospect was puzzled by certain aspects of the big leagues. While looking at the bat rack one day, Bottomley noticed a strange, slender bat and politely asked a veteran pitcher, "Pardon me sir, but who is this Mr. Fungo?"

Bottomley's biggest day in the majors came on September 16, 1924, playing in Brooklyn, when he drove in a major-league record 12 runs. He went 6 for 6 in the game, with two homers, a double, and three singles.

Waiting to oppose the Cardinals in the World Series were the Yankees again, and they remembered what had happened just two years before. The Yankees, on paper at least, did not look as formidable as the 1926 club, so it was a complete shock to Cardinals fans when the New York club won the Series in four straight games.

Not only did the Cardinals lose, they were not competitive in any of the four games. They lost by scores of 4–1, 9–3, 7–3, and 7–3. The biggest mistake the Cardinals pitchers made was in pitching to Babe Ruth, who hit .625 in the Series with three homers, four RBIs, and nine runs scored. Hornsby had ordered Ruth walked 12 times in the 1926 Series, but he was given just one walk in 1928. Gehrig also wore out the Cardinals pitchers, hitting .545 with four homers. Ruth repeated his three-homer game of 1926 in the fourth game of the Series.

The person most upset by the lopsided defeat was Breadon. He blamed the manager, McKechnie, and demoted him to the Cardinals' Rochester farm team. He brought in Billy Southworth, a former Cardinal who had been managing Rochester, to take over the team in 1929.

Southworth didn't make it through the season as manager.

When he had played with the Cardinals, he had been one of the boys. But as manager, he thought he had to be a strict disciplinarian, and the moves he made backfired. In spring training, the team had a trip scheduled from the Avon Park, Florida, base to Miami, and Southworth intended for the team to make the trip together by train. Some of the players wanted to drive in their own cars with their wives, and Southworth threatened to fine anybody who did so $500.

By July, Breadon decided he had made a mistake in rushing Southworth back to the majors, so he flipped him and McKechnie again, bringing McKechnie back to the Cardinals and sending Southworth to Rochester.

The move helped relax the atmosphere around the team but not enough to keep the team from doing better than a fourth-place finish.

The 1929 season brought to an end Alexander's great career. On an eastern trip in August, he was sent back to St. Louis because he had consistently been out of condition. Breadon, rather than criticizing him, paid him off for the rest of the season and sent him home to Nebraska.

The Cardinals had some other great players during the 1920s, including outfielder Chick Hafey and pitcher Jesse Haines, both of whom went on to the Hall of Fame. Haines pitched the first no-hitter in Cardinals' history, on July 17, 1924, against Boston, and won 210 games, the second highest total in team history.

Haines, who developed a knuckleball in 1922 that was a key to his success, once was thrown out of a game by umpire Bill Klem. Haines was ejected when he ran off the mound to protest a call, even before he had said a single word.

"Later, I was fined and I demanded that the league office tell me what kind of a report Klem filed on me," Haines said. "They told me he tossed me out for having a threatening look on my face."

Hafey, while still enjoying a Hall of Fame career, might

have been even better if not for constant medical problems. He developed sinus trouble that forced him to undergo an operation and wear glasses.

"I always thought that if Hafey had been blessed with normal eyesight and good health, he might have been the best right-handed hitter baseball had ever known," Rickey said.

The 1920s also was a decade of tragedy for the Cardinals. Within nine months in 1922, two players died. William "Pickles" Dillhoefer, who had been a catcher in the major leagues since 1917, died in February at age 27 of typhoid fever. Outfielder Austin McHenry, who had been with the Cardinals since 1918, began having trouble judging fly balls during the 1922 season, and Rickey sent him to a doctor, who diagnosed a brain tumor. An operation was not successful, and McHenry died in November, also at age 27.

But the lasting memories of the decade were of Alexander striking out Lazzeri and Hornsby tagging out Ruth to give the Cardinals their first World Series title. It had been a good decade for the Cardinals, but the 1930s would be even better.

3

Dizzy and the Gang

THE 1930s

◆

The new decade brought one immediate change for the Cardinals—another new manager. Gabby Street, who had been a coach with the team in 1929 but was most famous for once catching a ball dropped from the Washington Monument, was hired by Breadon and Rickey to succeed Bill McKechnie.

McKechnie likely could have stayed as the Cardinals manager, but he had seen how quick the team's hierarchy acted in changing managers. When he received a five-year contract offer to manage the Braves in Boston, he took the security and moved east. That left Street, who had spent 17 years laboring in the minor leagues, to become the Cardinals' fifth manager in five years.

The 1930 team was not highly regarded at the beginning of the season. The feeling was that the championship teams of 1926 and 1928 were breaking up because of age, although Rickey's farm system was still proving that it could continually provide good, effective replacements.

After seeing the Cardinals spend the first half of the season in the middle of the standings, Rickey swung a deal on the June 15 trading deadline that helped change the Cardinals' fortunes for the rest of the season. He sent Wee Willie Sherdel and Fred Frankhouse to Boston for Burleigh Grimes. When

Grimes joined the club, Rickey told him if he could win a dozen games, the Cardinals could win the pennant. Grimes would win 13.

Still, the deal didn't automatically deliver the pennant to the Cardinals. In the middle of August they were still one game under .500 and 12 games behind league-leading Brooklyn. The team caught fire, however, and from August 30 until September 26, the day they clinched the pennant, the team reeled off a 21–3 record. The team won behind an offense that saw every regular hit over .300 and rookie right fielder George Watkins hit .373, still the highest batting average ever for a rookie.

With the pennant already clinched, Street decided to pitch a 19-year-old rookie just up from the farm team in Houston in the season's final game against the Pirates. His name was Dizzy Dean.

Mayor Victor Miller, on hand to congratulate Street before the game, asked the Cardinals manager about the team's new pitcher as he was warming up.

"Is he going to be as good as they say?" Miller asked Street. Street replied, "I think he's going to be a great one, Mr. Mayor. But I'm afraid we'll never know from one minute to the next what he's going to do or say."

Probably never in his life did Street make a more accurate statement.

Dean won the game, pitching a three-hitter to stop the Pirates 3–1. But his legacy with the Cardinals wouldn't really begin for a few more seasons. The rest of the team, meanwhile, had a World Series to play against the Philadelphia Athletics.

The Athletics were back in the Series for the second straight year after winning the American League pennant. They had defeated the Cubs in five games to win the 1929 World Series and were counting on making it two straight. The opening game in Philadelphia's Shibe Park matched Grimes against Lefty Grove, and the Athletics used home runs by Al Simmons and Mickey Cochrane to beat the Cardinals 5–2.

Cochrane homered again in the second game, helping Philadelphia to a 6–1 victory and a 2–0 lead in the Series as the two teams boarded the trains and headed west to St. Louis. Street tried to get his team to forget those two games and remember how they had stormed from behind to win the pennant. His speech proved inspirational, and the Cardinals came back to win the next two games behind Bill Hallahan and Jesse Haines, 5–0 and 3–1, respectively, to even the Series at two games each.

The fifth game was a classic, with Grimes and George Earnshaw (relieved in the 8th by Lefty Grove) locked in a scoreless pitching duel into the ninth. But Jimmie Foxx connected for a two-run homer after Grimes walked Cochrane to open the ninth and the Athletics had a 2–0 victory and a 3–2 lead in the Series.

The Series shifted back to Philadelphia, where the Athletics clinched their second straight title with a 7–1 victory in Game 6.

One of the Cardinals who suffered most in the series was Bottomley, who was just 1 for 22, a miniscule average of .045. For Sunny Jim, there wasn't much to smile about.

"I have the reputation of taking things as they come and not worrying," Bottomley would say later. "True, I don't worry much. But I got tired of being referred to as a big bum and a batting bust, and I began to wonder if those Athletic pitchers hadn't got my number. They're great pitchers all right, especially Earnshaw and Grove. But it didn't seem to me reasonable that even great pitchers ought to make me swallow such a bitter dose as a .045 batting average."

As the team loaded the bus to head back to the train station and on to St. Louis for the winter, George Puccinelli, a backup outfielder who had played in just 11 games during the season, didn't realize how tough the defeat was for some of the veterans to take.

He started singing, "It's all over now . . . it's all over now."

Frankie Frisch didn't like it, and neither did Grimes. Grimes got to his feet and walked to where Puccinelli was singing in the back of the bus.

"Listen, you big SOB," Grimes said. "We know it's all over, but dammit, we don't want to hear about it."

Puccinelli was back in the minors in 1931, but it was a player who finally came up from the minors to stay that season who helped establish the beginning of the Gashouse Gang tradition, a young, scrappy center fielder who later would shift to third base—Johnny Leonard Roosevelt "Pepper" Martin.

Martin had earned his nickname "Pepper" while in the minors. Blake Harper, who would later become the head of concessions for the Cardinals, was at the time running the farm team in Fort Smith. After the Cardinals acquired Martin, they assigned him to Harper's team there.

"They just called him Johnny Martin, or Jack, but he was so full of life and energy that I started calling him Pepper," Harper said. "It fit like a glove, and has stuck ever since."

Martin was tired of life in the minors and thought he deserved a chance to play on a regular basis for the Cardinals. Early in the season, when he still was limited to pinch-hitting, he burst into Rickey's office one day.

"I'm tired riding that bench," Martin told Rickey. "I want to get into the game or I want you to trade me to some club that will play me."

Rickey, always one to admire the ambition of others, gave Martin his chance by trading Taylor Douthit to the Reds on June 15 for Wally Roettger.

Martin made sure Rickey never regretted the deal. He would later join with Dean to become the most vociferous members of the Gashouse Gang, but until Dean arrived, Martin proved he was more than capable of performing some hijinks by himself.

A typical Martin story relates how he got to the Cardinals' spring training camp. Martin, who had been bought originally by Rickey for $500 from the Class D Greenville, Texas, farm club, sometimes hopped freight trains to make the trip from Oklahoma to Florida. One year, he was picked up in Thomasville, Georgia, and spent a night in jail. He was fined five dollars and had to borrow the money from a local minister. When the minister asked if Martin needed more money, he asked for another dollar and bought cigarettes for his cellmates. The minister also bought a ticket to Florida for Martin. When he finally reported to the Cardinals' camp, wearing khaki trousers and a hunting jacket, he had a week's growth of beard and his face was smeared with dirt and oil. In May the minister received a letter from Martin, and the loan was repaid in full.

In his later years with the Cardinals, Martin's appearance oftentimes looked the same. One of his favorite hobbies was midget auto racing, and he usually spent mornings of home games tinkering with his car. Martin's secret ambition was to one day compete in and win the Indianapolis 500, a goal he never accomplished. Often Martin would show up at the ball park just in time to take batting practice, with his face, hair, and hands still covered with grease.

One day, he arrived after the rest of the team had taken batting practice. Before Frisch could reprimand him, Martin confessed he had been at the racetrack all morning, competing against several professional drivers. The stakes were a gallon of ice cream. Martin won.

Martin was superstitious and thought finding hairpins brought him good luck. Later on in Martin's career, J. Roy Stockton and Ray Gillespie one time deliberately scattered a packet of hairpins in the lobby of the team hotel in Cincinnati. Before Martin arrived, however, outfielder Joe Medwick came through the lobby and started picking up the hairpins.

"Hey, those are for Pepper Martin," Stockton said. Replied Medwick, "Let him find his own hairpins."

It didn't take long for Martin to become one of Rickey's—and the Cardinals' fans—favorites. The attitude and spunk he carried with him that day into Rickey's office carried over with him onto the field as well, whether he was batting, running the bases, or playing defense.

"Did you ever see a fellow like Martin," Rickey would say later on in Martin's career. "Tremendous enthusiasm, camaraderie, devil-may-care, and above all, genuineness. Nothing hypocritical about Pepper. I can give you his biography in four words: *He is as was.* He is a child of nature and never pretends to be anything he isn't."

Martin, who wore uniform number one, was the type of player who always had a dirty uniform. If he couldn't get to the base any other way, he would run or dive over the opposing fielder.

Veteran St. Louis baseball writer Bob Broeg, talking about Martin in his book *My Baseball Scrapbook*, said of all the Gashouse Gang members, none was more ahead of his time than Martin.

"Of all the players who were born too soon, none missed his era more than when Martin preceded television," Broeg said. "With that rugged face right out of a western movie, his expressive nasal twang, his music-fracturing Mudcat band, and his comic sleight-of-hand pepper game, the old Wild Horse would have been on TV more than he'd have been on base. And Pepper could get on base."

The Mudcats, a collection of Cardinals who played loud western music at nightclubs as a diversion from baseball, were behind many of the Gashouse Gang's practical jokes in later years. Some of Martin's favorite songs were "Willie, My Toes Are Cold," "Birmingham Cool," and "They Buried My Sweetie Under an Old Pine Tree." But he saved most of his talent for on-the-field performance, and he was good enough to help the Cardinals roll to their second straight pennant in 1931 and another date with the Athletics in the World Series.

Many longtime observers consider the 1931 Cardinals the greatest team in the history of the franchise. "I've seen a lot of great ball clubs in my day, but for pitching, hitting, spirit, and all-around balance, I would back my 1931 Cardinals team against any of them," manager Street said. On the infield, Jim Bottomley was at first, Frankie Frisch at second, Charley Gelbert was the shortstop, and Sparky Adams, Andy High, and Jake Flowers split the games at third. In the outfield, Martin was in center, flanked by Chick Hafey in left and either George Watkins or Wally Roettger in right. Jimmie Wilson and Gus Mancuso were the catchers, and the pitching staff included Paul Derringer, Bill Hallahan, Burleigh Grimes, and Syl Johnson. Five of those players would later be inducted into baseball's Hall of Fame—Bottomley, Frisch, Hafey, Martin, and Grimes.

The Cardinals became the first National League team in 18 years to achieve at least 100 victories, finishing with 101, and wound up 13 games ahead of the second-place New York Giants. Hafey won the batting title, beating out the Giants' Bill Terry and his teammate Bottomley by less than a percentage point, .3489 to .3486 for Terry and .3482 for Bottomley.

But the star of the World Series was Martin. Through the first five games, Martin collected 12 hits, including four doubles and a home run. The Wild Horse of the Osage, as he had been nicknamed by a Rochester writer when he was playing there in the minors, also stole five bases, drove in five runs, and scored five times.

Still, the Cardinals were having a hard time putting away the Athletics. Martin's home run and four RBIs led the Cardinals to a 5–1 victory in Game 5, after the Cardinals had lost the opener 6–2; won Game 2, 2–0; won Game 3, 5–2; and lost Game 4, 3–0.

In the sixth game, the Athletics won 8–1 to force the seventh and deciding game. George Watkins hit a two-run homer in the third inning off Earnshaw to help the Cardinals build a 4–0 lead; the team hung on for a 4–2 victory and their second world championship. Appropriately, with the Athletics threatening and the tying runs on base in the ninth, Hallahan got Max Bishop to fly out to Martin in left center for the Series's final out.

Commissioner Landis came into the Cardinals clubhouse to

congratulate them after the game and told Martin, "Young man, I'd rather trade places with you than with any other man in the country."

Martin didn't miss a beat. "Why, that'll be fine, Judge," Martin said, "if we can trade salaries, too."

Martin wasn't really worried about money. He was making $4,500 a year, compared with $60,000 for Judge Landis, but all he would do with the extra income would be buy more tools or new gadgets for his midget racer. He went on a vaudeville tour following the World Series, earning an extra $1,500 a week, but he quit the show with five weeks left on the schedule, saying he wasn't an actor and was cheating the public and the man who was paying him. It also was hunting season back home in Oklahoma.

Even though Martin had been the star of the World Series, the Cardinals' best player during the season had been Frisch, and he was rewarded by winning the MVP award. Even though he likely deserved it more when he finished second in 1927, the honor still was meaningful to him. Frisch was nearing the end of his playing career, and he knew it. He had proved he could still run when challenged the previous September to a race against Martin and Ernie Orsatti. Frisch nipped the duo in a $75 dash across the outfield.

But Frisch celebrated the World Series triumph and his MVP award by going on an All-Star tour of Japan, then took his wife on an around-the-world trip by boat. He came home overweight and out of shape and was one of several Cardinals whose performance level fell off greatly in 1932, when the team slumped to a sixth-place finish.

Frisch became agitated when he found out some people were saying that he was not giving 100 percent and that Street had not told the press he was playing on two very sore legs.

"I'm riding the worst charley horses I've ever had," Frisch said. "We're going lousy, but I'm playing because, even hurt, I'm better than anybody Street's got. I try to let it all out only when it really counts.

"I don't want the old man's [Street] job. But I'll tell you this, if or when I manage this club or any other and I've got to use a man who's under par, I'll certainly let the press know his condition, in all fairness to the player."

Frisch, who wouldn't have to wait long to get his chance to manage, had many interests besides baseball. He liked books, plays, and classical music. He was an amateur gardener, collected pipes, and enjoyed travel. When the Cardinals again played poorly in the first part of the 1933 season, Breadon and Rickey thought Frisch was the best choice to replace Street and become the team's new manager.

Street had been a good manager and had earned the respect of his players, probably to the point that they didn't appreciate him and took advantage of him. When Street, at age 68, died in 1951, those players recalled what Street had meant to them—especially Frisch, Martin, and Dean. All said one of the keys to his success was that he was able to lighten the atmosphere in tense situations.

"Many a time in a nerve-wracking [pennant] drive he'd relieve the tension and build our spirits with stories of his career," Dean said. "He always shared the troubles of the players."

Frisch was angry that some people said he had tried to take Street's job as the team's manager.

"That's not true," Frisch said. "When they asked me to take the job, I held back. I hated to see Street go out that way and I did not think I was ready yet to become manager."

Martin said Street may have been funny off the field but was serious when it was time to be serious.

"He had a lot of funny stories but was serious when it came to baseball," Martin said. "About the only time he was humorous was on the train during trips when we had a lot of spare time. He'd sit back, smoke a pipe I bet was 100 years old, and tell stories. His favorites were about his experiences as a sergeant in World War I."

Street had earned the nickname "Gabby" while in the minor

leagues, for the obvious reasons, and he fully justified the name during his years with the Cardinals. One of his favorite stories was about the night he kicked his coach and roommate, Buzzy Wares, out of bed because of a losing streak.

"Worried over the plight of the ball club, Street was walking the floor, smoking his pipe and pondering on what to do," the *Globe-Democrat* reported. "Sound asleep in his own bed and all oblivious of Street's mental sufferings, Wares was snoring with overtones. Finally, Street could stand it no more. He kicked Wares and kicked him again, until he had him out of bed, and then asked indignantly, 'Buzzy, how can you sleep so sound and snore so loud, with conditions the way they are?'"

Much like Street, Frisch had interests outside baseball but took the game very seriously. Frisch was a disciplinarian who knew the players had been taking advantage of Street and getting away with activities that he would not allow. In his first speech as manager, he laid down the rules—no heavy drinking or gambling, be in the hotel room by midnight, and no loafing on the field. Frisch knew that was the way he played, and that was the way he wanted his players to perform as well.

"I won't apologize for having wanted my players to be as good as I was supposed to be," Frisch would later say. "If intolerance of mediocrity is a crime, I plead guilty."

Frisch, a graduate of Fordham, also knew how to praise his players when they deserved it. One thing that had alienated Street from his key players—Frisch, Martin, and Jimmie Wilson—was when he started accepting the praise and credit for the Cardinals' victories in 1930 and 1931. When those players rebelled, Street wasn't strong enough to stop it.

Rickey had become one of Frisch's biggest fans ever since the 1927 season. At the Hall of Fame in Cooperstown, New York, is a letter Rickey wrote to Frisch after that season. "I wanted you to know how deeply and genuinely I appreciate the fine effort you made," Rickey said in the letter. "I want to tell you that nothing has been more gratifying than your attitude. You are not only to be congratulated on the character of your play, but the great influence for good sportsmanship. . . . This is not simply a formal note of appreciation, but is meant to be just a little personal expression of my own high regard for you as a player and as a man."

That feeling was shared by most of his players after Frisch became the manager, with the team quickly learning that Frisch would do whatever he could to help them win a game—whether it was outsmarting the opposition, fighting with the umpires, or modifying his own players to perform at the top of their game.

Frisch didn't like to lose. He admitted he was a better manager with a better team, and he admired perfection. One night, the Cubs and the Cardinals were leaving St. Louis together on a train ride for an eastern swing after the Cardinals had swept a doubleheader, winning the second game by 11 runs. As the train headed east, Frisch strolled into the car where Charlie Grimm, the Cubs manager, was playing cards.

The meeting, as recalled later by John Carmichael of the *Chicago Daily News*, started with Grimm saying hello. Without acknowledging the greeting, Frisch said, "Did you see that [Joe] Medwick get thrown out at the plate in the fifth? Great play, that was, on his part. Couldn't slide, huh? Cost us a run that did. . . .

"Grimm threw down his cards. 'Well I'll be. . . ,' he said. 'Lost a run, did you? Tough! If he'd a scored, you'd be ahead by 12 instead of 11. Get outta here . . .' and then ran Frisch back to his own team. But after he'd gone, Grimm growled, 'I guess that's why those guys [the Cardinals] play the way they do.'"

Frisch's clubhouse meetings were classics. One day before a game, he was running down the opponent's batting order when Martin interrupted him with a question.

"Frank," Martin said. "I can't decide whether to paint my midget auto yellow or red, what do you think?" People three blocks away could hear Frisch's reply.

Martin was one of the most fun-loving Cardinals, and it was

just a question of when he wanted to have fun that bothered Frisch. If it was away from the ball park, it was fine with him, such as the occasion in Philadelphia when the two men and some other Cardinals were leaving their hotel for dinner.

"As we stepped onto the street, a Rolls-Royce dream boat stopped in front of us, a snooty chauffeur got out and waved us aside like peasants, and escorted his lordship into the lobby," Frisch recalled.

"Our boys didn't relish the treatment. Two of them lifted the hood, and when that fine-feathered chauffeur got into his car, he sailed right out and high-balled down the street. One of our boys just happened to have a string of firecrackers in his pocket, and the noise and smoke was something terrific when they exploded under the hood."

Frisch's biggest challenge as a manager was controlling his players—especially Martin and a rookie pitcher who had finally stuck in the major leagues in 1932, Dizzy Dean.

Martin, even though his performance fell off in the 1932 season, was still a character off the field. One year he arrived for spring training driving an old car, with two bird dogs and a shotgun in it. While driving to Florida, he had stopped at a small hotel, where he walked up to the front desk in his overalls, carrying the gun, and signed the register as "Pretty Boy Floyd." It was a matter of minutes before the town's sheriff led an armed posse to Martin's door, where he shook his fist under Martin's nose when he learned his true identity.

Nobody was safe when it came time for one of Martin's pranks. One day in Boston, as Frisch was walking outside the team hotel, something exploded at his feet. Suspecting Martin immediately, Frisch charged up to Martin's room.

"When I saw the grin and the sparkle in his eyes, I knew I had my man," Frisch said. "Pepper said, 'Frank, that was a slip, honest to John it was, and if you'll just forgive me this once, I'll go out tomorrow and hit a home run and win a ball game for you.' And that's exactly what Pepper did."

Another time, a bandage on Martin's right thumb came off

as he fielded a hot smash and threw to first. Blood squirted out, and Frisch inquired as to how Martin had been injured.

"Well," Martin began, "I was sitting in my hotel room last night and I saw some ol' gals walking their dogs down below, so I figured I'd have some fun. I got a pitcher and filled it with water and . . ."

Frisch broke in. "The thumb, how did you cut it?"

"I was getting to that Frank," Martin said. "I hit the pitcher against the windowsill and it broke and cut my thumb."

Later, Frisch would laugh when he recalled some of Martin's more particularly outrageous activities.

"Never was a man like him anywhere," Frisch said. "When I want to feel happy I think of him. He used to sit on the bench, legs crossed, and you could see his shoes. Spikes all worn off and the sole cracked all the way across. But buy a new pair? Not him. He'd save up for a midget auto or a mouth organ instead. Then he'd get out in the field and his feet would start hurting and he'd hold up the game to rest his 'cramps.' What a guy."

It was players such as Martin—who gave an all-out effort all the time, playing the way Frisch played—who earned Frisch's praise and affection. He had no room for players who didn't give their best effort all the time.

"A man is up to bat four times a day as a rule," Frisch said. "He's out there from 2 to 5. Why can't he hustle? Why won't he run out everything? Why doesn't he want to give his best? The fans don't like to see a guy joggin' down to first and maybe carrying his bat with him. That looks lousy. I got a man on my club right now who could be a standout . . . a great player . . . the darling of the fans . . . but he won't bear down. He just goes through the motions."

Frisch had other challenges as the manager besides controlling his star players. The Cardinals' talented young shortstop, Charley Gelbert, had shot himself accidentally while on a hunting trip prior to the 1933 season. Frisch also had seen the team trade Jim Bottomley and Chick Hafey. But they had good players coming up to take their place, Ripper Collins and Joe Medwick. Another piece of the puzzle in quickly rebuilding the Cardinals into a contending club came when Rickey was able to acquire a shortstop from Cincinnati—Leo Durocher.

Reporters covering the Cardinals didn't know what was going on when they were summoned to Rickey's hotel room before breakfast. What they found was Rickey, clad in his pajamas, propped up in bed, where he had spent the night on the telephone. In between bites of his ham and eggs and before gnawing on a fresh cigar, he broke the news that he had traded Paul Derringer for Durocher.

At 27, Durocher was a good defensive shortstop, and his acquisition would allow Frisch to move back to second base after he had tried to fill in for Gelbert at shortstop.

Durocher was not happy about the deal. He had been with the Reds for three-plus seasons, and when he reported to the Cardinals, he burst into Rickey's hotel room and blurted out a flurry of insults about the Cardinals organization. Rickey relaxed in his bed and listened until Durocher was through. Rickey said that while some of what Durocher said might in fact be true, he also had heard some things about Durocher as well. He said that hadn't persuaded him not to make the deal, and leaning over and pointing his cigar at Durocher, said, "I made this trade because I think we can win a lot of pennants with you at shortstop. You can do it for us, you can be the spark. You can help us win pennants."

Rickey continued. "However, we have a shortstop who will play this afternoon's doubleheader if you don't choose to. If we lose, though, how will you feel at the end of the season if we lose the pennant by two games?"

That put Durocher in his place. He played that afternoon and became the shortstop Rickey knew he could be.

It wasn't known to some of the players at the time, but Durocher was a major force behind some of the pranks of the Gashouse Gang members and was an especially skilled double-crosser. He would often set up the pranks and then, while they were being played out, bring in the authorities to find out what all the fuss was about.

Durocher, who would later serve with Rickey in Brooklyn with the Dodgers, learned to admire Rickey, beginning with the moment he burst into his hotel room.

"You can acquire more knowledge from Rickey than from anyone in baseball," Durocher said. "He can talk about any phase of the game for hours at a stretch. Then he can show you how to do anything—throw a ball, field, bat, pitch, slide. He can tell in a moment how smart you are, and he's never wrong. Sometimes you'll get lost talking to him, all those long words, you won't know what half of them mean. But he'll send you scurrying to the dictionary. I remember he said something to me once about tranquility. I looked it up and it set me to thinking. Why, if you absorb only half of what Mr. Rickey says, you'll come out ahead."

While Durocher and Rickey learned to get along, with Durocher eventually being named captain of the Cardinals, there quickly developed a strained relationship between Durocher and Frisch. The two men started to have increasing differences on the field and often wouldn't talk to each other for weeks at a time. It got to the point where Rickey finally had to trade Durocher to the Dodgers in 1937 to placate Frisch.

Frisch didn't have that trouble with all his players. One who knew when to play and when to be serious, Frisch's type of guy was the versatile Collins, who played outfield and also replaced Bottomley as the first baseman in 1932.

Like Durocher, he was a key member of the pranks pulled off by his teammates even though he may not have received all the attention.

"Rickey always accused me of being the ringleader," Collins said. "I never could understand why he picked on me—unless it could have been because there was considerable truth in his allegations. Yet I'll wager that no ball club ever got more fun out of playing than we did. It wasn't that we broke training, because we didn't. It was merely anything for a laugh."

By the 1933 season, the Gashouse Gang was coming together, even though they were not called by that term until the next year. The writer generally credited with creating the name was Frank Graham of the *New York Sun*, who reportedly overheard a conversation at the Polo Grounds one day between Dizzy Dean and Durocher.

The Cardinals were in sixth place at the time, and Dean, always contemptuous of the American League, said, "I don't know whether we can win in this league, but if we was in the other league we could win."

Durocher, his uniform already soiled and a bulging chew of tobacco in his mouth, recalled the immaculate appearance of the Yankees and said, "They wouldn't let us in the other league. They would say we are a lot of gashouse ballplayers."

Graham quoted Durocher in the next day's newspaper; the term spread to St. Louis reporters and was quickly picked up as an appropriate name for the Cardinals.

The Cardinals finished the 1933 season in fifth place but were just nine and a half games out of first. The biggest moment to come out of the season was the first All-Star Game, in which the Cardinals had four starters—Martin, Frisch, Jimmie Wilson, and Bill Hallahan. Frisch hit the first home run in All-Star Game history, although it didn't help the National League, which lost the game 4–2.

A rookie outfielder came up from the minor leagues and had a big season. Joe Medwick hit .306 with 18 homers and 98 RBIs, giving an indication of things to come in future seasons.

When the 1934 season began, nobody was ready for a bigger year than Dizzy Dean.

Dean earned his nickname before he ever got to the Cardinals. Most of the stories of Dean's legendary feats started in the cotton fields in the South, where he lived and worked until he joined the Army. While Dean was in the Army pitching in an exhibition game against Chicago, White Sox manager Lena Blackburne saw him retire hitter after hitter and finally got frustrated enough that he yelled out at his team, "Don't let that dizzy rookie fool ya." The name stuck, primarily because of Dean's zany behavior on and off the field and his colloquial speech.

After Dean had made his Cardinals debut in the final game of the 1930 season, many people thought he would be with the team at the start of the 1931 season. But Dean was still living by his own rules, and when he overslept and missed practice one morning in spring training, Street told him he was sending him back to the minors. Dean talked himself into another chance but was in and out of Street's doghouse throughout spring training, finally losing in his attempt to stay in the majors.

Dean had other problems that spring, most of them financial. He had developed a knack in the minor leagues for spending more money than he was making, leaving IOUs all over town that eventually found their way to the Cardinals business office, which took care of them. One time when he was pitching in St. Joseph, Missouri, Dean had rooms booked at three hotels at the same time so he could stay wherever it was most convenient. That spring in Bradenton, Florida, Dean had continued his way of spending. He left signed chits all across towns, at the café, the druggist, and other stores, not only for himself, but for friends who happened to be with him. Finally, Clarence Lloyd, the Cardinals secretary, had more than he could take. He sent notices to all the Bradenton merchants that Dean's IOUs were not to be accepted. He also put Dean on a budget—one dollar a day, cash. No more, no less.

Dean was heartbroken when the Cardinals sent him back to Houston, but it likely was the best thing that ever happened to him. He met his wife, Patricia Nash, and she quickly became his stabilizing influence, especially in financial matters. Dean won 26 games, and when he came up to the Cardinals to start the 1932 season, he was in the majors to stay.

The son of a sharecropper, Dean didn't have an entire pair

of shoes until he joined the Army. He worked long, grueling hours picking cotton for 50 cents a day, so when he finally reached the major leagues and had money to spare, he was determined to enjoy himself. And he did.

Dean became a sensation around baseball, not only for his pitching ability, but for his homespun humor and spirit. Jack Newcombe, in a *Sport* magazine article in 1959, said part of Dean's legacy simply was a matter of timing.

"He was fortunate enough to come to the game when men showed an earthy zest for playing baseball for a living," Newcombe wrote. "Ballplayers were less cultured then, less controlled, and far more colorful. Winning games was serious business, but there was some freewheeling fun to be had, too.

"Born 20 years later, Dean might have been even more successful as a pitcher but he would have been far less a character. He would have made a lot more money, but he would have had a lot less fun doing it."

Dean himself noted that the game of baseball was changing, and he knew he had been in the right place at the right time.

"As far as color goes and things like that, they just don't do things as far as gags," Dean said in an interview after he retired. "We'd do anything. We'd give a kid from the bushes a key and tell him to open the pitcher's box. And we'd start a rhubarb just by walking down the line and saying something. If it rained, we'd put up an umbrella to show the umpire. Now you can't even open your mouth to the umpires. You never read anything in the paper about ballplayers having fun. You see the same thing in the paper every day. Baseball is strictly a business."

Make no mistake, it was a business to Dean, too. But he also knew how to have fun—like the time he and several teammates interrupted a luncheon at a hotel ballroom in Philadelphia, wearing overalls and carrying some carpenters equipment they had picked up in a pawn shop. They upended an empty table, then began shouting and pointing at each other, taking measurements, and pounding and disrupting the banquet in progress. The luncheon speaker stopped talking, and everyone turned to the bedlam in the corner.

"We're redecorating," said Ripper Collins. "But you go right ahead. You're not bothering us one bit."

The gag collapsed a couple of minutes later when one of the guests recognized Dean. There was a burst of applause from the crowd, and Dean was directed to the head table and asked to speak to the group.

Dean oftentimes would get himself in trouble, then be able to pitch his way out of it. Fined $100 by Street for missing an exhibition game—Dean claimed he fell asleep in the wrong train car—he got Street to rescind the fine by pitching a shutout against Brooklyn. Another time, Dean wandered into the Dodgers clubhouse the day he was supposed to pitch. Manager Max Carey was going over the Cardinals hitters. Dean sat down to listen, and when Carey was through, he turned to Dean and asked if he was right in how to pitch to the Cardinals hitters. Dean said yes, then proceeded to tell the Dodgers exactly how he was going to pitch to them that afternoon. When he was through, he got up, grabbed his glove, and said, "I've told you how I was going to pitch. Come on out now and see if you can hit." Dean then registered another shutout.

Dean would usually pitch to a hitter's strength, just to prove to himself and to the hitter that he was a better pitcher than the batter was a hitter. In one game at Boston, he and the catcher worked a game without signs, and all Dean threw were fastballs. He won easily.

In his biography of Dean, Curt Smith noted that what Dean possessed, and what made him such a star, was God-given ability combined with a God-given spirit that made him someone to whom common people could relate.

"More so than Ruth, or Stengel, or Gehrig, Dizzy Dean was pure Americana," Smith wrote. "That was the essence of his appeal. He spoke of an earlier era; his bearing was of a simpler, less abrasive age. To be sure, Dean could be insufferably vain. 'I may not have been the greatest pitcher ever, but I was amongst 'em,' he was fond of saying. Part egotist, part gambler, with the gall of a brass monkey thrown in, Dizzy Dean was a man of many dimensions—and all were overshadowed by the folksy, down-home charm which made Diz a long-running hit with middle America."

An example: Dean was riding in a car with a New York writer one day when they pulled into a corner gas station. Dean looked at the pump for several moments and finally said, "That's always puzzled me. I don't see how they do it."

The writer, baffled by Dean's comment, asked him what he meant.

"It puzzles me how they know what corners are good for filling stations," Dean said. "Just how did these fellows know there was gas and oil under here?"

As innocent as Dean was about many phases of society, he definitely knew what to do with a baseball. He won 18 games in his rookie season of 1932, had an ERA of 3.30, and led the league in strikeouts and innings pitched. In 1933 he won 20 games for the first time. On July 30, pitching against the Cubs, he set the then major-league record by striking out 17 batters. The last out came when Jim Mosolf was batting for the Cubs. With two strikes, he took a pitch, and umpire Bill Klem called it a ball. Mosolf had had enough, however, and walked away from the plate, telling Klem, "It was a strike, Bill."

Dean's greatest rival over the years was Carl Hubbell of the Giants. There were classic duels each time the two squared off, which was whenever possible because the owners of both teams knew the gate appeal the matchup would have for the fans. One time, pitching against the Giants, Dean fulfilled a promise he had made to some kids in a hospital—to strike out Bill Terry with the bases loaded. With runners on first and second and two outs in the ninth, Dean walked a batter just so Terry could come up to bat. He walked in from the mound and told Terry, "I hate to do this, Bill, but I done promised a bunch of kids I'd fan you with the bases loaded." And he did, on three pitches.

When Dean and three other players were caught out after curfew by Frisch, Dean was fined $400 and the other players $200 each. Dean complained, but Frisch told him, "Why Diz, you're not the same as those guys. You're the great Dizzy Dean. Everything about you has got to be bigger and better than anybody else. And that goes for fines, too." Dean couldn't argue.

If Frisch thought just having one Dean around was tough, he didn't know what was in store for him in 1934—the year the Cardinals promoted Dean's brother Paul to the major-league team. But Frisch and the rest of the baseball world quickly found out.

Dean was excited that his brother had finally reached the major leagues. Even though the two had similar pitching styles, their personalities couldn't have been more different. While Dizzy quickly boasted that he and Paul, two and a half years younger, would combine to win 45 games, Paul was quiet and reserved.

In his article on Dean in *Sport* magazine in October 1959, Jack Newcombe described the impact the Dean brothers had on the Cardinals in 1934, when Dizzy and Paul made sure Dizzy's prediction came true by combining to win 49 games—Dizzy 30 and Paul 19.

"The summer of '34 was the Deans' to gloat, boast, clown and laugh," Newcombe wrote. "They were nearly invincible on the pitching mound. Dizzy might have won 10 more games if he had been serious enough about it. Off the field, Paul usually went Dizzy's way, which was not always the way the Cardinals were going at the moment."

The year was not without incident, of course, as anyone who had chronicled Dean's career to that point would have suspected. The biggest disturbance came on August 12, when the Dean brothers lost a doubleheader to the Cubs. They then failed to show up at the St. Louis train station where the team was leaving for an exhibition game in Detroit.

While Dizzy was relaxing and eating dinner at a friend's

house, an angry Frisch announced that the brothers were being suspended and fined. It appeared the dispute could cost
the Cardinals any chance they had of winning the pennant. It
was mid-August, and the team already trailed the Giants by
six games.

Dean tried to talk Frisch into reinstating him and his
brother, but the Cardinals proceeded to win seven of their next
eight games without the Deans. Finally, Frisch agreed to rein-
state them, but the fines—$100 for Dizzy and $50 for
Paul—stood. Dizzy and Paul said they still wouldn't play.
Dizzy was so enraged he ripped up his home uniform. When
photographers appeared in the clubhouse, he ripped up his
road uniform just for their benefit.

It took the intervention of Judge Landis to finally settle the
dispute. He ruled the fines were appropriate and had to be
paid by the Deans. Dizzy was out $486—the $100 fine, $350
for the seven days of wages, and $36 for ripping up the two
uniforms. Paul was fined $100.

While the incident cooled relations between the Deans and
Frisch, it didn't affect the team's drive for the pennant.

Dean was not about to back down from his manager. Typical of Dean's behavior was what occurred on September 21 in
Brooklyn, when he and Paul were scheduled to pitch a doubleheader against the Dodgers as the Cardinals still were in fran-
tic pursuit of the Giants. At the daily clubhouse meeting
before the first game, Frisch was trying to go over the hitters
and tell the pitchers how to work the Brooklyn hitters. When
he got to Sam Leslie, whom Frisch said to pitch high and outside, Dizzy interrupted.

"That ain't the way I pitch to him," Dean said. "I give nothing but low, inside stuff. And he ain't got a loud foul off me
yet."

The next hitter on Frisch's list was Tony Cuccinello. He
noted that he was a dead fastball hitter and instructed his
pitchers to throw him nothing but curveballs.

"That's mighty funny," Dean said, interrupting again. "I ain't never bothered to dish him up a curve yet, and he ain't never even beat out a bunt on me."

Frisch continued, but not without more challenges from Dean, who said he pitched every hitter differently than Frisch was suggesting. "Frank," Dean said finally, "this really is a silly business. I win 26 games already this season and it don't look exactly right for you, an ordinary infielder, to be telling a star like me how to pitch."

Frisch exploded, ending the meeting and telling Dean to pitch however he wanted to and he didn't care if he got hammered.

Dean carried a no-hitter into the eighth inning and was just four outs away when it was broken up. Dean likely was telling the truth later when he said he wasn't aware he was working on a no-hitter.

He was watching, however, as his brother pitched the second game and did complete the no-hit game.

"Shucks, Paul, why didn't you tell me you was gonna do that," Dean said afterward. "I'd have pitched one, too, and that would have been something."

In between games, Dean had visited the Dodgers clubhouse, where manager Casey Stengel wanted to know if there were any more Deans at home. Dizzy said yes, they had a brother, Elmer, who was at Houston and was burning up the Texas League. Stengel was so excited he informed reporters the Dodgers were going to try to sign the third Dean brother. But when he made inquiries, he found out Elmer was burning up the league as a peanut vendor.

Dean was also not afraid to stand up to opponents. On another day, he happened to wander into the Giants clubhouse before a game in New York when manager Bill Terry was going over how to pitch to the Cardinals' lineup.

Terry asked Dean to leave, but Dean said to go ahead, he already knew all the St. Louis hitters' weaknesses.

Another sign of Dean's cockiness came a couple of years

later in a game in Boston against the Braves. One devoted Cardinals fan, Johnny Perkins, had accompanied the team to the series in Boston, and Dean and Perkins ended up arranging a bet that Dean could not strike out Vince DiMaggio four times in the same game.

The first three times up, DiMaggio struck out. On his fourth at bat, the Cardinals were leading 2–1 with a runner on second. Dean quickly got two strikes when DiMaggio hit a foul popup behind the plate. As catcher Brusie Ogrodowski circled under the ball, Dean came racing in from the mound. "Drop it, drop it," Dean yelled. "If you want to catch me again, drop it." The young catcher did.

Frisch was so upset that as he attempted to leap from the dugout to find out what Dean was doing, he hit his head on the roof. Only after Dean fired the next pitch past DiMaggio for the fourth strikeout did Frisch find out about Dean's 25-cent bet.

Dean had already picked up his 20th victory of the 1934 season, on August 7 over Cincinnati, before his dispute with Frisch. He would go on to win 30, including his last four wins in the final nine days of the season, but even now there is some controversy about whether Dean should have been credited with all 30 victories. Dean was awarded victories in two games that under more modern scoring rules would have been credited to other pitchers. On June 23, he was awarded the victory for "effective relief work" in a 5–4 win over Brooklyn. The win had originally been credited to Bill Hallahan. On June 27, Dean was awarded the victory in an 8–7 win over New York even though he left the game when the score was tied.

In a *New York Times* article in 1968, Leonard Koppett said that the scorers were following the rules of the day, which were basically none. The modern-day rules about crediting wins to pitchers came into existence in 1950.

Despite all their antics off the field and bragging about how good they were on it, the Cardinals didn't actually move into first place until the last week of the season, thanks in large part to Dean's four wins in the season's last nine days. The Cardinals' efforts were also aided by the Giants, who were ahead by seven games on Labor Day before they collapsed.

When Dean wasn't pitching, he was carrying on some prank, usually with Pepper Martin. On hot July days, with the temperature more than 100 degrees Fahrenheit, the two would build a fire in front of the dugout. Armed with blankets, they would mock the sun by sitting Indian-style in front of the fire. On other occasions, the two would throw bags of water out hotel windows onto the sidewalk below, narrowly missing people walking by. In hotel lobbys, Martin would hide sneezing powder in some newspapers, then walk in front of a fan. Other times, each would fill his mouth with popcorn before entering the hotel lobby, then get into a staged fight. Each would spit out the popcorn kernels, which looked suspiciously like teeth.

Dean was not about to change his behavior just because the Cardinals' pennant had put them in the World Series against the Detroit Tigers.

Dean and his teammates showed up at Navin Field in Detroit for a workout the day before the series was to open. The Tigers already were on the field, taking batting practice, when Dean, still wearing his street clothes, walked up and took the bat away from Hank Greenberg, the Tigers' future Hall of Famer. Dean proceeded to hit a shot into the left-field bleachers, showing Greenberg how it was supposed to be done.

The next morning, before the opening game, the Dean brothers were invited to have breakfast with automobile pioneer Henry Ford, whose company was sponsoring the Series broadcasts on radio. Accompanying the Deans to Ford's house outside Detroit were Will Rogers, a friend of Dean's, and Ray Gillespie, a young St. Louis writer.

While in the car on the trip to Dearborn, Rogers was instructing Dean on how to greet Ford. He informed Dean that he needed to be formal and polite, saying when he introduced them, "Mr. Ford, I would like you to meet Dizzy Dean and his brother Paul." Ford responded, just as politely, "How are you, Mr. Dean?" as they shook hands.

Everything Rogers had told Dean in the car was quickly forgotten. Dean pumped Ford's hand, saying, "Put 'er there, Henry. I'm sure glad to be here 'cause I heard so much about you, but I'm sorry I'm a-gonna have to make pussycats out of your Tigers."

When he got back to the ball park, Dean was true to his word. He beat the Tigers in the opener, 8–3. Frisch selected Bill Hallahan to pitch the second game over Paul Dean, thinking the younger Dean would be more effective in the third game in the friendly atmosphere of Sportsman's Park. Hallahan pitched well, carrying a 2–1 lead into the ninth. But the Tigers tied the game and then won it 3–2 in the 12th.

The series then shifted back to St. Louis, and as Frisch had expected, Paul Dean pitched effectively at home, winning 4–1. The Tigers came back to rout the Cardinals 10–4 in Game 4, evening the series at two games each, but the biggest play came when Dizzy Dean was sent in to pinch-run for catcher Spud Davis.

Martin hit a slow roller to Detroit second baseman Charlie Gehringer, who flipped it to shortstop Billy Rogell, who tagged second to force Dean. Dean did not slide, however, and Rogell's throw to first in an attempt for a double play hit Dean on the head. Dean had to be carried off the field on a stretcher and was taken to the hospital for X rays. Afterward, reporters crowded around Paul to find out about his brother.

"Diz wasn't hurt bad," Paul said. "All he was doing was talking, just talking."

One reporter asked what Dean had said. "He wasn't saying anything," Paul said. "He was just talking."

The famous headline in the newspaper the next morning could have carried a double meaning: X RAYS OF DEAN'S HEAD SHOW NOTHING.

The incident didn't prevent Dean from getting the ball to

pitch the fifth game. But Dean lost to Tommy Bridges, 3–1, putting the Tigers ahead 3–2 with the series returning to Detroit. It was up to Paul Dean to keep the series alive in the sixth game, and he did, beating Schoolboy Rowe, 4–3, and even got the game-winning hit in the seventh inning to drive in Durocher.

Using a little psychology, Frisch said after the game he wasn't sure whether Dizzy Dean or Hallahan would start the decisive seventh game. Frisch hinted to several writers that he was leaning toward starting Hallahan, a World Series veteran who had been rested since the second game, while Dean would be pitching on one day's rest. Frisch then waited for the news to get back to Dean—and for Dean's reaction.

Dean found Frisch in the showers.

"You wouldn't dare pitch any of those bums tomorrow, not after I've brought you this far already," Dean yelled. "You won't need any runs tomorrow, I'll shut them out. You know, I ain't failed you yet."

Dizzy pledged to Frisch that he would get plenty of rest, and Frisch conceded. Dean would start the seventh game.

The date was October 9, and the festivities began innocently enough. Dean was on the field before the game, posing for pictures with Rogers. Dean joked with Tigers manager Mickey Cochrane and with Eldon Auker, Cochrane's choice to be his starting pitcher. The game was scoreless until the third inning, when Dean came up with one out and hit an apparent single to left. But Dean ignored the stop sign of coach Buzzy Wares and took off for second, where he eluded Gehringer's tag and was safe with a double. Martin beat out a grounder to first and stole second, and after Jack Rothrock was intentionally walked, Frisch came through with a bases-clearing double that put the Cardinals up 3–0.

The Cardinals went on to score seven runs in the inning, and the rout was on. The excitement hardly was over, however. In fact, it was just beginning.

In the sixth inning, with the Cardinals leading 7–0, Medwick hit a shot off the wall in right center to drive in Martin. Medwick slid hard into third base, and his spikes went hard into third baseman Marv Owen.

The two went down in a heap in the dirt and exchanged some angry words, but order was restored, and when the inning ended, Medwick picked up his glove and went out to his position in left field.

The fans in the stands, no doubt angered by the lopsided score and the thought that the Cardinals were embarrassing their Tigers, let Medwick have it, first with boos, then with anything they could find to throw onto the field—bottles, oranges, apples, bananas, tomatoes, rolled-up newspapers, and various other kinds of garbage. Medwick was amused at first and used the apples to play catch with Ernie Orsatti in center and Martin at third. Attendants had to clear the field three times, and after about 10 minutes, Durocher came out to talk to Medwick.

"Don't worry kid, they can't hurt you," Durocher said. Medwick replied, "Leo, we're leading 9–0, why don't you stay out here and play left field and I'll go into shortstop?" Durocher didn't say anything but turned and went back to his position.

When the disturbance showed no signs of abating, Commissioner Landis summoned Medwick, Owen, and the two managers to his box. He asked Medwick if he had tried to spike Owen, and Medwick said no, he had just slid in hard like he always did. The commissioner then issued his ruling and ordered Medwick out of the game.

"I've often wondered what he would have done if the score had been 0–0," Medwick would say years later. "We'll never know, but I wonder."

Even though Landis's ruling had no bearing on the outcome of the game, it did deprive Medwick of a chance at setting the record for most hits in a World Series. He had 11, one shy of the mark, with at least one more at bat to come.

The Cardinals added two more runs in the seventh after Medwick was ejected, and they finished with an 11–0 victory.

Medwick didn't even get to join his teammates in the postgame celebration. He was confined to his hotel room with
seven bodyguards from the Detroit police force.

Dean celebrated by donning a pith helmet and playfully
holding a rubber tiger doll. He chewed the tiger's tail, twisted
its head, and mangled its tail. When the celebration reached
St. Louis the next day, in a rally at Union Station before the
parade through the city, Dean pointed to the tiger's tail, which
contained four knots, one for each of the Tigers' losses. Holding the tiger aloft, Dean choked it by the throat, to the roars
of the crowd.

In his biography of Dean, Curt Smith noted what winning
the World Series meant for Dean:

> "For Dizzy Dean, the series of 1934 was a God-sent
> prize; he became the nation's predominant sports figure,
> willing to be merchandized, able to command almost any
> wage," Smith wrote. "During the next five months Ol' Diz
> earned more than $40,000 for endorsements, personal ap-
> pearances, and banquet speeches; memories of Dean's
> barren background were fleetingly shunted aside. Poverty
> was out, the gold rush on. A flood of Dean-related prod-
> ucts was unfurled. Consumers could buy a Dizzy Dean
> candy bar, Dizzy Dean overalls, a Dizzy Dean shirt and
> Dizzy Dean watch. His name was imprinted on fielders
> gloves, on baseball shoes, on uniforms and hats. Dizzy
> and Paul received $5,000, a higher fee than even Ruth had
> gained, for a one-week vaudeville stint at the Roxy The-
> ater in New York."

It was almost anticlimactic weeks later when Dean was
named the National League's Most Valuable Player.

Of course, the Dean brothers were not the only ones who
had played key roles in helping the Cardinals win the pennant
and the World Series. Leading the offense was first baseman
Ripper Collins, who tied Mel Ott for the league lead in homers

with 35 and was second in the league in RBIs with 128, while hitting .333. Four other regulars also finished the year with a .300 average or higher; Frisch, center-fielder Ernie Orsatti, catcher Spud Davis, and Medwick, who hit .319 with 18 homers and 106 RBIs in just his second full major-league season.

Nobody was more pleased with the Cardinals' success than Breadon, but that success presented him with a challenging situation. Lew Wentz, an oil millionaire from Oklahoma, was interested in buying the Cardinals from Breadon. Breadon remembered his boyhood vow never to be poor again and knew if he sold the club, he wouldn't have to worry about that ever happening. Negotiations reached the point where the two sides had agreed upon a price for the Cardinals ball club but broke down over what Breadon thought his farm club affiliations were worth. In the late 1930s the Cardinals had 39 different farm teams in various leagues.

Finally, a deadline imposed by Breadon for reaching an agreement passed, and he retained ownership of the Cardinals.

With virtually the same team returning in 1935, Breadon, Rickey, and Frisch thought the Cardinals could be headed for another big season. They were right, as the team won 96 games, one more than in the previous year. It wasn't enough to beat the Cubs, however, who used a 21-game winning streak in September to knock off the Cardinals, who had held a two-and-one-half game lead on Labor Day. While the Dean brothers combined to win another 47 games (28 by Dizzy, 19 by Paul), the offense was led once again by Medwick, who improved his average to .353, his home run total to 23 and his RBI total to 126.

Much of Medwick's success was a result of his scrappy and fighting nature. He never backed down to anyone, including his own teammates. Oddly, he was a terrific bad-ball hitter, which frustrated pitchers trying to figure out a way to pitch to him. At times, however, Medwick's fielding in left field could best be described as indifferent. One day in Pittsburgh, with Dizzy Dean on the mound, a fly ball that Dean thought should have been caught dropped inside the foul line. Three runs scored, and when Dean got to the dugout at the end of the inning, he griped to brother Paul, who quickly joined in loudly enough to get Medwick's attention.

As the Dean brothers walked down the dugout toward him, Medwick picked up a bat and told them to keep coming, he would separate them. Cooler heads prevailed, and an inning later, Medwick delivered a grand slam. Walking into the dugout, he went first to the water cooler and filled his mouth with water. He then walked over to the spot where Dizzy was sitting. Medwick spit the water on Dean's shoes and said, "All right, you big meathead, there's your three runs back and one extra. Let's see you hold the damned lead."

It didn't take long for Frisch to be amazed at Medwick's performance, which included winning the Triple Crown in 1937—when he hit .374 with 31 homers and 154 RBIs.

"I just wonder what he would have hit if he didn't go for those bad pitches," Frisch said. After thinking for a moment, he added, "He might not have hit as well as he did, you know."

Medwick earned the nickname "Ducky" while playing in Houston—where he briefly roomed with Dean—in the minor leagues when a female fan commented that he walked like a duck. He preferred the nickname "Muscles," but not many people called him that.

Medwick should have learned all he needed to know about Dean while they were in the minors and the team went on its first road trip. For the 16-day trip, Dean brought with him a large traveling bag, but as the two checked into a hotel in Dallas, Medwick noticed that the only thing Dean carried inside the bag was a carton of cigarettes.

"What are you going to do for clothes?" Medwick asked Dean.

Dean replied, "Huh, busher. Why do you suppose I picked you as a roomie? You wear the same size as me." By the time the team hit the next stop on its trip, Medwick had a new roommate.

Medwick also was involved, although indirectly, in one of the funniest events of Frisch's career. In a game against the Giants at the Polo Grounds, Don Padgett was on first when Medwick singled to right. Frisch was coaching third. Padgett took off on Medwick's hit and was headed for third, and it appeared the play was going to be close. Frisch was wildly waving the runner on, then signaling for him to slide. Finally, Frisch got so caught up in the play that he forgot he was the coach. He took two quick steps toward the bag, then flung himself toward the bag. Padgett, sliding in at the same time, was out. Frisch had made a beautiful hook slide, reaching the base before the throw, but to no avail.

The 1935 and 1936 seasons were notable, if for no other reason, than for the debut of two Cardinals greats, Terry Moore and Johnny Mize. Moore, still viewed as one of the greatest defensive center-fielders in history, took over for Orsatti in 1935 and Mize, who would develop into one of the game's best home-run hitters, took over first base from Ripper Collins in 1936.

Unfortunately, neither player's addition could help the Cardinals to more than a second-place finish. The 1935 club's chances were derailed, not only by Chicago's record winning streak, but also by a broken leg suffered by Moore in September. In 1936, very few things went right for the Cardinals, but they still managed to tie Chicago for second place behind the Giants.

When the careers of Paul Dean and catcher Bill DeLancey should have just been entering their peak years, both were over. Dean was a spring training holdout, then tried to get in shape too quickly and hurt his arm. He won only five games, and even though he hung on for a few more years, he never was the same pitcher again.

DeLancey was struck down by tuberculosis. He sat out the 1936 through 1939 seasons, then returned to play just 15 games in 1940. He died in 1946 on his 45th birthday.

The Cardinals also were witnessing the end of the great

playing career of Frisch, who took himself out of the lineup in 1937, never to return. The Gashouse Gang was running out of gas.

In a game in Philadelphia, Frisch was in the lineup and was at second base, with Moore on first, when Medwick lined a shot into the right-field corner. By the time Frisch reached third, Moore had already rounded second and was headed his way. Third-base coach Mike Gonzalez, in his broken English, tried to send Frisch to the plate and tell him Moore was in hot pursuit.

Just as Frisch slid into the plate, Moore slid in under him, Frisch was embarrassed, and when he got to the dugout said, "Anytime they can run down the Flash, it's time to quit. You, [Jimmy] Brown, go to second base."

Frisch never played in the field again, and it was considerably later in the season when he did bat again. Looking for a pinchhitter, he was spurred to bat by a heckler in the stands at Sportsman's Park with the bases loaded, two outs in the ninth, and the Cardinals losing by a run.

"Why don't you hit, Grandma?" the heckler yelled at Frisch.

That was all the inspiration Frisch needed. He went up to the plate and hit the first pitch thrown to him by Braves reliever Jim Turner for a two-run single, winning the game for the Cardinals. That would have been an appropriate way to end his playing career, but Frisch tried to repeat the magic the next day, grounding into a double play in his final at bat in the major leagues.

Just as the playing career of Frisch was over, so too was the career of Dizzy Dean coming to an end. After winning 24 games in 1936, Dean's win total fell off to 13 in 1937 and worse, he suffered a broken toe when he was struck on the foot by a line drive hit by Earl Averill in the All-Star Game in Washington, D.C.

"Your big toe is fractured," a doctor told Dean.

"No it isn't," Dean replied. "It's broke."

Dean, citing his disdain for exhibition games, had wanted

to refuse the trip to the All-Star Game but was talked into going by Breadon and his wife, Pat. After he was hurt, he tried to come back too soon, against the advice of Dr. Hyland, because the Cardinals were in the pennant race. He altered his pitching motion because of his injury, and that hurt his arm. In the spring of 1938, the Cardinals traded Dean to the Cubs for pitchers Clyde Shoun and Curt Davis and $185,000.

Even though Dean was hurt, Rickey was not trying to pull anything over on the Cubs. Rickey told Phil Wrigley that Dean, still only 27, did in fact have a sore arm. Wrigley wanted him anyhow and likely felt the price was worth it when Dean won seven games and helped the Cubs reach the World Series. Dean would win just nine more games in his career.

The next star to go was Durocher, traded to the Dodgers after the 1937 season. Frisch lasted as manager until September 1938, when Rickey finally decided he had to make a change. Gonzalez, the coach, took over for the rest of the season and former Cardinals outfielder Ray Blades returned to take over the managing duties in 1939.

But while the late 1930s marked the end of many great Cardinal careers, it also marked the beginning of the Moore and Mize years and saw some of the greatest performances in baseball history from Medwick.

It was during Medwick's great 1937 season that Leo Ward, the Cardinals' traveling secretary, noticed that only Medwick and Pepper Martin carried trunks on the road. Medwick's ample wardrobe was evidence as to why he needed the trunk, but Ward wondered what Martin needed his trunk for, knowing that Martin would many times start and end a trip with the same suit and sometimes even the same shirt. Ward went to Martin one day and asked him about the trunk. Martin opened it, revealing an electric motor and other parts for his farm equipment back in Oklahoma.

Perhaps it was putting up with players such as Martin that gave Frisch his appetite. Martin Haley of the *Globe-Democrat* wrote in a 1932 story that Frisch did not have many faults, but one of them was that he liked to eat, and it didn't make any difference what time of day or night it was.

"Like everything else that is a little out of the ordinary," Frisch told Haley, "my eating has been exaggerated. I do love to eat, no doubt about it, but during the season I usually eat only two regular meals a day, one at 10:30 in the morning and another at 7 at night. Sometimes I do eat heavily at hours that seem out of reason to many, but it seems to be natural for me. I have that kind of an appetite. I enjoy food and so far it doesn't seem to have done me any harm."

Frisch and the Cardinals got a break when they attempted to trade Mize to the Reds in 1936, but the Reds returned him, saying he wasn't physically fit to play because of a spur in his groin. After surgery by Dr. Hyland, Mize was ready to play and turned in several solid seasons for the Cardinals, including setting the team record for most home runs in a season, 43, in 1940, that still stands today.

Commissioner Landis had called Hyland the surgeon general of baseball because of his growing reputation of being able to treat player's injuries. Even though he worked mainly in private practice in St. Louis, he earned a lot of his notoriety for his work in baseball.

"All of the players came to see him," said his son, Robert Hyland. "He loved it; he was an athlete himself. It was truly remarkable what he did because he didn't have any of the modern techniques or facilities. Some guys made some miracle recoveries after people thought they wouldn't be able to play again."

That the Cardinals were not winning brought an end to Pepper Martin's Mudcat band, another sign that the Gashouse era was nearly over. Frisch grimaced one day when the Cardinals arrived in Rochester, New York, for an exhibition game and the sign noted that Martin's Mudcats would be appearing there that day. Even though the band had picked up a new member in pitcher Lon Warneke, acquired in a deal with the

Cubs, Frisch put an end to the sideshow because he thought it was keeping the team from being successful on the field.

Three players who were producing were Mize, Medwick, and Moore. In 1939, Mize hit .349 with 28 homers and drove in 108 runs. Rickey wasn't impressed, however.

"Rickey said, 'You should hit more homers,'" Mize later recalled. "So the next year, I hit the 43 homers, drove in 137 runs, and hit .314. And when I went in to talk about my contract, he said, 'Your batting average is down 30 points. Would you be willing to take a cut in salary?'"

Mize narrowly failed to win the league batting title in 1938, when the race between him and Reds catcher Ernie Lombardi came down to the final day. The Cardinals were playing in Chicago, and the outcome of the game would have no bearing on either team's final place in the standings.

"The Chicago pitcher came to me before the game," Mize said.

"He told me he'd have the third baseman play back and that he'd cover first. He said, 'Just bunt the ball. You'll get the hits.'

"Tony Lazzeri was playing second base for them. My first two times up, he played me way over in the hole. If I hit routine grounders, I would have had base hits. But I hit the ball right at him both times for outs. The same kind of balls in July or August would have been base hits. I went 0 for 4 and Lombardi won the title."

Mize also contributed to the team by being Moore's roommate, which meant helping Moore control his anger when he found he wasn't in the lineup one day in Chicago and he had some unflattering things to say about Frisch.

"Mize grabbed me by the arm, took me out in the front of the dugout," Moore said later. "Said he wanted to play a little pepper. I didn't think much of the idea, but he didn't give me much choice. He just grabbed a bat, handed me my glove, and there we were. Besides, he was bigger."

Mize said, "I just wanted to relax him. I bunted the ball

back to him, and he wouldn't use his glove. Just grabbed the ball barehanded and fired it back at me. It got to be a contest. I started hitting the ball a little harder, and Terry still refused to use his glove, just the bare hand. The first thing you know I was really smashing the ball at him."

After this went on for a few minutes, Mize stopped and asked Moore if his hand was OK. Moore acknowledged that it was hurting, both laughed, Moore's anger was forgotten, and he was back in the lineup the following day.

Despite the hitting of Medwick and Mize, the Cardinals fell to sixth place in 1938, and on September 11, Frisch was fired as the team's manager. Frisch was informed of the news by Breadon before the game but managed one last time as Paul Dean came back from the minors to beat Pittsburgh 6–4. After a year of broadcasting in Boston, Frisch returned to managing with the Pirates, and two incidents there showed he had not left any of his spark in St. Louis.

He was coaching third, as was the custom for managers then, when a heckler would not stop bothering him from the box seats behind the dugout. Frisch began talking to the man—what would he like to see in this situation, how about a bunt, etc. Frisch then went over and asked the man where he worked. The man responded with a downtown business address but wondered why Frisch wanted to know.

"Because," Frisch said, "I'm going to be down at your office tomorrow morning, flannelmouth, and tell you how to run your blankety-blank business."

Another day, playing the Dodgers at Ebbets Field, Frisch could not believe the umpires were allowing a game to be played in a cold, steady rain. It was a scheduled doubleheader, and Frisch was moaning and complaining, but the umpires wouldn't call the game because they knew that was what Frisch wanted.

When the first game ended, Frisch thought the day was over. He couldn't believe it when the umpires said they were going ahead with the second game as well. At the suggestion of Ripper Collins, the former Cardinal who had joined him with the Pirates, Frisch borrowed an umbrella and began walking toward home plate. Frisch got only a few steps from the dugout before he was kicked out of the game.

Off the field, the Cardinals suffered another major loss when Commissioner Landis, who was never fond of the team's farm system, ruled the organization had secret agreements with various minor-league clubs that allowed them to protect too many minor-league players. He ruled 74 of those players were immediate free agents and eligible to sign with other clubs. The biggest plum that got away was outfielder Pete Reiser, who went to the Dodgers, where he won the 1941 NL batting title.

Replacing Frisch as the manager of the Cardinals in 1939 was Ray Blades, who had been a member of the 1926 championship team. Even though Blades was an unconventional manager, constantly shuffling the lineup and making substitutions, he kept the Cardinals in the pennant race until the final week of the season. They wound up second to the Reds, winning 92 games.

But that was Blades's one season of glory; he was fired in June the next year with the Cardinals in seventh place.

Many outstanding players had appeared in Cardinals uniforms during the 1930s—Dean, Martin, Frisch, Medwick, Mize, and others. But as the new decade of the 1940s dawned, nobody could foresee that the greatest player in the franchise's history was about to make his debut—Stan Musial.

4

A Legend Arrives

THE 1940s

◆

When the 1940 season began, not even the most zealous Cardinals fan knew Stan Musial was alive. Numerous people within the organization knew him only by the uniform number on his back, as undistinguished as the rest of the more than 200 minor leaguers in the spring training camp.

Musial was a left-handed pitcher who had signed with the Cardinals only after crying when his father turned down the team's scout's offer. His father wanted his oldest son to go to college, and Stan indeed did have a basketball scholarship offer from the University of Pittsburgh. The crying swayed him, however, and Lukasz Musial finally agreed to let his son try to make his life away from the steel mills in Donora, Pennsylvania, through baseball.

Musial had gone through two undistinguished years in Williamson, West Virginia, in the Mountain State League in 1938 and 1939 when he was assigned to Daytona Beach, Florida, in the Class D Florida State League in 1940, a year that was going to change his life and the fortunes of the Cardinals forever. Under manager Dick Kerr, Musial began to play some games in the outfield when he wasn't pitching.

The day his life changed was August 11, while he was in center field. He tried to make a shoestring catch, and after catching the ball, he fell heavily on his left shoulder. A big knot formed there, and he would pitch in just two more games. Having recently married and learned he was about to become a father, Musial, who had been making $100 a month, asked Kerr if maybe the best thing Musial could do was forget about baseball, go back to Donora, and enter the business world.

Kerr, who had won two games for the White Sox in the 1919 World Series against the Reds, while his "Black Sox" teammates were trying to throw the series, wouldn't let Musial quit.

"You can't let the game down, or your team," Kerr told him. "And you've got a great future ahead of you."

Kerr even went beyond reassuring Musial about his future. He rented a bigger house, then had the Musials move in with him and his wife. Despite Kerr's help, however, Musial wondered again what his future would be when he came to spring training in 1941.

Musial's arm was still bothering him and affected his throwing, even from the outfield. Although he could hit, most of the managers in the Cardinals farm system were skeptical about his chances for success because of his poor arm. He was dropped from the camp in Hollywood, Florida, and assigned to the camp for lower-level minor-league players in Albany, Georgia. Branch Rickey was not ready to give up on him, however, and finally persuaded Ollie Vanek, the manager of the Class C farm team in Springfield, Missouri, to take Musial.

In the team's first three games, Musial hit a home run and two doubles. He was on his way. After 87 games, he was hitting .369 with 26 home runs and 94 RBIs. The Double A team in Rochester, New York, was looking for an outfielder; Rickey knew he was asking the 20-year-old Musial to make a big jump but told the young man to pack his bags for Rochester.

The jump didn't slow Musial down. His first at bat produced a home run. After 51 games he was hitting .327, and suddenly many people in St. Louis knew all about him, especially Billy Southworth, who had taken over as the Cardinals manager midway through the 1940 season. A year after wondering if he should give up baseball, Musial found himself in the major leagues.

The Cardinals had finished third in 1940, and now they were battling with the Dodgers for the pennant, a rivalry that would continue through the decade. The Rochester season had ended, and Musial had gone home to Donora when the Cardinals sent word they were promoting him to the major leagues. Even though he was overjoyed by the news, Musial's trip was delayed slightly when his wife, Lil, drove him to Pittsburgh, only to arrive too late for the train to St. Louis.

Musial caught the next train, however, and walked into a major-league clubhouse for the first time on September 17, 1941. With him were Rochester teammates Erv Dusak and Whitey Kurowski. The Cardinals were two games behind the Dodgers.

Rickey signed Musial for $400 a month for the rest of the season and for 1942 at the same salary. Musial recalled nothing memorable coming out of his meeting with Rickey, thinking then as well as now that the player the Cardinals were the most interested in of the trio coming up from Rochester was Dusak, a right-handed power-hitting outfielder. What Rickey didn't know at the time was that Dusak would prove to have too much trouble hitting the breaking ball to be anything more than a journeyman performer.

It was sheer luck that clubhouse manager Butch Yatkeman handed Musial uniform number 6, thinking it was the size that would fit him best. Musial never wore any other number, and nobody would ever wear it again after he retired 22 years later.

The Cardinals' opponent in a doubleheader that day was the Boston Braves. With Enos Slaughter out with a broken collarbone, manager Billy Southworth—who had replaced Ray Blades—put Musial in the starting lineup for the second game.

Musial's first at bat in the majors produced nothing more than a weak popup to third off Jim Tobin. His second at bat, however, was more memorable—a two-run double off the wall in right center that started the Cardinals to a 3–2 victory. With a week to go in the season, the Cardinals boarded the train headed east just percentage points behind the Dodgers.

As the train chugged along, Musial plopped down in one of the seats next to team captain Terry Moore and commented about how fast things had happened to him during the season, starting from the point when Moore had homered off him in spring training.

Musial remembers Moore looking at him and staring, first in disbelief, then in laughter. "It can't be," Moore said. "You're not that kid left-hander."

Musial nodded that yes, indeed, he was the one.

Moore called across the train car to where Johnny Mize was playing cards. "Hey John," he said. "You won't believe this. Musial is the left-hander who threw us those long home-run balls at Columbus this spring."

The Cardinals, who had signed Musial away from the Pirates before the Yankees or the Indians could make an offer, couldn't quite catch the Dodgers that year, even with the dazzling debut of Musial. He hit .426 in his first 12 games in the majors. The Cardinals finished with 97 wins but still were two and a half games behind the Dodgers.

Billy Southworth was a good enough judge of baseball talent to know immediately what kind of player he had in Musial.

"That kid," he said, "was born to play baseball."

Southworth had learned a lot about handling players and handling the pressures and responsibilities of being a manager since his first failed attempt a few years before, in 1929.

In his 1943 history of the Cardinals, Fred Lieb discussed Southworth's relationship with his players:

"He is the friend of every man on the team, and they know it," Lieb wrote. "They come to him with personal problems, as well as those concerning baseball. Even if a man has made a stupid blunder, Billy doesn't bawl out the player until [the] next day. Then both he and the athlete have had a night's sleep on it. He is a strict disciplinarian, but not in the sense that McGraw and George Stallings were clubhouse despots.

"The Cardinals just don't step out of the traces, because that wouldn't be playing fair with Billy. He is known as baseball's 'little gentleman,' but he can carry an iron fist in his velvet glove. No one puts anything over on him, and one of his first rules on the club was that no Cardinal should go into the front office except to get his paycheck. That rule wasn't always in effect."

Southworth, the same man who had refused to let some of the players drive their own cars to a spring training game so their wives could accompany them, showed how much he had changed by offering to let his players stay over in New York one night, instead of going on to Boston, so they could attend a championship fight.

Another observer who noticed the change in Southworth was Bob Burnes, writing in the *Globe-Democrat*, "Southworth is not the raucous type manager. He's the quiet, friendly type. No player has ever been roundly upbraided in the presence of other players. If Southworth has something to say to a player, he says it quietly when the other boys aren't around.

"Even when he's trying to help a player who is making the same mistake constantly, he usually waits until that player is by himself."

Southworth's good relationship with his players showed in such decisions as scheduling additional spring training workouts, at the players' requests, so they could get more batting practice. It also was in evidence during one game at Boston when the Cardinals were losing 3–1 in the ninth inning.

The team was rallying, with runners at first and second and one out, when Southworth was selecting a pinch hitter to bat for Marty Marion. It was at this point that the runner at second, Johnny Hopp, was motioning wildly, trying to get Southworth's attention.

"I called time and rushed out to him," Southworth related

the next day in the *Globe-Democrat*. "'You were too busy hit-ting to the infield during batting practice,' Hopp whispered. 'I don't think you've had a chance to notice [Ray] Sanders. He's hittin' like a fool, knockin' the cover off every time up. I thought I ought to tell you.'"

Southworth called back Ken O'Dea, whom he had originally selected to hit, and sent up Sanders, who promptly drilled a single to drive in Hopp and send the other runner to third. O'Dea then did hit and followed with a squeeze bunt that pro-duced the tying run. The rally went on to produce four more runs and a Cardinals victory.

"We stress emotional steadyness on the Cardinals," South-worth said in a *Saturday Evening Post* article in 1943. "It is our most important factor in team success. Sportswriters take good-natured pokes at my theories now and then. They call me a Pollyanna, a Boy Scout manager and so on, but I know that individualism in baseball is a thing of the past. Cohesive thinking and coordinated movement of an intelligent team will always beat a team of individual stars."

One of the other things Southworth learned with experience was that he enjoyed the victories more, though the losses didn't get any easier to take.

"I guess most people don't think managers take it [the game] that seriously," he said in an interview in the *Post-Dis-patch* in 1941. "I suppose they think of us as happy-go-lucky fellows—if we win all right, and if we lose all right. But let me tell you, it makes a difference. Nights we win, we have dinner out somewhere, and somehow the food always tastes better. After dinner, we read books, magazines, and keep up with the news. If we lose, dinner's not very good, and there's no reading at all. I just can't get interested."

Fortunately for Southworth and the Cardinals, the team was entering a period during which they would win many more games than they would lose, even though Southworth, like all managers in the major leagues, faced a challenge of having to find replacement players for those lost to a larger cause—go-ing off to war.

World War II had begun, and like men from all walks of life, baseball players were being called to serve their country. Southworth not only watched his players leave, he saw his own son, with a promising baseball career ahead of him in the minor leagues, sign up to join the fight in Europe. Billy Southworth eventually worked his way up to the rank of major, and his proud father said he took more pride in his son's war achievements than in the Cardinals' success. But he also had to suffer the tragic death of his son, who was killed in 1945 when the B-29 he was piloting crashed as he was attempting to land in New York.

The Cardinals were somewhat protected from the loss of players to war duty by their farm system. By 1940 the Cardinals' minor-league empire included 23 teams, 14 of which were owned outright by the major-league team. The next richest farm system had 10 teams. The Cardinals had the most scouts of any team, conducted the most tryout camps, and signed the most players, usually youngsters they could get for small salaries.

As the 1942 season began, it was just months after the bombing at Pearl Harbor, and the war movement was beginning to affect baseball. The Cardinals' most promising rookie pitcher, Johnny Grodzicki, was inducted into the Army, but the team managed to keep all its other star players, at least for that season.

Some observers still consider the 1942 club one of the best in franchise history. With Musial up to stay, he joined an outfield of Terry Moore and Enos Slaughter that was as good as any in the game. Whitey Kurowski also stuck as the regular third baseman, joining Marty Marion at shortstop, Jimmy Brown at second base, and the platoon of Johnny Hopp and Ray Sanders at first base. Walker Cooper took over as the regular catcher, and the pitching staff included Walker's brother Mort, Johnny Beazley, Max Lanier, Howie Krist, Harry Gumbert, and Howie Pollet.

"Terry Moore was the captain and if you had any problems

you went to him and he settled them," Musial said. "We had a great spirit on that ball club. We had great determination and we wanted to win."

Moore earned a reputation of being one of the best defensive outfielders in baseball despite using the smallest glove in the majors—the fingers were just about three inches long. He hit .300 only once, and admitted he worried more about his defense than he did his offense.

"I was just learning how to hit when I went into the service," Moore said. "When I came back I wasn't as good of a player as I had been before."

The only three of the group who were more than 30 years old were Brown and Gumbert, each 32, and the team captain, Moore, who turned 30 during the season. Despite all that talent, however, the Cardinals didn't know in midseason if they were going to be good enough to catch the Dodgers, who won 71 of their first 100 games.

The *Sporting News,* on August 6, wrote, "As the situation now stands, the Cardinal death notice is likely to be released around September 15."

On August 15, the Cardinals found themselves nine and a half games behind. That's when the charge began, however, and the Cardinals won 30 of their next 36 games, finished with 106 wins, and beat the Dodgers by two games. Their victory total was the highest by an NL club since 1909.

"Pass the Biscuits, Mirandy," had become the team's victory song, and it blared on the clubhouse phonograph through the last two months of the season.

Part of the reason the Cardinals were able to catch and pass the Dodgers was the pitching of Cooper, who had never before won more than 13 games at any level of his professional career. He had asked for uniform number 13 in 1940, hoping it would "bring me above 13." In his first two years afterward, he posted 11 victories and 13.

So when Cooper reached the 13-victory mark again in 1942, he knew he had to do something to change his luck. Catcher

Gus Mancuso had been traded to the Giants, so nobody was wearing number 14. Cooper put it on and won. He then proceeded to borrow the uniform shirts of his teammates, whether they were the proper size or not, all the way up until his 20th victory. Cooper finished the year with a 22–7 record, an ERA of 1.77, and the league's Most Valuable Player award.

It was a sight watching Cooper wearing his brother Walker's 15, but that wasn't as good as seeing him squeeze into Ken O'dea's number 16. When the jersey switch kept working, however, Cooper kept doing it.

The other pitcher who carried the Cardinals down the stretch was Beazley, a 24-year-old rookie right-hander who had moved into the rotation when Lon Warneke was sold to the Cubs for $15,000. The night before he was supposed to pitch a key game in Philadelphia, however, he got into an argument with a redcap at the train station, not wanting the redcap to carry his bag. The argument heated up when Beazley said the man cursed him, and Beazley threw his bag at him. The redcap pulled a knife, and Beazley raised his arm in self-defense, only for the knife to slash his right thumb. The wound turned out to be deep though not serious, but Musial and his teammates didn't know how he would be able to pitch the next day.

Beazley pitched, however, and carried a 1–0 lead into the ninth before the Phillies rallied for a 2–1 victory. The Cardinals won the second game behind a homer from Terry Moore and actually picked up a game in the standings when the Dodgers dropped a doubleheader to Cincinnati.

The Cardinals went into the final day of the season needing only a split of the doubleheader against the Cubs to clinch the pennant. The Dodgers beat the Phillies, but the Cardinals swept the Cubs and were headed back to the World Series again.

The opponent once again was the Yankees, led by Joe Di-Maggio, who had easily won the American League title. Even though it had been only eight years since the Cardinals' last trip to the World Series, there was nobody left who had been a member of that club.

Musial was particularly excited about his first trip to the World Series. He had had a very good rookie season, hitting .315 with 10 homers and 72 RBIs. He didn't know enough to appreciate that the Yankees were heavy favorites.

"We weren't awed by the Yankees because we had played them five times during spring training," Musial said. "Also, it wasn't like we were coming to New York for the first time, because we came there all the time to play the Giants and Dodgers. We felt we could beat them."

The Yankees took the opening game, behind Red Ruffing, who had a no-hitter until the eighth, when Moore broke it up with a single. The Cardinals rallied for four runs in the ninth before finally losing, 7–4, but that last-inning burst gave them inspiration that was to last for the rest of the series.

An RBI single by Musial in the eighth inning of the second game drove in Slaughter, who had doubled, to break a 3–3 tie, and Slaughter then turned in a great defensive play in the ninth to preserve the Cardinals' 4–3 win and even the series at one win each.

The series shifted to New York, where the Cardinals outfielders again excelled defensively and Ernie White came through on the mound, shutting out New York for a 2–0 victory. The fourth game also went to the Cardinals, who blew a 6–1 lead before rallying to win 9–6 and move ahead of the Yankees three games to one.

When Moore came out to home plate to exchange lineup cards before the fifth game, Yankee coach Art Fletcher, representing manager Joe McCarthy, had an unusual request. The Yankees wanted the Cardinals' equipment manager, diminutive Butch Yatkeman, removed from the dugout. Fletcher called him "that little guy"; he was so short that the Yankees didn't believe he had anything to do with the Cardinals.

Moore said, "You don't mean little Butch? He's in the dugout for all our games."

That was whom Fletcher meant. The umpires had to go along with the Yankees' request, so Yatkeman had no choice but to return to the clubhouse and listen to the game on the radio. Before leaving the pregame meeting, however, Moore told Fletcher, "This is just one more reason why there's going to be no tomorrow in the World Series."

Moore was right. With the score tied 2–2 in the ninth, Kurowski pulled a shot down the left-field line for a two-run homer that gave Beazley and the Cardinals a 4–2 victory and another world championship.

It was a big moment for the Cardinals and for Kurowski, who had overcome some physical and emotional scars to become the star of the moment. Kurowski, whose real first name was George, had learned to play baseball as a kid while overcoming osteomyeletis, a disease that left him without part of the ulna bone in his right forearm. To compensate, Kurowski had to develop powerful muscles. His right arm was shorter than his left arm, and that forced him into a crowded stance at the plate, which made him especially vulnerable to high and inside pitches.

Emotionally, Kurowski had to survive the death of his brother, Frank, who was killed in a mine cave-in just before Kurowski left his hometown of Reading, Pennsylvania, in 1937 to begin his baseball career. In the spring of 1942, as Kurowski was trying to make the Cardinals, his father had died of a heart attack.

It figured to be an exciting train ride home from New York for Musial, but knowing finances were still a bit tight, he decided he could save some money and skip the ride back to St. Louis and just meet wife Lil and their family in Donora. Lil and most of the other Cardinals' wives had stayed behind in St. Louis when the series shifted to New York, thinking the end would not come there but after the games returned to St. Louis.

As Musial accompanied his teammates to the train station, then had to watch them get on the train to leave, he couldn't help but burst into tears.

The Cardinals didn't know it at the time, of course, but the next season, they would have a much easier time repeating as NL champions, winning 105 games and earning another World Series appearance against the Yankees, this time without DiMaggio, who had been inducted into the service.

The Cardinals also were feeling more of the war's impact, however, having lost Slaughter, Moore, Beazley, and Creepy Crespi, the starting second baseman in 1941 who had lost his job to Jimmy Brown in 1942 but had remained a key reserve.

Of all the Cardinals who went off to the war, Crespi's story was one of the saddest. Just 24 at the time, he figured to have plenty of time left in the majors. Then the orders calling for him to report to the Army arrived.

"Some people told me that I could have protested because my brother had already been killed and because I was the sole support of my mother," Crespi later recalled in an interview with Bob Burnes in the *Globe-Democrat*. "But I didn't want any part of that. So when they called, I went."

While playing for the Army team at Fort Riley, Kansas, Crespi injured his leg. He was training in a tank, waiting to be shipped out, when the tank overturned and Crespi broke his already injured leg. He was sent to an Army hospital in Indianapolis, where more trouble was to follow.

As Burnes reported, Crespi and another private with a similar injury were being treated at the same time. "Orderlies were pushing our wheelchairs, and they decided to have a race down a long hall," Crespi said. "A door opened suddenly, and my orderly put on the brakes and I slid right out of the chair—and broke the leg again."

The tragic development that followed next was a nurse misreading the medication that was prescribed for the leg. One of the ingredients was to be one-tenth of one percent of acid, but she added 10 percent, eating everything off the leg down to the bone.

"It almost had to be amputated," Crespi said.

As it was, both his military and baseball careers were over. He missed qualifying for his baseball pension by less than 50 days. More than 40 years later, he still walked with a limp.

"You wonder how great a ballplayer he might have been if World War II hadn't come along," Burnes said.

The Cardinals still had many talented players in 1943, led by Musial, who won his first batting title, hitting .357, and Howie Pollet—who was drafted in July. Pollet, Lanier, and Cooper finished 1–2–3 in the league in ERA.

The other major defection from the Cardinals was in the front office, where Rickey and Breadon finally parted company, with Rickey moving on to become the general manager of the Brooklyn Dodgers. His departure didn't have as much of an effect on the players already in the major leagues as it did on those who were hoping to get there one day. When Rickey left, he took his great baseball knowledge and his ability to find a blue-chip prospect in a tryout camp with him. It was no small coincidence that the Dodgers under Rickey flourished just as the Cardinals had in his days of running the team. Part of the reason the Cardinals were so successful during the war years and were able to withstand losing so many players to the service was because of Rickey's foresight in signing so many minor-league players and having such a deep farm system.

Some of the players knew they would miss Rickey, especially when it came time to negotiate a new contract with him. One of those players who recalled his sessions with Rickey was Marion, in an interview with William Mead in his book *Baseball Goes to War*.

"Mr. Rickey and Mr. Breadon were very tough bosses," Marion said. "You knew they owned the ball club but that was it. They didn't even talk to you; the only time you ever saw them to talk to was at contract time. I had quite the conversations with Mr. Rickey. He was a great orator, Mr. Rickey was, and a great writer. No matter what you did, he would always send you a nice, three-page letter, and he would explain to you in no uncertain terms that although you may have fielded well, you didn't do this right or that right. There was always something you didn't do right; you were not the complete ballplayer.

"Mr. Rickey was a genius at selling you just after you passed your peak. He didn't believe in sentiment. Take a player these days like Bob Gibson, who hung on too long; Rickey would have sold him a long time ago. Gibson, Lou Brock, those kind of ballplayers, he'd have sold them. Probably would have sold Musial, too."

Breadon proved he could be just as stubborn as Rickey when it came to negotiating contracts, offering Musial only a $1,000 raise after his 1942 season, when he finished third in the league batting race. After writing letters back and forth from St. Louis to Donora, the two finally agreed on a compromise offer, and Musial reported to spring training in Cairo, Illinois.

"Breadon was a very tough negotiator," Musial said. "He wasn't very liberal with his money. When he talked about a contract, he always brought up how much money we made in the World Series, but that was supposed to be a bonus.

"As a player, you never saw him very much. He was at every game, but he wasn't one to come and visit with the players and socialize. Maybe some of the veteran players saw him more, but he didn't come by the clubhouse very much."

Because of the war, teams were ordered to train closer to their home city. For the Cardinals, that meant Cairo, and trainer Doc Weaver advised players to wear long underwear during the workouts and to wear hats and topcoats to camp. The warmth of the Florida sun seemed a long way away.

The path back to the World Series was relatively easy, as the Cardinals used an 11-game winning streak in July to break away from the Dodgers and go on to win the pennant by an 18-game margin over the Reds. Unfortunately, they would not be able to repeat the previous year's success against the Yankees.

The Yankees won the Series opener 4–2. The morning of the second game, word reached New York that Robert Cooper, a mail carrier in Independence, Missouri, and the father of Mort and Walker Cooper, had died of a heart attack.

The news came in an early-morning telephone call to their hotel room that Walker answered. Walker, knowing his older brother was supposed to pitch that afternoon, debated whether he should break the news to him. Finally, he called his brother and Southworth and told them of the news he had received in the telephone call.

"Walker said he wanted to tell me before any of the newsmen or anybody else did," Mort later recalled. "But I told him and Southworth that I wanted to pitch that game because it was what my father would have wanted me to do. I pitched with everything I had, and the Cardinals were leading 4–1 in the ninth inning. I was rapped for two runs, when Southworth came out to the mound to reassure me that everything was okay. I felt better, and began to cut loose. I set down the next three batters in order. I'll never forget that game."

The 4–3 victory evened the series at one win apiece, but the Cardinals didn't win again. After a 6–2 loss, the Series moved to St. Louis, where Harry Brecheen got beat 2–1, and the Yankees then finished off the series victory with a 2–0 victory on a sixth-inning homer by Bill Dickey off Cooper.

There were other brothers playing in the major leagues, but none were as famous as the Coopers. If one didn't know they were brothers, however, their actions might not have indicated they were related.

"The Cooper boys are as unlike as brothers could be," one newspaper report said in 1944. "Mort has thick, dark hair, a round, reddish and somewhat battered face and is on the fleshy side. Walker's blonde hair is thinning out, and his lantern-jawed face is pale and he is lean and stringy.

"Mort is nervous, restless, and quick-tempered. He is a ready talker and sociable, and likes to go places and do things. Walker is quiet and unemotional, talks rarely, and smiles even less often. As his mother says, 'He never seemed to be having a good time but he always was. It was a great event in our house when Walker smiled."

Musial remembers Walker Cooper as being a great prankster, however. One time, he caught a man in a New York hotel lobby trying to eavesdrop on a conversation between the two of them and Cooper walked over, took the man's straw hat, and pulled it down over his ears.

The Coopers had injuries that they thought would keep them out of the war. Mort was classified 4F because of a bad back injured in a fall from a ladder. Walker was 1A, available for limited service, as a result of a shoulder injury suffered in a home-plate collision in 1941. It turned out that Walker was drafted, and he missed almost all of the 1945 season.

Like all brothers, Walker had tremendous pride in Mort's ability and accomplishments.

"Mort was a shutout pitcher, a great asset any time and particularly in a big game when you might run into a low-run effort yourself," Walker said in a *Sporting News* interview in 1956. "Another thing, if he said he was going to pitch to a hitter one way, you could set your defense accordingly. He wouldn't miss. He had the guts, too. I remember when the bone chips in his elbow were so painful that he'd chew an aspirin between innings so he could keep going."

Like Mort Cooper, another player who didn't have to fight in the war was Marion, the talented shortstop who also had a childhood injury that prevented him from being drafted.

"When I was nine years old we were playing cowboys and Indians down in the woods," Marion recalled in Mead's book. "I jumped off about a twenty-foot bank and hit wrong and broke my leg. My bone was sticking out, and the kids I was playing with ran off and left me. When my Daddy got home, he asked the kids, 'Where's Martin?' And they said, 'The last time we saw him he was laying down in the gully.' So Daddy came down through the woods and found me. I had been laying there a couple of hours. I remember him picking me up and taking me to the hospital. It was Grady Hospital, a charity hospital in Atlanta, where we lived.

"They set it, and I guess I was in the hospital about two and a half months. Then they X-rayed my leg and found out it was about an inch and a half shorter than the other leg. So they put me on the operating table, and for two hours and a half, they cut my leg. So my right leg is wired together, and I have forty stitches up the thing. I walked on crutches for about a year. Although the broken part of my leg never bothered me playing ball, the knee was injured, too. All through my high school days, when I'd play ball, all of a sudden my knee would slip out, you know? I'd lay down on the ground, they'd jerk it back in, and I'd get up and play again. The docs said, 'Marty, it will get stronger as you get older.' And it did. I didn't have any trouble with my knee in pro ball until I was, oh, 30 or 31 years old, maybe."

The Cardinals hero in 1944, Marion won the league MVP award, becoming the first player to win that honor primarily for his defensive accomplishments. Six players on his own team hit more home runs, five of the regulars hit for a higher average, and six players drove in more runs—but nobody played a bigger role in the Cardinals' success.

Marion might not have even gotten into baseball if it hadn't been for a childhood friend, Johnny Echols. Rickey wanted Echols to travel to St. Louis for a tryout, but he wouldn't come unless the Cardinals brought along Marion, his buddy, at the team's expense. Rickey finally agreed, and one person who remembered Marion from his tryout was Frankie Frisch, the manager at the time.

"He was a major-league shortstop, even then, a master fielder, but," Frisch added, "he was the worst, the weakest hitter I ever saw."

Marion improved enough to make it to the majors. One theory suggests that Rogers Hornsby was responsible for making him a better hitter; another says it was Southworth. In an interview in the *Post-Dispatch* in 1949, Marion said neither was the case.

"I'd like to go along with those stories if they were true, but they aren't," Marion said. "I improved at the plate by changing around on my own, hitting more to right field, studying pitchers, and overcoming a complex. When I came up, a poor hitter and good fielder, the older players told me, 'You worry about the fielding; we'll take care of the hitting.' I believed them for a time, but now I'd rather hit than field."

By 1944, playing in the World Series was becoming the norm for the Cardinals. For the third straight year, they blew through the National League, even though they had again lost more players to the war—Harry Walker, Lou Klein, Howie Krist, Murry Dickson, and Al Brazle. Musial again was lucky, missing the draft notices for another year.

Mead recalled why Musial was able to remain with the Cardinals when players older and with bigger families were being drafted:

"Stan Musial's deferment illustrated the uneven character of draft calls from one community to another," Mead wrote. "There was no hint that Musial sought or received special consideration; he was just lucky. Age, number of children conceived before Pearl Harbor, and occupation were weighed by each local draft board in deciding who should be drafted and who should be deferred. Some draft boards had to take virtually every able-bodied man between the ages of 18 and 38; others had more eligible men and had to make choices.

"Musial was healthy and 23. He had one son born before Pearl Harbor, and supported his parents as well; Musial's father had contracted black-lung disease while working in the Pennsylvania coal mines. Musial worked during the off-season in a war plant. He was deferred again until after the 1944 season. Again, purely by luck, the draft took many players who were older than Musial and had larger families."

Musial hit .347 during the season to help the Cardinals win

105 games for the second year in a row and finish 14½ games in front of Pittsburgh. The margin could have been greater. On September 1, the Cardinals were 20 games in front. No doubt because they knew they already had the pennant won, the team lost 15 of its final 20 games and coasted in for its third straight title.

The difference this season was that it wasn't the Yankees who were waiting for them. On the final day of the season, the St. Louis Browns beat the Yankees for the fourth straight game and clinched their only American League pennant. The World Series would be an all–St. Louis affair, and while it might not have mattered to the rest of the country, in St. Louis the rivalry was the only thing on people's minds. The first problem the all–St. Louis World Series presented for Billy Southworth was finding a place to stay. With housing at a premium because of the war, Southworth and Luke Sewell, the manager of the Browns, had agreed before the season began to share an apartment. One team was always on the road when the other was at home, so there was never an overlap or a debate about who was staying at the Lindell Towers apartment—until the World Series.

As Mead reported, "However admirable this display of inter-league cooperation might have appeared during the season, it would never do for the opposing managers to sit in the same living room after a World Series game, sipping bourbon and chatting politely with their wives. Besides, Sewell wanted to invite his mother, and Mrs. Southworth could hardly be expected to put up with a mother-in-law from the wrong family and indeed, the wrong league."

A controversy was avoided when another resident of the building, out of town, agreed to allow the Southworths to use his apartment.

The problem for the Musial family wasn't where to stay—it was all the noise being created by the Browns fans. The Musials had lived for two summers at the Fairgrounds Hotel, close by Sportsman's Park, and whenever the Cardinals would

leave town and the Browns returned home, the area was relatively quiet—until the Browns put on their late-season charge
to the pennant. Musial said his wife, Lil, called the atmosphere surrounding the World Series her "rude awakening"
and complained that St. Louis had become a Brownie town.

Even though everybody likes an underdog, not all the town's
residents had switched their allegiance to the Browns. The
most avid Browns fans knew the Cardinals were the stronger
team and should win the Series, and some of the Cardinals
players—in the Series for the third straight year—admitted
they had to guard against overconfidence coming into the first
game.

"We thought we were going to walk through them," Marion
said in a later interview. "Who in hell's the Browns, you know.
By the time we got in that first game, we found out they were
a pretty good ball club. Yes, sir, we had a hell of a time beating those boys. They were tough. If they'd have beat us in that
second game, we'd have probably been in trouble. We had a
good ball club but it wasn't great. They had quite a bit of
pride.

"That Streetcar Series . . . if the Browns had beat us, that
would have been really a disgrace."

The Browns did in fact win the opening game, 2–1, on a
homer by George McQuinn off Mort Cooper. The second game
went to the 11th inning, and the Browns might have gone up
2–0 if not for a great fielding play by Cardinals reliever Blix
Donnelly, who pounced on a bunt and forced the Browns runner at third. Ken O'Dea's RBI single as a pinch hitter in the
bottom of the inning gave the Cardinals the victory.

Sewell had his mother at that game, coming up from her
home in Alabama. Devastated by the loss, he went back to his
apartment and found her sitting in a rocking chair.

"Mom, what did you think of that game today?" Sewell
asked her. "Oh," she said, "I was awfully glad when someone
won because I was getting mighty tired." Sewell said, "It just
broke my heart."

Sewell got a little rejuvenation when the Browns came back to win the third game, 6–2, but Harry Brecheen stopped the Browns in Game 4 as Musial hit a two-run homer to lead the Cardinals to a 5–1 victory that once again tied the series.

Cooper came back to put the Cardinals ahead for the first time in the series, with a 2–0 victory in Game 5, striking out 12 and riding the home runs of Ray Sanders and Danny Litwhiler. The world championship went to the Cardinals for the second time in three years the following afternoon when Max Lanier and Ted Wilks combined on a three-hitter in the Cardinals' 3–1 victory.

One of the reserves on that Cardinals team, brought back for insurance because of all the players lost to the service, was Pepper Martin. He showed he hadn't changed a bit as he grew older when he lined up to play right field one day, with Musial next to him in center.

Musial lost a fly ball in the sun, and it hit him on the head and bounced away. Musial remembers Martin picking up the ball, getting it back to the infield, then coming over to find out if he had been hurt.

Musial said he was OK, and later recalled, "Pepper put his hands on his knees, doubled over, and said, 'Then you won't mind if I laugh.' They had to hold up the game until he stopped laughing."

For Musial, the World Series victory was extra special because that winter, he found out his luck had run out and it was his turn to go into the service, in his case the Navy. He wasn't alone, as the Cardinals also lost Walker Cooper, Max Lanier, and Danny Litwhiler, and even though the Cardinals came up with another 22-year-old replacement from the farm system—a kid from Germantown, Illinois, by the name of Albert "Red" Schoendienst—the team's victory total in 1945 fell off to 95, and they finished second, three games behind the Cubs.

Schoendienst had risen through the minor leagues after attending a tryout camp in 1942. He and a boyhood friend, Joe

Linnemann, had heard that anybody coming to the camp would be allowed to stay and watch the Cardinals game against Brooklyn. That was all the incentive they needed. They hitchhiked to St. Louis, then spent the night sleeping in a park across the street from Union Station because they didn't have enough money for a hotel room. In the tryout camp, Schoendienst's natural ability immediately impressed the scouts. Because Schoendienst was still under age, he couldn't sign a contract without his parent's permission, so scout Joe Mathes raced to Illinois, where the elder Schoendienst, a state employee, was helping paint a bridge. He stopped his work, signed the contract, and his son became a Cardinal. Mary Martin, Breadon's private secretary, gave Schoendienst five dollars so he and Linnemann could get something to eat. Without getting to see that game against Brooklyn, Schoendienst found himself on a bus headed to Union City, Tennessee, a Class D farm club, where he began his professional career.

From Union City, he moved up to Lynchburg, Virginia, and then when the top farm club in Rochester was in need of a shortstop, the word went out for Schoendienst to move up again. Schoendienst knocked on the clubhouse door, and manager Pepper Martin answered and told the youthful looking Schoendienst that the team didn't need a batboy. Schoendienst said no, he had been told to report there from Lynchburg to play shortstop.

"John Brown," said Martin, "You must be that Shone . . . er, something or other. Criminy, I'm in last place and they send me batboys."

But Martin found out that Schoendienst could in fact play, before he too went into the service; when he returned, it was on to the Cardinals, where he broke in as the team's left fielder.

Schoendienst turned in a solid rookie season, hitting .278 and leading the league with 26 stolen bases. As the war ended and the Cardinals veterans began returning to the club, with players like Schoendienst waiting for them, the future looked very promising. But as the players came back, they found out they were getting a new manager.

In what would now be viewed as a severe case of tampering, Southworth was lured away by the Boston Braves even though he was already signed to manage the Cardinals for 1946. As Stockton reported in his *Sport* magazine article in 1951, "The new owners of the Boston Braves probably didn't know there was any rule to interfere with their buying what they wanted, what they considered the best. They looked around and decided that Southworth was the most successful manager in baseball."

Southworth reported the offer to Breadon and asked if Breadon would release him from his contract. Breadon knew that if he said no, he would have an unhappy manager, and that would not be a good situation. He asked for a little time to look for a replacement, then gave Southworth the OK to take the Boston job.

The man to whom Breadon turned to replace Southworth was Eddie Dyer, a veteran of the organization who had gotten out of the game to go into the oil and insurance business in his hometown of Houston. After Rickey had left for Brooklyn, Dyer had been running the Cardinals farm system, so Breadon knew he would be familiar with the team's personnel.

One player who was all too familiar with Dyer was Walker Cooper, who announced immediately after Dyer was selected as the manager that he wanted to be traded. It seems Cooper had not cared for Dyer when Dyer was managing a farm team a few years earlier that included Cooper.

Dyer, however, tried to talk Breadon into at least letting him see if he could work things out with Cooper, then in the Navy, before he made a trade.

"I wouldn't get rid of Cooper," Dyer told Breadon. "He's the best catcher in baseball and the organization would be set for several years with Cooper behind the plate."

Breadon had the excuse he needed, however, because he had

not forgotten the bitter salary strike waged by both Cooper brothers the previous year. Upset when they found out Marty Marion was making more money then they were, both threatened not to play until they got a raise. Walker Cooper's case ended when he was drafted into the Navy, but the dispute with Mort continued into May. He left the club in Boston the day he was scheduled to pitch against the Braves, and a week later he walked into Breadon's office, where the Cardinals owner had a surprise announcement for them—he had just traded Cooper to the Braves for pitcher Red Barrett and $60,000.

Before Dyer could talk Breadon out of it, the Cardinals sold Walker Cooper to the Giants for $175,000, at the time a record transaction for a player-for-cash deal in which no other players were involved. When the Coopers signed as minor leaguers with St. Louis, the combined cost was $75.

"If we hadn't sold Mize, Cooper, and Dickson, we might have won 10 pennants in a row," Musial said.

Even without those players, however, the Cardinals made it four pennants in five years in 1946, but this one was a lot tougher to win than the previous ones had been.

The Cardinals, like all teams, had been strengthened by the return of their players from the service. Like all teams, however, some of the players weren't as good when they came back as they had been when they left. Johnny Grodzicki, who had been one of the Cardinals' top pitching prospects, was never the same because of a dropped foot, a result of a gunshot wound. He pitched just 19 games over the next two seasons, with an 0–1 record, and his career was over.

Beazley had hurt his arm while pitching in the service and never was the pitcher he had been before the war. He won seven games for the Cardinals in 1946, then was dispatched to Boston but won just two more before his career came to an end. Ernie White also had hurt his arm, and Terry Moore was not able to run as well as he had three years earlier.

Still, the Cardinals began the 1946 season with a ball club

loaded with talent, the offense led by Musial and Slaughter and the pitching staff led by Pollet and Brecheen.

The Cardinals and the Dodgers had been battling since the beginning of the decade. On June 12, 1940, the Cardinals traded Joe Medwick and Curt Davis to the Dodgers for Ernie Koy, three minor leaguers, and $125,000 cash. Six days later, Medwick was beaned by the Cardinals' Bob Bowman at Ebbets Field in the second game of a doubleheader, beginning what would turn out to be years of fighting almost every time the two teams got together.

There was never any evidence that Bowman had beaned Medwick intentionally. Bowman, however, had to be escorted from the park by policemen, and Brooklyn's president Larry MacPhail wanted him banned for life. There were reports that Bowman and Medwick, along with the Dodgers' Leo Durocher, had been involved in a heated argument at a hotel, but Bowman's roommate, Max Lanier, said he didn't think that had any bearing on what happened on the field.

Medwick had to spend several days in the hospital, and even though he returned to play, he never again was the feared hitter he had been in the 1930s.

Lanier, in an interview with Donald Honig in *Baseball When the Grass Was Real*, said he thought Medwick was beaned because Dodgers' coach Chuck Dressen had tried to call Bowman's pitches, had guessed curveball, and had told Medwick, when in reality the pitch was a fastball.

"Bowman was upset about it, I know," Lanier said. "He never showed up in the room that night. He was supposed to be in at 12, and he didn't come in. I thought, gosh, maybe something's happened to him. I didn't want to call the manager, because there was the chance Bob might be out having a couple of drinks and I didn't want to get him in dutch. So I called Pepper [Martin], and he told me that they'd sent Bowman on to Boston. They wanted to get him out of town because they were afraid some of those very rabid Dodgers fans might try something the next day."

Cartoon from *The Sporting News,* satirizing St. Louis owner Chris Von der Ahe by comparing his chute-the-chute sideshow ride with the Browns' slide in the standings. (*The Sporting News*)

Roger Bresnahan. (National Baseball Library, Cooperstown, N.Y.)

Rogers Hornsby with Miller Huggins, after Huggins had left the Cardinals for the Yankees. (St. Louis Mercantile Library)

Grover Cleveland "Pete" Alexander. (St. Louis Mercantile Library)

Sportsmans Park. (St. Louis Mercantile Library)

The 1926 World Champion Cardinals. (St. Louis Mercantile Library)

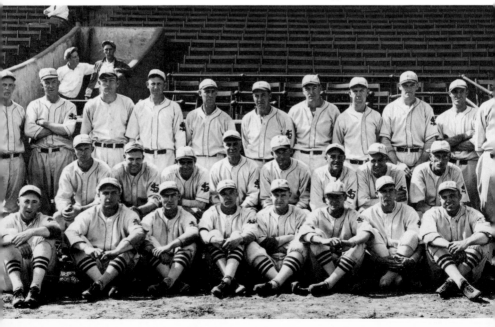

Hall-of-Famer Chick Hafey starred from 1924–31. (St. Louis Mercantile Library)

"Sunny Jim" Bottomley and Frankie Frisch, 1928. (St. Louis Mercantile Library)

Dizzy Dean. (St. Louis Mercantile Library)

Manager Frankie Frisch and Dean, celebrating Cardinals' win in Game 7 of the 1934 World Series. (St. Louis Mercantile Library)

Burleigh Grimes. (St. Louis Mercantile Library)

Pepper Martin, one of the Cardinals' great players and all-time characters. (National Baseball Library, Cooperstown, N.Y.)

Martin's trademark: diving into third base.

The 1934 Gashouse Gang. (St. Louis Mercantile Library)

Center fielder Terry Moore, sliding into third in a 1939 game. (St. Louis Mercantile Library)

Frankie Frisch (left) after leaving the Cardinals for Pittsburgh, and new manager Billy Southworth. (St. Louis Mercantile Library)

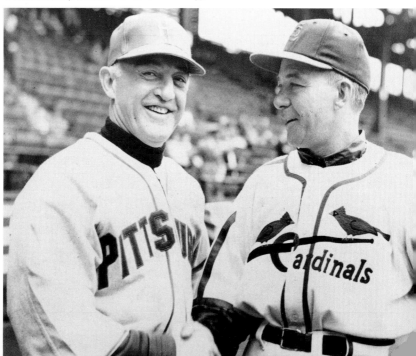

Enos "Country" Slaughter, safe at home. (*Associated Press*)

Slugger John Mize. (National Baseball Library, Cooperstown, N.Y.)

The Cardinals' 1946 infield: 3B Whitey Kurowski, SS Marty Marion, 2B Red Schoendienst, 1B Stan Musial. (George Dorrill/ *The Sporting News*)

Team president Sam Breadon (at microphone), introducing Gabby Street (at left), field announcer Charlie Jones, and radio announcer Harry Caray. (St. Louis Mercantile Library)

Branch Rickey (left) with Fred Saigh. (St. Louis Mercantile Library)

Front row: George Silvey, Walter Shannon, Bing Devine, and Solly Hemus. Back row: Eddie Stanky, Johnny Keane, and Harry Walker. (Courtesy of Bing Devine)

os Slaughter (left) and Red Schoendienst kiss pitcher Harry Brecheen after his victory in the 1946
orld Series. (St. Louis Mercantile Library)

Schoendienst in action, turning a double play in 1952. (Courtesy of Red Schoendienst)

Eddie Stanky, Slaughter, owner August A. "Gussie" Busch Jr., Schoendienst, and Musial, 1953. (*The Sporting News*)

More than one member of the Cardinals thought the biggest instigator of the battles with the Dodgers was the former Gashouse Gang shortstop, Leo Durocher. Over the next six years, there were at least five documented brawls between the two clubs.

"Somebody would start throwing close, or there would be some jockeying from the dugout, and that would start it off," Lanier said. "Durocher was a great one for that. You could hear him in the dugout: 'Stick it in his ear. Knock him down.' Stuff like that. You never knew when he meant it. You take that kind of thing, some mean pitchers, a great rivalry, and put it in the middle of a tense pennant race, and you're going to have some fun out there."

The mild-mannered Musial got so mad at one Brooklyn pitcher, Les Webber, after two knockdown pitches, that for the only time in his career even he charged the mound.

Enos Slaughter recalled that one national magazine quoted a Dodgers player as saying that Slaughter was the dirtiest player in the league. Slaughter didn't deny the charge but said he merely was playing hard because that was what it took to win.

"I had friends on the Dodgers," Slaughter said in an interview in 1976. "I liked [Pee Wee] Reese and [Duke] Snider and those guys. But when we were on the field I'd knock the daylights out of them if I had to win the game. That's the way I played.

"Pitchers would throw at hitters a lot back then—especially when the Dodgers played the Cardinals. When a pitcher hit me, that was all right, because I got to first base and you can't win unless you get to first base.

"But I never forgot who hit me, and at some point in the season there'd be a time when he'd be covering first base and I'd run right up his back, cut him off if he got in my way."

The Cardinals had to fight another opponent in their attempt to win the pennant—some uninvited guests from Mexico who were trying to break up the Cardinals ball club and lure some of its stars into taking big money for jumping from the major leagues to a rival league that was being set up in Mexico.

Lanier recalled that he was first contacted one night as he was leaving the ball park in Philadelphia. Bernardo Pasquel told Lanier he was interested in talking with him and would contact him again at the Cardinals' next stop, in New York.

Pasquel and his brother had been involved in Mexican League baseball for years, and being millionaires, they had decided to invest some of their own money into signing players out of the major leagues to improve the level of play in their league.

While in New York, Lanier learned that two of his teammates—second baseman Lou Klein, upset about losing his spot to Schoendienst, and pitcher Freddie Martin already had agreed to jump to Mexico. They tried to talk Lanier into it, and then another meeting with Pasquel was set up. Lanier told Donald Honig he was still hesitant, but he had been having some trouble with a sore elbow, and thought if his elbow was indeed hurt, maybe it wouldn't be such a bad idea to take the money when he could.

After raising their offer to a $25,000 bonus and a five-year contract for $20,000 a year, Lanier signed.

"I couldn't turn it down," Lanier told Honig. "I said I'll pitch the rest of my life for the Cardinals and come out with nothing. I think the highest-paid guy on the ball club made $14,000, and I'm talking about a ball club that had won three out of the last four pennants and had a lot of top stars on it."

The three jumped the club immediately, went back to St. Louis, packed up, and left for Mexico.

More players left other teams, and the Mexican raiders decided to try to go after the best players they could find. On the Cardinals, that meant Musial, Moore, and Slaughter.

The Mexicans' offer to Musial kept going up. At one point, Pasquel dropped five cashier's checks for $10,000 each on a hotel bed and told Musial he could consider that a bonus if he agreed to jump. In addition, Musial would receive a five-year contract for $25,000 a year. Lanier even telephoned from Mexico to try to talk Musial into it.

It was Eddie Dyer who gave Musial the speech that talked him into turning down the offer; Dyer asked him how it would sound to his children if they knew their dad had broken his contract with the Cardinals.

The town had been buzzing with the news that Musial might jump, and when reporters gathered outside Musial's hotel they found six-year-old Dickie and asked him what his dad was doing. The child answered, innocently enough, that his father was packing—and that sent the reporters scrambling. In fact, Musial was packing—to move to a new house in St. Louis, not to Mexico City.

Breadon decided at that point that he had to do something to stop the Mexicans from coming after his players. Against the wishes of Commissioner Happy Chandler, Breadon flew to Mexico City and met with the Pasquel brothers. He put on a great performance, pleading with them not to sign any more of his players. The brothers were so moved by his speech that they agreed.

Chandler wasn't pleased. He was also concerned about the raids on major-league players, but he didn't want one team making a separate deal with the Pasquels that didn't apply to the rest of the teams as well. He fined Breadon $5,000.

The Mexican league, of course, failed to make enough inroads to survive. All the players who jumped, however, were banned from the majors for five years. That ban was later rescinded, however, and Lanier, Martin, and Klein came back to play for the Cardinals. Lanier had the most impact, winning 11 games in 1950 and also in 1951.

If the Cardinals had had Lanier for the entire 1946 season, their race with the Dodgers might not have been so close. For the first time in history, the race ended in a tie at the end of the regular season.

Musial had tried to do his part to make sure the Cardinals

won—he even moved to first base against his will when Dyer thought it would help the ball club. It was in Brooklyn that season that Musial earned his famous nickname, when the crowd moaned, "Here comes that man again" as Musial strolled toward the plate. The press picked it up, and the legend of Stan "the Man" Musial was born.

Musial won his second batting title, hitting .365, and would be honored after the season with his second MVP award.

The Cardinals had a chance to win the pennant on the final day of the season and avoid the playoff, but they lost to the Cubs at the same time that old teammate Mort Cooper was beating the Dodgers. A coin flip was used to determine the site of the opener of the best-of-three playoff, and Durocher, representing the Dodgers, won the toss and chose to host the final two games, opting to play the opener in St. Louis.

Dyer had both Howie Pollet and Murry Dickson warm up for the game because he wasn't sure if Pollet's injured muscle in his back would allow him to pitch. But Pollet said it was OK, and he started the game—and finished it, too. His 4–2 victory put the Cardinals in command of the short playoff, and after taking the train ride back to New York, they clinched the pennant with an 8–4 win. They had built an 8–1 lead going into the ninth before the Dodgers rallied, but Harry Brecheen came out of the bullpen to strike out the final two batters with the bases loaded.

Once again it was on to the World Series, this time against the Boston Red Sox, where the big showdown was supposed to be Musial against Ted Williams. As usually happens, the script didn't work out the way it was planned, but it turned out to be even more exciting.

Harry Brecheen, a personal favorite of Dyer's, emerged as the pitching hero of the Series by becoming the first pitcher since 1920 to win three games in the same Series. He and the other Cardinals pitchers managed to limit Williams to five singles in 25 at-bats, thanks in part to a shift ordered by Dyer that had all the infielders actually playing shallow in the outfield.

The Series did not start out well, for the Cardinals, when Rudy York's 10th-inning homer off Pollet gave the Red Sox a 3–2 victory. Musial recalled that he never saw Dyer lower than he was after that game, primarily because he felt sorry for Pollet, whom he had scouted and signed and managed in the minor leagues.

Brecheen pulled the Cardinals even by winning the second game, 3–0. The Red Sox went back ahead with a 4–0 victory in Game 3, after the Series had shifted to Fenway Park, fueled by a first-inning three-run homer by York. The Cardinals finally broke out offensively in the fourth game, winning 12–3 as they tied a Series record with 20 hits, including four each by Slaughter, Kurowski, and rookie catcher Joe Garagiola.

But a 6–3 Boston victory in Game 5 put the Red Sox one win away from a World Series victory. The other bad news for the Cardinals was that Slaughter had been hit on the right elbow with a pitch, and even though trainer Doc Weaver worked with hot and cold packs all night on the train ride back to St. Louis, it didn't appear likely that Slaughter would be able to play for the rest of the series.

Dr. Hyland recommended that Slaughter not play out of fear that a blood clot at the elbow might move. Slaughter knew the risk he was taking, but he played anyway and contributed a base hit in Brecheen's 4–1 victory that set up the seventh and deciding game.

Earlier in the Series, third-base-coach Mike Gonzalez had held up Slaughter on a play when Slaughter thought he could have scored. Slaughter had complained to Dyer, and the manager had told him that if it happened again and Slaughter thought he could score, to go ahead and try.

This conversation would prove crucial. The Red Sox had rallied from a 3–1 deficit to tie the seventh game in the eighth inning. Slaughter led off the bottom of the inning with a single to center but stayed on first as the next two Cardinals batters were retired. With Harry Walker at the plate, Slaughter broke for second, and Walker lined a hit into left center. Remembering his conversation with Dyer, Slaughter didn't even notice if Gonzalez was trying to stop him at third.

"I never considered stopping," he would say later.

Catching shortstop Johnny Pesky by surprise because his back had been to the infield, Slaughter's dash to the plate beat Pesky's hurried throw, and the Cardinals were back in front.

Walker's hit was eventually scored a double but would have been nothing more than a single except for Slaughter's daring baserunning. When Brecheen retired the Red Sox in the ninth after allowing hits to the first two batters, the Cardinals had another championship banner to fly above Sportsman's Park.

Challenging the decision by his coach and Pesky's arm was nothing for Slaughter, who had overcome bigger obstacles simply in getting to the major leagues.

During the winter of 1938, Slaughter had gone hunting for rabbits with his father near his home in North Carolina. They handled infected rabbits, and by the next morning his father was dead of tularemia. Slaughter also became ill and nearly died. When he reported to spring training, Slaughter was still experiencing occasional dizzy spells, but he beat off the disease and opened the season as the Cardinals' regular right fielder.

Slaughter never forgot the lesson he learned from Dyer back in the minor leagues in 1936, when Dyer caught him walking into the dugout from the outfield at the end of an inning. "He said to me, 'Kid, if you're tired, I can get you some help.'

"After that I never stopped running, from the time I left the top step until I got back there, from 1936 until I retired. And I ran whether I felt like it or not."

It was Slaughter's hustle, even on routine plays in the middle of games in July, that was his trademark with the Cardinals. That his most famous play was a dash from first base to home was truly appropriate.

In a column for the *Globe-Democrat* in 1976, Bob Burnes admitted that he was a member of the Enos Slaughter fan club.

"His enthusiasm, his constant hustle typified more than any other player, past or present, the image of the Cardinals," Burnes wrote. "He never walked. He always ran. He never ducked an argument, a fight, or a tag. He was in some dandy brawls in his time. He didn't always win but he never ran away from them."

Slaughter recalled one game in Pittsburgh when he slid hard into second base, attempting to break up a double play. The fans got on him, and the next time the Pirates came to St. Louis and Slaughter was on first base, they made several attempts to hit him with the ball on throws from second to first.

"[Danny] Murtaugh is covering but he's late and I'm on top of him," Slaughter said. "I come in with my right foot high and I get him with my spikes right in the belly button. It cut off his uniform. He was standing there with his shirt in shreds. After that there wasn't any more trouble."

Slaughter may not have been a surprise star for the Cardinals in the World Series, but they did get an unexpected boost from their 20-year-old catcher, Garagiola, who hit .316 and had four RBIs. Garagiola had joined the Cardinals in May, and he never was to forget his introduction to the major leagues, which came at a hotel in Philadelphia, when he arrived at 2:30 A.M. and was told by the desk clerk he was rooming with Marion, the team captain. Garagiola had to walk up and down the hall outside his room trying to gather enough nerve to wake up Marion and tell him he was his new roommate.

Arriving in the big leagues almost caught Garagiola as off guard as when he was in an Army mess hall in the Philippines listening to the radio and heard the commentator say the Cardinals were excited about a young catcher they had in the minor leagues who almost was ready to join the major-league team.

"I listened to him and said, 'I'll never get out of Columbus,'" Garagiola said. "Then the guy stumbled over my name and I almost fell off the bench."

When Garagiola did get to the major leagues, he was quick to begin practicing for his second career, as a broadcaster, at the same time. He would start talking about the hitter coming to the plate, and it became a really annoying habit to a lot of hitters.

"Here's Roy Campanella," Garagiola would say, "hitting .320 and so he's just about hitting his weight. If Campy would shed about 20 pounds, he'd be hitting better."

One player became so upset by Garagiola's constant banter that he stepped out of the batter's box and asked the umpire to tell Garagiola to be quiet. Garagiola continued the habit even after he was traded by the Cardinals in 1951, but one player he couldn't rattle was Musial.

"One day in Pittsburgh, Musial stepped up and I said, 'How's the family Stan?'" Garagiola said. "The next thing I knew he was crossing home plate with a homer and saying, 'They're all fine, Joe, how's your family?'"

Garagiola and Musial had known each other for a long time, having first met when Garagiola was 15 years old and went to work for the Cardinals as the assistant grounds keeper for their Springfield, Missouri, farm team. That was the season Musial was playing there, and one of Garagiola's jobs was the laundry. He also cut the grass and caught batting practice.

The Cardinals had designs on Garagiola's playing ability, however, and he proved them correct in 1946 and in later years. Even though he now cracks jokes about his career, he was a solid player, finishing his nine-year career, five-plus with the Cardinals, with a .257 average.

Musial, Slaughter, and the rest of the Cardinals received a smaller share for winning the World Series—because they had voted to waive the $175,000 in broadcasting revenue to help establish the players' pension fund.

The idea of shortstop Marty Marion and trainer Doc Weaver, the fund called for matching financial contributions from the players and ball clubs, along with profits from the All-Star Game and the radio receipts from both the All-Star Game and the World Series, to be used to fund the plan. Players who spent five years in the major leagues would be able to draw $50 a month at age 45, and 10-year men would receive $100 a month.

"In my opinion, Marion's plan, if it had been in effect before, might have stopped Max Lanier and others from jumping to Mexico," Terry Moore said at the time. "Certainly, I believe it would help prevent such things in the future. It would be a reward for loyalty to an employee of long service. Actually, it would be an investment for which the player's own skill and effort would provide most of the dividends."

The system has changed some over the years, obviously primarily from the inclusion of television revenues, but remains basically the same as was originally mapped out by Marion and Weaver. The pension plan is one of the biggest perks in baseball and is the best plan in any professional sport.

As the Cardinals were basking in the glow of another World Series triumph, they didn't know this one would have to last a while. It would be 18 years before the team would return to the Series again, in 1964.

In 1947, the team got off to a slow start. Breadon made a special trip to New York to try to find out what was wrong, and he sought the advice of Moore and Marion on whether he should replace Dyer as manager. Only when they assured him that the problems weren't Dyer's fault was his job saved.

The players had learned to respect Dyer quickly in 1946, even those who had not approved of his selection as the successor to Southworth. Dyer had earned a reputation in the minor leagues for developing young players, and his major-league players also knew he was in control of the club. He even went to the team's management and convinced Breadon to give the players an extra $20 a month for tip money when they were on the road. It was not a major event, but it convinced the players Dyer was looking out for them.

"As manager you're not in a popularity contest," Dyer said in an interview in 1949. "Most of your men will appreciate what you do for them and the consideration you show them, but there's always someone who will misinterpret that as a sign of weakness. That's when you crack down."

Dyer did get the team to play better, but it wasn't enough. The Cardinals finished second to Brooklyn, five games out. The biggest news occurred off the field, after the season, when Breadon sold his beloved Cardinals to St. Louis businessman Fred Saigh and Robert Hannegan, who had been the U.S. postmaster general, for a little more than $4 million.

Breadon, now 70 years old, already knew his health was failing, and he was worried about what would happen to the team if he died. Within two years, he would be dead of cancer. Hannegan had been Breadon's longtime neighbor in St. Louis, and they began talking about the sale of the ball club after Hannegan had sent Breadon a congratulatory telegram for his 70th birthday.

"It is unpleasant for me to dispose of the Cardinals but I believe, in the interest of the Cardinals, a man of the character and ability of Bob Hannegan, a young man, will be able to do more in keeping the Cardinals in the position they are today than I could do from now on," Breadon said.

There was some speculation at the time that Breadon had delayed selling the Cardinals for several years because he wanted to prove the team could win without Rickey, who had received much of the credit for the team's success prior to his departure in 1942. The team did win in 1943, 1944, and 1946, but primarily with players who had been acquired when Rickey was in charge.

That the Cardinals missed Rickey's expertise, primarily in the acquisition of young players, was quite evident during the last few years of the 1940s and the early 1950s, when the Cardinals were slow to sign black players while Rickey broke the color barrier by signing Jackie Robinson for the Dodgers and quickly added more black players.

When the Dodgers first signed Robinson, there were unsubstantiated reports that the Cardinals had voted to boycott games against the Dodgers. Musial said that never happened, and he also didn't know what all the fuss about Robinson was anyway.

"I had played against him in some exhibition games, and watched him take ground balls and he seemed kind of stiff to me and not real graceful," Musial said. "Watching batting practice, I thought he had a short, choppy swing and I wasn't too concerned about him as a major leaguer. I guess my scouting talents proved wrong. He turned out to be a very exciting player."

Hannegan lasted just a year with the Cardinals, however, before he also became a victim of poor health. He sold his interest in the team to Saigh, and he would die less than a year later from the effects of high blood pressure.

The 1948 season probably was the finest of Musial's career, even though he couldn't lead the Cardinals to more than a second-place finish, six and a half games behind the champion Boston Braves. Musial won MVP honors again and missed winning the Triple Crown by just one home run. He led the league with a .376 average and 131 RBIs. His 39 homers were just one less than former teammate Johnny Mize and Pittsburgh's Ralph Kiner had hit. He set career highs in hits, homers, runs, RBIs, batting average, and slugging percentage.

It was during that season that a couple of pitchers said they had figured out how to pitch to Musial. Preacher Roe of the Dodgers interrupted a Cardinals pregame meeting one day with his plan on how to pitch to Musial. "Walk him on four pitches and pick him off first," Roe said. On another occasion, Brooklyn's Carl Erskine revealed his strategy on pitching to Musial. "I just throw him my best stuff, then run over to back up third base," he said.

For Cardinals fans who had been used to seeing the team come from behind to win close pennant races, 1949 was a tough season. Instead of coming from behind to win, the

Cardinals went from a two-and-a-half-game lead with 10 games to play and lost, finishing one game behind the Dodgers.

The race came down to the final day, with the Cardinals having to win and the Dodgers needing a loss to force another playoff. The Cardinals did their part, beating Chicago, but the Dodgers pulled out a 10th-inning victory over the Phillies to clinch the pennant.

Dyer said he thought the team's downfall simply was a case of running out of gas.

"I don't want anyone blaming the ball club for our downfall," Dyer said at the time. "I don't want anyone to think that they quit, that they didn't have the stuff in the clutch or that any internal problems hurt them.

"I know, better than anyone else in the world, that the boys gave me everything they had. Some of them were exhausted, and that, more than anything else, accounted for the defeats and the slump at the end of the season."

The 1940s had been a great decade for the Cardinals. It would be another story in the decade to come.

5

Gussie Takes Over

THE 1950s

◆

The Cardinals' struggle during the last few years of the 1940s were nothing compared to the troubles the team would face in the decade of the 1950s. The trouble began with owner Fred Saigh's indictment by the federal government on charges of income tax evasion, extended through the many front-office changes and bad trades made during the decade, and even reached the playing field, where several would-be stars failed to fulfill their promising potential.

For nine consecutive years, starting in 1941, the Cardinals had either won the National League pennant or finished second. The only time they even came close to winning in the 1950s was in 1957, when they stayed in the race with the Milwaukee Braves (the team had moved from Boston in 1953) until September before slumping, finishing in second, eight games out. During the rest of the decade, nobody in St. Louis had to worry about catching pennant fever.

Saigh was convinced the Cardinals could field a competitive team at the start of the decade. The interest in the team was high, partially from the expanding radio network that was now broadcasting all games, home and away. With the Cardinals the southernmost and westernmost franchise in the majors, they were the team of choice for a great many fans all over the country. When the broadcasts later shifted to power-house radio station KMOX, heard in many states at night, the interest increased even more.

In at least one area, Saigh was a little ahead of his time. He wanted the Cardinals to play more games at night than they were scheduled for, believing there would be more interest in the games, both from fans coming to the ball park and others listening at home on the radio. He even had the Cardinals play the first opening day night game in baseball history in 1950, beating the Pirates 4–2.

The idea was novel at the time, and Saigh had a hard time convincing his skeptics, including *Globe-Democrat* sports editor Bob Burnes, that he was right. Wrote Burnes, "We just seem to have the feeling that while night baseball is a wonderful thing, there can be too much of it. Night baseball was invented for the sole purpose of providing baseball at a time when working people could see it. That it has been a financial boon can never be denied. To extend it to Sunday night, however, seems to be going a bit too far, seems just a little too much like grasping for an extra dollar."

While Saigh turned out to be right about night baseball, he turned out to be wrong about a plan to build an arch along the St. Louis riverfront. In 1949 the arch already was being discussed, as was building a new stadium for the Cardinals, and Saigh said he thought the stadium should have priority.

"The argument that it will become a trademark for St. Louis and a landmark for generations of the future is a rather empty one to me," Saigh said about the arch. "St. Louis has gradually lost ground in maintaining its standing in population. It hasn't been so many years since we were the fourth largest city in the country, and the fifth and sixth largest in terms of population, in the country.

"How could a stainless steel arch, costing anywhere from $8 million to $12 million, recapture the glory that made St. Louis the outstanding city in the Middle West? Practical men say 'no,' the longhairs say 'yes.' I side with those who keep practical and yet create something beautiful in so doing.

"There are many things that can be done on the riverfront which would be practical, have a great deal of utility and yet have beauty. It may not be a stadium, but certainly it should not be a useless arch."

Worrying about whether the city should build the arch or whether the Cardinals should play more games at night or during the day didn't turn out to be Saigh's biggest problem. On April 22, 1952, Saigh was indicted by a federal grand jury on five counts charging evasion of income taxes through the filing of false returns. Saigh was charged both personally and as head of the Cardinals with evading $49,620 in taxes on unreported income of $108,823.

Saigh eventually pleaded no contest to two charges of income tax evasion. He was sentenced to 15 months in prison and fined $15,000. When he was sentenced on January 28, 1953, he was given until May 4 to wind up his business affairs, including selling the Cardinals, and turn himself over to begin serving his sentence.

Saigh, who complained that he received too stiff a sentence, knew as soon as his legal troubles began that he likely would be forced to sell the Cardinals, but he didn't have much time left to find a buyer. He naturally was hopeful a local person or company would come forward, but nobody did, and it appeared he was going to have to sell the franchise to groups that would have moved it to Milwaukee or Houston.

That was when August A. Busch, Jr., the head of Anheuser-Busch and a St. Louis civic leader, if not a baseball fan, stepped forward. His company bought the Cardinals for $3.75 million for the primary reason of keeping the team in St. Louis.

"When it became apparent that an out-of-town group was ready to purchase the Cardinals at a price which I felt was a fair value for the club, I informed Mr. Busch and his associates of the impending sale," Saigh said at the time. "They again expressed serious interest in having the club remain here. For the past several days we have been working out the details.

"As sorry as I am to part with the club, I am genuinely happy that St. Louis fans will now continue to see the kind of baseball that only their Cardinals can play."

James Hickok, executive vice-president of the First National Bank in St. Louis, was one of Busch's two key representatives in the negotiations, which concluded with the brewery buying the team on February 20, 1953.

"We all felt that if the Cardinals were moved out of St. Louis, this community would have lost a great civic asset and that St. Louis would never be the same without them," Hickok said.

Before Busch stepped forward, the sale negotiations with the Milwaukee group had reached the point where front-office employees of the Cardinals were told that if they wished to move with the club to Milwaukee, their expenses would be paid and the club would compensate them for any losses in selling their homes.

Busch said he had not seen a Cardinals game in the previous two or three years when he bought the team; his friends said he was exaggerating, that he had not seen two or three games in his life. It didn't take long for Busch to develop a love for the game and for the Cardinals, however. Just weeks after buying the club, he was in St. Petersburg, Florida, for spring training, and after donning a uniform shirt and a cap, he strode proudly to the plate and took some swings and pitches from Eddie Yuhas, who was standing about 30 feet away.

"When Busch missed a few swings [Eddie] Stanky warned Yuhas that if Busch didn't get to hit the next one, Yuhas would find himself on his way to some other ball club," J. Roy Stockton reported.

It didn't take long for Busch to learn that one of the secrets to a successful team was in drawing fans, and as he had learned in the brewery business, the secret was in giving people what they wanted.

"There is one important thing I know about running a ball club, and that is: Do not challenge the customers," Busch said in an interview with J. G. Taylor Spink in the *Sporting News* on May 29, 1953. "Do not set up inconveniences for them to hurdle. Baseball must be sold, not merely displayed with a sort of off-hand invitation, 'Come and get it, if you can, and if you want it.'

"Selling beer and selling baseball entail the establishment of friendly relations between the buyers and the sellers. That much I know about baseball."

Busch's big hobby growing up had been show horses, not baseball. Before Saigh got into trouble and the Cardinals almost moved, Busch said he had "no more intention of becoming involved in baseball than I had of buying a trans-Atlantic liner."

Busch was a quick learner, however. One of his first lessons came when he realized that the best way to develop players was through the minor leagues.

"I am convinced that buying a pennant is impossible," he said in the same 1953 interview. "I did not go into this proposition without some study. I noted that many men and organizations of considerable wealth had dashed into the major leagues with the belief that money lavishly spent could turn the trick. I have no such ideas.

"I am alive to the tremendous importance of the farm system, and the necessity for 100 percent co-operation among those who run our subsidiary clubs."

Busch carried his philosophy of running Anheuser-Busch with him to the Cardinals—work hard, love one's work. What he found out, however, was that it took more than hard work and a love for the job to be successful.

The first year that Busch owned the team, the Cardinals finished tied for third. The disappointment was just beginning.

Busch had been surprised and upset by the condition of Sportsman's Park, and he decided it would be cheaper than renting for the Cardinals to buy the stadium from the Browns.

He paid an extra $800,000, since the Browns didn't have the money to make the repairs Busch thought were needed, and took over ownership of the facility.

As part of the sale, Busch changed the name from Sportsman's Park. He first wanted to call the stadium Budweiser Park, but was convinced that was too commercial a name. He compromised on the name Busch Stadium.

Even though Busch had said he knew he couldn't go out and buy a championship, he certainly tried to do so. Over the next four years, the Cardinals made either cash or player offers for the Cubs' Ernie Banks, the Dodgers' Gil Hodges, and the Giants' Willie Mays, only to be turned down each time.

The first target was Hodges. After Stanky said he might be available, Busch instructed a team official to contact Dodgers owner Walter O'Malley to find out how much it would cost to acquire Hodges. He came back and reported O'Malley's price was $600,000.

Even Busch wouldn't go that high. Later, O'Malley said he had quoted that figure, but only because he didn't expect the Cardinals to accept. "I don't know what I would have done if they had accepted the price," O'Malley said. "Brooklyn fans would hang me and burn me and tear me to pieces if I traded or sold Gil Hodges."

The next target was Banks. During a 1957 interview, Busch said he still had not learned that baseball was different than any other business.

"In industry, when you're putting together a factory and you need something, you just go out and buy it," Busch said. "I figured that building a team wasn't much different from building a factory, but in a few days I was reminded again that this wasn't so. [Frank] Lane called to tell me we couldn't get Banks.

"What did you offer for him," Busch asked.

"I went up to $500,000," Lane said.

"And you couldn't buy him?" Busch exploded.

"Mr. Busch," Lane said, "I was told politely that Mr. Wrigley needs a half million dollars just about as much as you do."

By 1957 the price for a superstar ballplayer had gone even higher, Busch learned. The target of his affections that summer was Mays—and the offer was $1 million. Apparently, the offer was considered by the Giants before the decision was made by the team that it would move from New York to San Francisco. That killed any possibility of Mays going to the Cardinals.

"[Chub] Feeney told me the last time we talked about a Mays deal that it was out of the question," Lane said. "As I recall, Chub told me that if they traded Mays and then moved to San Francisco, the people out there would throw them into the bay."

Bing Devine, who spent a long time working as a general manager under Busch, said it took those lessons for Busch to learn that running a baseball team was different from running a brewery.

"He came into baseball with the idea that he could run the team the same way he ran his corporation," Devine said. "He thought he could take the same approach to baseball and that it would work. He was shocked when other owners told him no offer would be good enough. He didn't understand it. But he was still used to a corporate way of thinking instead of a baseball way of thinking. He learned the hard way, but he learned rather quickly."

Even though Busch had trusted people working under him, he found out it wasn't easy building a successful team. It became even harder when the team changed managers, changed general managers, made bad trades, and had players whom it thought would be productive but failed to develop.

The Cardinals went through seven managers in the 1950s. Eddie Dyer left after the 1950 season. Marty Marion retired as a player and became the manager in 1951.

Saigh had been impressed with Marion, who would casually drop into Saigh's office from time to time while the owner was reviewing about 25 candidates for the job.

"I think I was impressed most by two things about Marty, aside from his intelligence, personality, and examples of leadership I had already seen," Saigh said in an interview. "One was his orderly thinking processes. He's a man of mental detail, the same as I am. Second, he's a man of exemplary conduct—not prissy—but a clean-living man who has handled his own affairs smoothly. I had the confidence I could trust him to handle my affairs—my ball club—too."

Unfortunately, the relationship between Marion and Saigh quickly soured. Despite guiding the Cardinals to a third-place finish, eight games above .500, Marion was fired when Saigh decided he wasn't forceful enough as the field boss. Marion's other major crime was the Cardinals' trouble in beating the Dodgers (they were 4–18 against Brooklyn that season), a problem that would continue plaguing the Cardinals in years to come. Ironically, Marion would immediately be hired to manage the hometown rival Browns in 1952.

Marion was replaced by Eddie Stanky, the first time in more than 20 years the Cardinals picked a manager who had not played for them (though Stanky would play for the Cardinals in 1952 and 1953). Saigh wanted an aggressive field boss, and that's exactly what he got. Stanky feuded with his players, he feuded with the press, he feuded with umpires.

In one game in Chicago, after Musial was forced to leave the game because of a twisted left knee, the officials in the press box contacted the Cardinals dugout, as was the customary procedure, to get a report on his condition. Not only would Stanky not respond, he told the reporters to go to hell.

Later, Stanky said he had been upset because he had had to fine one of his players earlier in the day, pitcher Harry Brecheen, for permitting a hitter to bunt on what was supposed to be a pitchout. It perhaps was more painful to Stanky because he considered Brecheen a close friend, since the two had first met in the minor leagues years before. Stanky did lift the fine in a subsequent clubhouse meeting.

It was Brecheen in fact who had taken Stanky in on the day

Stanky first arrived in Greenville, Mississippi, in the Class C East Dixie League, treated him to dinner, and found him a place to stay. Stanky claimed he was so homesick that if it hadn't been for Brecheen's kindness, he might have said good-bye to professional baseball after one day and turned around and went home to Philadelphia.

Some of Stanky's other fines also were cause for trouble. In spring training, if a player didn't come to camp at the weight that had been prescribed for him, Stanky fined him one dollar for each pound over the requested weight. He also fined players if they weren't in the dugout for the first and last pitch of a game and if a hitter failed to get a man in from third with no outs or one out, along with fines for other various reasons.

Busch got along well with Stanky and admired his aggressiveness. When the team struggled and there were suggestions for Busch to dump Stanky, he refused.

"I am a Cardinals fan myself and I want to win, too," Busch said. "As a matter of fact, one of the reasons I like Stanky is because he has the same will-to-win spirit. He is a tenacious little scrapper and if we all give him and the team support and a chance to make good, I don't think they will fail us."

One of Stanky's most celebrated run-ins was with umpire Scotty Robb during a game in Cincinnati in 1952. Solly Hemus was called out on strikes by Robb, then threw his bat. After he was ejected, Stanky took up the argument, and Robb also kicked him out of the game. While the two were arguing, Robb began shoving Stanky.

Stanky and Hemus were both fined by NL president Warren Giles, but Robb got a stiffer fine that Giles said well exceeded the combined totals of the fines assessed Stanky ($50) and Hemus ($25). Robb was so upset by the whole situation that he resigned his umpiring position.

Stanky lasted until the early part of the 1955 season, when his temper finally got the best of him and he was fired. He was replaced by Harry Walker.

Walker lasted just through the rest of the 1955 season, being replaced by Fred Hutchinson at the start of the 1956 season when Frank Lane took over as the team's general manager. Hutchinson remained until 10 games from the end of the 1958 season. Stan Hack replaced him on an interim basis, and when the 1959 season began, Solly Hemus was in place as the seventh manager of the decade.

The confusion caused by the constant shuffling of managers wasn't all that was wrong with the organization during those years. There was a shuffling of players as well, as general managers Dick Meyer, Frank Lane, and Bing Devine tried to pull off the one deal they thought would make the difference between a winning and losing club. Unfortunately, at least until near the end of the decade, almost every deal the Cardinals attempted turned out to be a mistake.

In 1951 the Cardinals packaged Joe Garagiola, Howie Pollet, and Ted Wilks and sent them to Pittsburgh for Wally Westlake and Cliff Chambers. The trade backfired when Garagiola, destined for more fame as a broadcaster, turned in several good seasons for the Pirates, while neither Westlake nor Chambers turned out to be as effective as the Cardinals had hoped.

The trade that produced the biggest shock and fan reaction came on the day of the Cardinals' final exhibition game before the start of the 1954 season. Outfielder Enos Slaughter was traded to the Yankees for four young players—only one of whom, pitcher Mel Wright, was identified at the time of the deal.

The 37-year-old Slaughter, who had come up through the Cardinals system and had played for the major-league team for 13 years, did the only thing he knew to do after general manager Dick Meyer informed him of the deal—he cried.

Stanky said the trade was made to create a spot in the Cardinals outfield for rookie Wally Moon, who had been impressive in spring training and would go on to win the 1954 Rookie of the Year award.

That didn't matter to the legions of Slaughter fans, who flooded the Cardinals' switchboard with the greatest reaction to a trade since Sam Breadon had traded Rogers Hornsby for Frankie Frisch. Callers threatened to cancel their season tickets, and some cried as much as Slaughter. Busch had to take his phone off the hook at his Grant's Farm estate.

Slaughter vowed that he still had some productive years remaining in his career and did not agree that the Cardinals needed to make the trade as part of a youth movement.

"I'll be around when a lot of these guys are gone," Slaughter said. "I'm not finished. I'll prove it to them. I can't see this."

As Slaughter left the stadium and headed for his car in the parking lot, he bumped into Musial. No words were spoken before both of them broke into tears again.

The Slaughter trade left Musial as the senior member of the Cardinals, and it also meant that only nine players on the roster at the start of the 1954 season had been there when Stanky had taken over as manager two years earlier.

In his column in the *Globe-Democrat,* Burnes wrote that the reaction was natural for a player who had been as popular as Slaughter had been with the Cardinals.

"From a strictly baseball point of view, the sale, trade, or otherwise dismissal of Enos Slaughter by the Cardinals to the Yankees can be defended," Burnes wrote. "If the Cardinals wanted to explain why it was done, they could find seven or even 70 reasons. But there is one problem.

"All of the reasons could be sound. They still would not satisfy the normal baseball fan, the much hackneyed 'man in the street' who pays at the gate. Enos Slaughter was more than a ballplayer, as any Cardinals fan could tell you. He was an institution—not only among the fans, but among the players as well. To be trite again, Enos was the ballplayers' ballplayer—he played the game the way it should be played.

"No matter how sound the reasons, fans are going to be upset when a player like that goes somewhere else."

One of the players the Cardinals ended up receiving for Slaughter was outfielder Bill Virdon, and he turned out to the Rookie of the Year in 1955, hitting .281 with 17 homers and

68 RBIs. But just as he was winning over some of the Slaugh-
ter-faithful skeptics, he too was gone, traded to Pittsburgh in
1956. Virdon was sent to the Pirates for outfielder Bobby Del
Greco and pitcher Dick Littlefield in another deal the
Cardinals would live to regret.

Just a month later, shortly before the June 15 trading deadline, general manager Frank Lane topped that deal by working
out an eight-player trade with the Giants that sent Red
Schoendienst to New York.

The public reaction to the deal wasn't as vocal as it had
been for the Slaughter trade, maybe because the fans had
grown more calloused. The *Globe-Democrat* reported that fans
calling the newspaper's switchboard had the general attitude
of "What's next?"

Schoendienst was critical of the deal, but not for a personal
reason. Also included in the deal was young outfielder Jackie
Brandt, one of the top prospects in the game at the time, although he didn't develop into a great player. The only notable
player the Cardinals received in the trade was shortstop Alvin
Dark.

"This is no reflection on a fine guy like Al Dark, but Brandt
alone, counting what he can do now and what he'll do in the
future, is worth all the players the Cardinals got in the deal,"
Schoendienst said at the time.

Schoendienst said he thought the trade cost the Cardinals a
chance to win the pennant in 1957, the year he helped the
Braves win after he was traded there by the Giants.

"I figured the combination [of young players] was so good
that no matter where the club finished this season, we would
have a good chance to win the flag next season," Schoendienst
said. "Lane made several good moves, but then he just
wouldn't let well enough alone."

Lane also traded Hemus to Philadelphia in 1956 for infielder
Bobby Morgan, whom Lane expected to take over as the
Cardinals shortstop, but who was really a second baseman. He
also sent shortstop Alex Grammas to Cincinnati that same

year for Chuck Harmon. When Morgan couldn't play short-stop, the Cardinals turned to Al Dark, who played well but not spectacularly until he was traded to the Cubs in 1958.

Lane likely wouldn't have stopped there if he had had his way. He wanted to make two more deals that Busch over-ruled—one that would have sent Musial to Philadelphia for pitcher Robin Roberts and another that would have moved Ken Boyer to Pittsburgh.

Lane had bucked tradition from the moment he arrived in St. Louis and changed the team's uniforms, taking the popular birds-on-the-bat insignia off the uniform and changing the stockings' base color from red to blue. He quickly learned that he had made a mistake.

"To me, as I told them in St. Louis, tradition meant the men who wore the uniform, not the uniform," Lane said. "I was wrong . . . you know, when I was with the White Sox we re-ceived lots of letters from fans who still wanted us to go back to the old white stockings. They were convinced that Fielder Jones's stockings had been more important than Fielder Jones.

"I wasn't kidding when I explained that we took the bird insignia off to make the Cardinals uniforms lighter; those in-signias were all backed up by canvas. I wanted a light uniform because of the hot summers we have in St. Louis."

But the reaction to that decision paled in comparison with what Busch had to say when he found out Lane, who had been given total authority over player moves, was thinking about trading Musial.

Musial and Schoendienst had been the two players Busch had known, on a social basis, before he had bought the team. He had not wanted Lane to trade Schoendienst, but he had understood the reasons for the move and hadn't blocked it.

Musial's business partner, Biggie Garagnani, had received a tip that Lane was in the process of completing the Musial deal. For confirmation, he called J. G. Taylor Spink at the *Sporting News*, and after making a couple of calls, Spink called back and said yes, the deal was in the works.

Garagnani tried to call Busch directly, but the owner wasn't available. He reached other top officials at the brewery and told them that if the trade did in fact go through, Musial wouldn't report; he would quit.

Musial didn't know anything about any of the conversations until he saw Garagnani at their restaurant. As Musial recalled in his autobiography, Garagnani told him that he normally didn't meddle in Musial's baseball affairs, but he couldn't stand by and watch him get traded to the Phillies.

"Fed up with rumors as well as watching our clubhouse filled with a stream of strangers, I told Biggie he'd been right, absolutely," Musial said. "However, if I had really been faced with the choice of ending my career, giving up a game I enjoyed so much, particularly with the 3,000-hit goal in sight, I well might have reconsidered. Fortunately, I was spared that critical decision."

When word finally reached Busch about what was going on, Busch called Lane and in no uncertain terms told him Musial would not be traded. He also stripped away Lane's carte blanche authority and told him any future moves had to be cleared through Dick Meyer at the brewery.

Lane's deals and would-be deals got him into hot water with Busch, who was half-serious and half-joking when he suggested at a dinner before the start of the 1957 season that if the Cardinals didn't win by 1958, Lane would be out of a job.

"I expect the Cardinals to scare the daylights out of a lot of clubs this year," Busch said at the Knights of the Cauliflower Ear dinner. "If we don't win this year, I know we will win next year. If we don't, Frank Lane will be out on his ear."

Lane also admitted that he expected the Cardinals to win and said, "Mr. Busch, if I don't produce that winner by the end of 1958, I'll believe that I have failed and I'll leave the ball club."

As it turned out, Lane was gone after the 1957 season, taking a job as the general manager of the Cleveland Indians. That allowed Busch to promote a young front-office executive who had grown up in the Cardinals organization by advancing through the front offices of minor-league clubs: Bing Devine.

One of Devine's first moves was a nonmove; he made a committment that the Cardinals would not trade Ken Boyer. Lane had been considering offers to deal Boyer to Pittsburgh, and after Devine took over, he received what he considered a fair offer from Philadelphia—outfielder Richie Ashburn and pitcher Harvey Haddix.

Although Boyer had been shuffled between third base and the outfield, Devine saw enough talent there that he decided Boyer would remain a Cardinal.

"I'll stake what little baseball reputation I might have that Boyer, out of position this year in center field, will become a standout third baseman, maybe the best the Cardinals ever had, and the kind of player on whom we can build for the future," Devine said after taking over the GM job in 1957.

Boyer was 26 at the time and had been in the major leagues for three years. The decision, as it turned out, was a correct one. Boyer was the first important piece of the puzzle that eventually would become a world champion team in 1964.

Bad trades aside, part of the reason for the Cardinals' struggles during the 1950s was the failure of several players who had been counted on heavily and didn't come through. The three biggest flops were Tom Alston, Von McDaniel, and Steve Bilko.

Alston had the distinction of being the first black player in Cardinals history. A tall, gangly first baseman, his contract was purchased from the San Diego club in the Pacific Coast League for more than $100,000 shortly after Busch bought the Cardinals.

Alston, 22 years old at the time, had hit .297 with 23 homers and 101 RBIs for San Diego in 1953. Unfortunately, he never was able to translate that success in the minors into success in the majors. He lasted only parts of four seasons with the Cardinals, hit a total of four home runs, and played just 91 games.

"He was overmatched," Devine said. "He probably was pushed too fast, and he was under a lot of pressure. Everybody was guilty."

Alston said in a later interview that his problem was physical; he couldn't play more than a week at a time without getting exhausted and needing a few days of rest. Trainer Bob Bauman said Alston was mentally ill as well as physically sick. Alston later spent 10 years in a mental institution in North Carolina after his baseball career ended.

Alston didn't think the pressure of being the first black player on the Cardinals was the source of his problems.

"That didn't bother me as much as my own worries about myself," Alston said in an interview with Bob Burnes in 1977. "Headaches, nausea, things like that got me down. I don't think that the pressure of making the team was the cause.

"They gave me every chance. I just want them to know I'm grateful. It wasn't their fault that I didn't make it."

The first really good black player in Cardinals history turned out to be a right-handed pitcher, Brooks Lawrence. He was 15–6 for the Cardinals in 1954, but then went 3–8 the next season and was traded to Cincinnati. He had two good years for the Reds, winning a combined total of 35 games.

Steve Bilko also failed to live up to his minor-league credentials.

"He had played for me in Rochester, but he just wasn't able to be anything more than be an outstanding Triple A player," Devine said. "He wasn't able to show the ability at the major-league level that he had shown at Triple A."

Bilko had one good season, in 1953, when he hit 21 homers and drove in 84. He was traded to the Cubs the next year, however, and bounced around the majors until his career finally ended in 1962.

What happened to Von McDaniel was no doubt one of the

strangest stories in the history of the Cardinals franchise. Signed out of high school in Oklahoma at the request of his brother Lindy, already pitching for the Cardinals, McDaniel reported to the team in 1957.

Manager Fred Hutchinson didn't intend to pitch the 18-year-old very often. He was on the major-league roster because the rules in those days dictated that anybody who received more than a $6,000 signing bonus was frozen on the major-league roster for two years. McDaniel, like his brother did, had received a bonus of $50,000.

With the Cardinals way behind in a game in Philadelphia, however, Hutchinson brought in McDaniel in relief. A funny thing happened—he pitched four scoreless innings.

It was during that game that Musial, who had missed meeting him after he had joined the team, went over from first base to introduce himself and tell McDaniel he would be playing off the base.

"Darned if Von didn't take off his cap, look wide-eyed at me and say, 'Gosh Mr. Musial, you've been my idol for years,'" Musial said. "It's sure good to meet you.' Then he shook hands. That's the kind of a kid he was."

Three days later, playing the Dodgers in Brooklyn, the Cardinals were behind when Hutchinson again inserted McDaniel into the game. After a rally put the team in front, most observers expected Hutchinson to switch to a more-experienced pitcher. But he left McDaniel in, nursing a one-run lead in the ninth.

With a runner on first and Duke Snider coming to the plate, shortstop Alvin Dark called time and ran in to talk to McDaniel. Dark asked him if he knew who was coming up to bat.

"Sure," he said. "It's Mr. Snider."

Snider grounded out, and the Cardinals won the game. By the time the Cardinals came back from the road trip, McDaniel's legend was building. The Cardinals needed a starting pitcher for a game against the Dodgers, and hoping not to get McDaniel too excited, Hutchinson tried to conceal that Mc-

Daniel was going to start. The ball park was packed anyway, and the fans got a bonus when they learned McDaniel was going to start.

They weren't disappointed. McDaniel carried a no-hitter into the sixth, when the Dodgers loaded the bases with no outs on two hits and an error. McDaniel calmly pitched out of the jam without allowing a run. When he came to bat in the eighth, he received a standing ovation. McDaniel pitched a complete game, winning 2–0, allowing just the two hits.

Writing in the *Globe-Democrat*, Burnes said, "Young Von is remarkable, almost unbelievable. We have some books around here someplace that prove conclusively and beyond doubt that it is a physical, mental, and mathematical impossibility for a youngster of 18 to pitch with the poise and effectiveness and aplomb and savvy and know-how that Von McDaniel has shown. And if we ever find those books, they'll wind up in the nearest waste basket."

One of the people watching, and marveling in McDaniel's success, was Devine.

"I went to the clubhouse after the game and asked Hutchinson what McDaniel had that I couldn't see," Devine said. "Hutch looked at me and in a very down-to-earth fashion said 'Not a damn thing.' That made me feel better, because I didn't think I had lost the ability to judge people. The hitters obviously didn't know him, and I guess they were looking for more, too."

Unfortunately, the legend of Von McDaniel was over almost as soon as it began. He finished the year with a 7–5 record and pitched in only two more games in his career. In 1958, he tore a muscle in his right shoulder, developed control problems, and never again pitched in the major leagues. He tried to make it as an infielder but never again got out of the minor leagues.

In addition to these disappointments, the Cardinals spent $90,000 on a Mexican pitcher, Memo Luna, who had been at San Diego; He pitched one game in his career, lasting just two-thirds of an inning.

There were some good moments in the decade as well, however, and most of them centered around Musial.

Perhaps the greatest comeback the Cardinals ever made came on June 15, 1952, when they fell behind the Giants 11–0 in the first game of a doubleheader. Stanky thought about pulling out his regulars and getting them some rest, but he decided to wait. The Cardinals began to rally, and by the eighth inning, they had closed the gap to 11–10.

Solly Hemus led off the eighth with a home run to tie the game, Slaughter added his fifth RBI later in the inning, and Hemus's two-run homer in the ninth capped the dramatic 14–12 victory.

Musial's best day of the decade came two years later, on May 2, 1954, also against the Giants, when he set a major-league record by hitting five home runs in a doubleheader.

Musial smashed three home runs in the opener, then came back with two more in the second game. Perhaps the longest ball he hit all day, however, was a harmless fly to Willie Mays in deep center field.

Musial's other biggest moments were setting a then NL record for consecutive games and collecting his 3,000th career hit.

Musial's streak, which eventually reached 895 games, could have ended earlier at a couple of points without fortunate breaks. Musial had hurt his back on opening day in 1957 and likely would have seen his streak end the next day—at 775 games, short of Gus Suhr's record of 822—except that the game was rained out. Earlier, in a game in 1955, the streak had been extended when Musial was listed in the starting lineup but, because of an injury to his hand, didn't play. The rules at the time credited Musial with a game played because he had been in the lineup, but that rule was later changed so that a player had to have either an at bat or play half an inning in the field defensively to get credit for a game played.

Musial hoped to record his 3,000th career hit in front of the home fans, and manager Fred Hutchinson tried to give him that chance. With Musial sitting at 2,999 hits and the Cardinals playing a game in Chicago before returning home, Hutchinson knew how Musial felt—and left him out of the starting lineup, telling him he would only call on him if he needed a pinch hitter.

Hutchinson called the St. Louis writers together and told them honestly what he was doing.

"I could say Stan has a bellyache and nobody would question this, but I'm not going to lie," Hutchinson said. "We'll use him if we need him, but I just hate to see the guy get the big one before three or four thousand when his closest fans, the ones back home, can have the chance a day later."

As luck would have it, however, the Cardinals were trailing the Cubs 3–1 in the sixth inning when Hutchinson sent word out to the bullpen, where Musial was watching the game, that he wanted him to bat.

Musial delivered, lining a double to left field off Moe Drabowsky, and had his 3,000th hit.

The celebration that followed spread all the way from Chicago to St. Louis, with the occasion also marking the last time the Cardinals traveled by train. As the train pulled into various Illinois towns, crowds had gathered and were shouting for Musial to make an appearance—in Clinton, then in Springfield.

When the train pulled into Union Station in St. Louis at close to midnight, hundreds of people were waiting, including Devine and other Cardinals officials who had not been at the game.

"I remember my wife and I meeting the train, and the fact that I was the GM had nothing to do with it," Devine said. "I was there as a fan. I lived that moment as a fan, not as an executive of the club. It was breathtaking. More than 30 years later, I can still pretty well draw a mental picture of it today."

Devine already knew what having Musial on the Cardinals meant to the team and the community, but the crowd at the impromptu rally only intensified that feeling.

"One of the key factors about Stan, over and above what he meant to the club, above his own personality, was that nobody on the club wanted to look bad in front of him," Devine said. "He had such an overwhelming reputation that he made the other players on the team play better, so they wouldn't be embarrassed in front of him."

One of Musial's other significant moments came off the field, when Busch awarded him the first $100,000 contract in National League history. That came out of an initial contract conversation between Musial and Devine, before the 1958 season, when Devine asked Musial what he wanted for the year. Musial replied that he would like to be the highest-paid player in NL history, noting that Ralph Kiner of the Pirates was making $90,000. Moments later, the two verbally agreed and shook hands on a contract calling for Musial to receive $91,000.

Before the contract could formally be signed, however, Devine called Musial back into his office and said, after talking it over with Mr. Busch, that they had decided to make him not only the highest-paid player in the league but the first to make $100,000.

Musial's friend and roommate, Red Schoendienst, had a chance to win the batting title in 1953 but finished .002 percentage points behind the Dodgers' Carl Furillo, .344 to .342. Furillo won the title despite missing the last three weeks of the season, suffering from a broken hand. It was the closest Schoendienst would come to leading the league in hitting.

Even though the careers of Musial and Schoendienst were nearing an end at the end of the 1950s, moves were being made that would quietly form the Cardinals into a contending team once again.

Prior to the 1958 season, Devine engineered a deal with Cincinnati that brought a 20-year-old outfielder—Curt Flood—to

St. Louis. A year later, he swung a deal with San Francisco—for 25-year-old Bill White. In 1960, yet another trade brought Julian Javier from Pittsburgh.

Meanwhile, in 1959, two players were coming up from the minor leagues who showed some promise as well—a 23-year-old right-handed pitcher, Bob Gibson, and a 17-year-old catcher—he would be 18 only days after the season was over—Tim McCarver. Both made their major-league debuts in the 1959 season.

The dark days were about to end.

6

Flying High Again

THE 1960s

◆

All Bing Devine had to do to see that the Cardinals were becoming a better team was look at the improved level of talent that was assembled on the field. By the end of the 1960 season, four regulars were in place who would play key roles on a championship club—White at first, Javier at second, Boyer at third, and Flood in center field.

The pitching staff was coming together as well. Gibson was ready to blossom, Ray Sadecki came up from the minors, and Curt Simmons was acquired from Philadelphia.

The Cardinals finished a respectable third in 1960, winning 86 games, and Devine and the team had reason for optimism at the start of the 1961 season. But midway through the season, with the team lagging below .500, Devine decided he had to make another change—he fired Solly Hemus as manager and promoted Johnny Keane to the job.

"We are committed to a policy of going with young players and Keane has a background of lengthy experience in the handling and managing of younger players," Devine said the day the change was made. "We feel he has the qualifications to do the job."

Keane had been working for the Cardinals in some capacity for more than 30 years. He had almost been named the manager a decade earlier, before owner Fred Saigh picked Marty Marion.

Keane had interviewed with Saigh and thought he was going to get the job to replace Eddie Dyer. An hour later, he found out Marion had been hired.

"Something happened between 11 A.M. and noon, when Mr. Saigh said he was naming Marion," Keane said. "He said I could have any other job in the organization."

Keane picked managing the Cardinals' top farm team in Rochester, and 10 years later, he finally got his chance with the major-league club.

Keane had been born a Cardinals fan; as a boy he went to Sportsman's Park at 5:00 A.M. to wait in line for bleacher seats for the 1926 and 1928 World Series. Keane's own playing career stopped when he suffered a skull fracture in the minor leagues, but his ambition then turned to managing in the majors, a goal he finally realized.

Keane may have been ahead of his time in one aspect of his managerial philosophy, admitting that he thought a big part of his job was how he handled his team when it wasn't on the field.

"Things are pretty routine on the field, but I think that possibly the most important parts of a manager's job now come off the field of play, in the clubhouse or in his office," Keane said. "By that I mean the handling of men, talking with them and advising them."

One of Hemus's problems as a manager had been how to handle the end of the Stan Musial era. Less than two months into the 1960 season, Hemus had decided to bench Musial, trying to find a way to improve the team's struggling offense.

It was a tough decision, with Hemus saying he considered Musial his "idol." But Musial had slumped to .255 in 1959 with 14 homers, and when he got off to another slow start the next season, Hemus wasn't the only one who thought Musial's great career might be coming to an end.

"Stan took it as if he wasn't good enough anymore," Hemus said. Musial did admit that as he got older, he had to work harder to reach the same level of performance that had come naturally only a few years before.

"I had to work harder, and the reflexes were slowing down a little," Musial said. "But I hated to give it up."

Musial also wanted to prove to Hemus and his other doubters that he could still be an effective player. He finished the 1960 season with a .275 average and 17 homers and came back the next year to hit .288 with 15 homers. Musial was even stronger in 1962, aided by the addition of two expansion teams, and hit .330 with 19 homers. But he knew his career was almost over.

With six weeks to go in the 1963 season, Musial announced he would retire at the end of the season. He received a grand send-off as he made his last visit to every city in the league, as the fans paid tribute and thanked him for all the great memories he had provided during his career.

Musial said he had only one regret, and that was that he never got to play in the major leagues with a good arm, thinking back to the day in Florida when he was just a kid in the minor leagues.

"The best break I ever got in baseball was when I hurt my arm, but I really think I could have been a complete player if I had been able to play in the majors with a good arm," Musial said. "It didn't bother me when I played first base, but anytime I had to make a long throw in the outfield it would hurt like a toothache."

Musial's final game was against Cincinnati, on September 29, 1963, 22 years after he had made his major-league debut. He got two hits, including an RBI single in his final at bat in the sixth inning, the 3,630th hit of his career. Musial left the game for a pinch runner, to a roaring ovation.

Playing second base that day for the Reds was a rookie named Pete Rose, who would go on to break not only Musial's National League record for hits but also Ty Cobb's major-league mark of 4,192.

Trying to help Musial go out a winner, the Cardinals had chased the Dodgers in September, reeling off a 19–1 streak that brought them within one game of Los Angeles. That was as close as they could get, however, and they finished the season six games behind despite winning 93 games.

Another key player who had been added to the lineup that year was shortstop Dick Groat, picked up by Devine in a trade with Pittsburgh. He solidified the infield, which was anchored by White at first base and Boyer at third.

White, Boyer, and Groat were elected to start the All-Star Game that year in voting by the players, and the fourth infielder, second baseman Julian Javier, was named to start after the Pirates' Bill Mazeroski was unable to play because of an injury. Branch Rickey called the Cardinals infield "the greatest hitting infield I have ever seen." They were often the top four hitters in the Cardinals lineup, and the arrival of Groat was just another factor in the team's improvement.

The Cardinals had been without a quality full-time shortstop since Marty Marion departed in 1950, and in getting Groat, the Cardinals had picked up a player who was only three years removed from his 1960 MVP season for the Pirates.

Groat, who was acquired for pitcher Don Cardwell and infielder Julio Gotay, had been an all-American basketball player at Duke University before signing with the Pirates. Because he was an experienced player, the younger players on the Cardinals were willing to listen whenever Groat had something to say. He was especially helpful in the development of his double-play partner, Javier.

"I was very fortunate to come to the Cardinals in 1963," Groat said. "I was hitting in front of Musial, and it was very special for me to end up playing with him. Kenny [Boyer] and I were close friends. He took care of me when I first came to St. Louis and helped me find a home. On the road we would hang around together all the time.

"I've said before I thought I was the luckiest shortstop in the history of baseball because I got to play between Don

Hoak and Mazeroski in Pittsburgh and between Boyer and Javier in St. Louis. You can't play with better people than those four guys."

Devine said he thought that the acquisition of Groat was another key move in the development of the ball club.

"He made the plays that had to be made," Devine said. "He didn't make any mistakes, and he brought offense with him."

As the club continued to come together, a closeness was building that was another reason the team was headed for success. White, who would later go on to become president of the National League, thought the closeness started to develop in spring training in 1961.

"We were the first team to integrate spring training," White said. "Some of the guys like Boyer and Musial had been staying someplace else, but they decided to come in and stay with everybody else. The Cardinals were determined not to let their black players be treated like second-class citizens, so they basically took over a hotel and everybody stayed there.

"We had cookouts every night and the players got to know each other, the wives were together and the kids all played together. Anheuser-Busch would take them on trips together all over Florida, and everybody became good friends."

White thinks the Cardinals were successful in 1964 not only because they were friends off the field but because they had respect and an appreciation for each other's abilities on the field.

"We didn't have any superstars," he said. "Everybody had a job to do. The lineup was basically the same every day. We were a team of professionals."

To Devine and Keane, however, there was something missing as the 1964 season reached the month of June. Musial had retired, Charlie James was struggling in left field, and it seemed to both Devine and Keane that the team needed an offensive spark. The development of Gibson and Sadecki had given the Cardinals a little pitching depth, so they thought maybe they could trade a couple of pitchers for an outfielder.

As the team flew from Los Angeles to Houston shortly before the trading deadline of June 15, Devine sat down next to Keane and said, "I can make the Chicago deal." Keane said calmly, "Make it."

On June 15, the deal was made. The Cardinals traded pitchers Ernie Broglio and Bobby Shantz and outfielder Doug Clemens to the Cubs for pitchers Paul Toth and Jack Spring and a 25-year-old outfielder—Lou Brock.

"No one knew how that was going to turn out," Devine said.

The Cardinals were in seventh place at the time, but Brock ignited the fire that Devine and Keane thought the team had been lacking. On July 7, Mike Shannon was called up from the minor leagues. On August 1, veteran reliever Barney Schultz was promoted to the major leagues. All would play key roles as the Cardinals headed down the stretch.

Keane wasn't sure how well Brock would play, but the manager was not hesitant to stick him in the lineup on a regular basis and find out.

Later that season, Keane would say, "I knew Brock was good, but I didn't think he would be this good this quick."

The reaction at the time of the trade, from Chicago and St. Louis, was mixed. Cubs fans liked the deal, Cardinals players did not.

"This deal puts us in as a contender," said one Chicago player.

Said White, "I didn't think it was a good trade. Most of us were upset. We traded three guys for a guy who was very raw and didn't know how to play. I didn't like it. If anybody tells you they approved of that trade, they're lying."

Said McCarver, "Ernie Broglio was a 20-game winner. We couldn't believe we'd give up a quality pitcher for an unproven guy like Lou Brock. But it didn't take long."

Brock was considered a defensive liability, and even though everyone knew he could run fast, there were questions as to whether he could hit well enough to take full advantage of his speed. But Brock thrived on the opportunity to play on a regular basis. The Cardinals began to climb back into the race.

One person who wasn't around to enjoy the ride back into contention was Devine. When Gussie Busch belatedly found out about a problem that had existed between Groat and Keane, he wanted to know why he wasn't told sooner. The simple reason was that neither Keane nor Devine considered it important enough to tell him, especially since all parties considered the matter resolved. But Busch thought the dispute, over whether Groat could hit-and-run at his own choosing, had been hidden from him. Devine was fired.

Busch was growing impatient for a winner, and it likely was his frustration that prompted him to dismiss Devine. Three weeks before Devine was fired, Busch had said he was "disappointed as hell" about the way the team had been playing. He criticized the team's attitude and promised changes if things did not improve.

Nobody knew he would take action so quickly, however, and everyone was shocked when Devine and business manager Art Routzong were fired on August 17.

"I felt it was time for a change," Busch said at the time. "Bing has been in charge for seven years. We have not won a pennant in that time and we are nine games away from one right now. It was my feeling that we are not making any progress.

"I'm convinced we cannot trade our way to a pennant. We must depend on production out of our own system and I have been disappointed with the operation of the farm department."

Busch added, "There's just one thing I want. I want a pennant for St. Louis. And I know our fine fans here in St. Louis have been denied a pennant too long."

At that point in the season, it looked as if that desire for a pennant would have to wait at least another year. Second place looked like the best the Cardinals could hope for. Even with two weeks to go in the season, the Cardinals trailed the Phillies by six and a half games.

One indication that things might go right for the Cardinals was a game in Chicago on September 13, when the Cardinals became only the second team in history to score at least one run in all nine innings.

"We needed a break to keep it going in the ninth inning," Boyer said. "It looked like we weren't going to score in the ninth but somebody on the Cubs dropped a pop fly with two out. Then Bill White, the only starter who hadn't had a hit, lined a double and drove in the final run.

"The thing that stood out was that everybody on the team did a perfect job that day. The whole month was exciting because everybody on the team did a job."

Still, the odds were against the Cardinals.

"We were six games back with eleven left," White said. "The only way we were going to win it was if their plane went down. But we kept hacking. The Phillies had been playing people out of position all year, and they were trying to go with two pitchers down the stretch."

Those moves caught up with them. The Cardinals swept the Phillies in a three-game series. The Phillies lost 10 in a row. The Cardinals won nine of 10. With three games to play, the Cardinals found themselves in first place by a game.

The Cardinals' last series was at home against the Mets, who had lost more than 100 games again. But Al Jackson outdueled Bob Gibson and won 1–0 in the opener, and the Mets came back the next day and pounded future Met Ray Sadecki in a 15–5 victory. If San Francisco had not lost that day, four teams would have gone into the season's final day with a chance to win.

The Cardinals and the Reds were tied, the Phillies a game behind. The Phillies were playing the Reds, and they broke their losing streak with a 10–0 rout. Curt Simmons started for the Cardinals, and while he wasn't sharp, the offense was. Curt Flood homered and Boyer and Brock each had a couple of hits. Bob Gibson came out of the bullpen to win the game, 11–5, with Barney Schultz getting the final out on a foul popup to McCarver.

After 18 years, the Cardinals had won another pennant.

A major factor, in addition to the Phillies' collapse, had been the play of Brock. After joining the Cardinals, he hit .348 and stole 33 bases in 103 games. The other big seasons were turned in by Boyer, who would be named the league MVP after hitting .295 with 24 homers and 119 RBIs, and White, who hit .303 with 21 homers and 102 RBIs.

"We didn't have a leader on that team," White said. "Basically, we had nine leaders everyday. That team was full of leaders. Most of those guys have gone on to be successful elsewhere after their playing careers were over."

Groat said one memory he had about the 1964 team was how well the team played defensively.

"We never made mistakes," Groat said. "It's often overlooked, but it also was an excellent baserunning team. It was a very unselfish team. We didn't have a lot of power, but if you couldn't hit .260 you couldn't have played on that club.

"It was a really competitive ball club. Nobody ever wanted out of the lineup. It was a very durable bunch. There also were a lot of characters on the club, led by Bob Uecker and McCarver."

Uecker was the backup catcher on the team, and perhaps practicing for his future career as a broadcaster, he was the one who kept everybody loose. He did impersonations and mimicked almost everybody, including Bob Howsam, who had succeeded Devine as general manager, and broadcaster Harry Caray.

Uecker would sit in the back of the bus when it was going between the airport and the hotel or the hotel and the ball park and keep everyone entertained.

"He was great," Shannon said. "One day in Pittsburgh we were going from the airport to the hotel and he really did a job on Howsam. I think that may have been what got him traded. I couldn't wait to get to the hotel because I was laughing so hard my side hurt."

It came as absolutely no surprise to anyone that Uecker

didn't stop his entertaining act just because the Cardinals were playing the Yankees in the World Series. Before one game, before a band was to perform on the field, Uecker appeared in the outfield with a tuba and proceeded to catch fly balls with the tuba during batting practice.

The rest of the Cardinals, however, were serious about the World Series. It opened in St. Louis, with Sadecki opposing Whitey Ford. The Cardinals fell behind 4–2 but went ahead with a four-run sixth, highlighted by a home run by Shannon, and won 9–5.

"A lot happened to me in about a week," Sadecki said. "I won my 20th game, then we won the pennant and I pitched in the opening game of the World Series—all within about 10 days. A lot happened at age 23.

"I was still very raw as a pitcher, more of a thrower than a pitcher. I was still at that point where, in meetings, when they told you how to pitch to a hitter, they'd tell me not to pay attention. 'Just throw strikes, kid.'"

The Yankees came back to win the second game 8–3, scoring four runs in the ninth inning after Gibson was removed for a pinch hitter. The series moved to New York, where Simmons and Jim Bouton were locked in a 1–1 tie through eight innings. Simmons left for a pinch hitter and was relieved by Barney Schultz, who had saved Game 1. Schultz wasn't as fortunate in this game, surrendering a home run to Mickey Mantle on his first pitch, giving the Yankees a 2–1 win.

The Yankees were ahead in the series by the same 2–1 margin and threatened to take a commanding 3–1 lead the next day. With Al Downing pitching, New York jumped to a 3–0 lead in the first and held it into the sixth. The Cardinals loaded the bases, and Boyer came through with a grand slam into the seats in left field. The Cardinals suddenly were in front 4–3.

As Boyer rounded third, he had to pass by his younger brother Clete, playing third for the Yankees. It was all Clete could do not to smile, but he did manage a quiet "that-a-boy" as his brother headed for the mob scene at home plate.

The Cardinals, behind the relief pitching of Roger Craig (who got the win) and Ron Taylor, held on for the 4–3 victory that evened the Series at two wins each.

Boyer, who probably also would have been a great center fielder had he stayed at that position, won five Gold Gloves at third. Except for that moment when he hit the grand slam, and his MVP award, Boyer never got the recognition he deserved.

"He never popped off or complained about anything as a player," Devine said after Boyer's death from cancer at age 51. "That's part of the reason he never got much attention. He wasn't somebody the fans could relate to well because he didn't play with a flair. Everything came so easily for him that he appeared to be a casual player. He was quite unassuming ... he was a somber, sober player and, because of that, he didn't get much attention."

Boyer later would recall that the grand slam was the highlight of his career.

"I can't remember anything in my career that had more impact," Boyer said. "But I felt happiest because it brought us back even in the Series. If we had lost that game, we would have been down three games to one. I can remember, as I ran around the bases, that the uppermost thought was that this might square the series. It did."

With the Series tied, the Cardinals had Gibson ready to pitch the fifth game in a rematch with Mel Stottlemyre, and he carried a 2–0 lead into the ninth. Just one out away from the win, Gibson surrendered a game-tying homer to Tom Tresh that sent the game into extra innings.

The tie was short-lived, however, as McCarver delivered a three-run homer in the top of the 10th that gave the Cardinals a 5–2 win, putting them ahead in the Series three games to two as it moved back to St. Louis.

McCarver had turned down a football scholarship to Tennessee to sign with the Cardinals for a $75,000 bonus and in 1959 made the same jump that Musial made—from Class D to the majors in the span of a season. It took him a little while to break into the lineup on a regular basis, but he was to play a key role in the Cardinals' success for a long time to come.

The Yankees stormed back in Game 6, however, behind home runs by Mantle and Roger Maris, and a grand slam by Joe Pepitone to even the Series and force a seventh and deciding game.

Gibson was ready to pitch for the Cardinals and the Yankees again went with Stottlemyre. The Cardinals built a 6–0 lead, but New York cut the margin in half on a sixth-inning three-run homer by Mantle. Ken Boyer answered with a home run in the seventh that increased the lead to 7–3, and that's where it stood entering the ninth.

Keane decided he was going all the way with Gibson, even after Phil Linz and Clete Boyer homered, cutting the lead to 7–5. Bobby Richardson who had already set a Series record with 13 base hits, was the batter, and Gibson didn't mess around. Richardson hit a pop-up to second baseman Dal Maxvill, and the Cardinals had won the Series.

The euphoria that usually goes with winning the World Series didn't last long this time, however. The next day, Keane dropped a bombshell on Busch. He quit.

It was not a closely guarded secret that Busch had been unhappy with Keane, and about the time he had fired Devine, he had begun discussions about whom he should pick to manage the Cardinals in 1965. He had apparently settled on Leo Durocher, at the time a coach with the Dodgers, and the two reportedly had a handshake agreement that would be announced shortly after the season was over.

That plan was threatened, however, when the Cardinals got hot and won the pennant and the World Series. Busch couldn't get rid of Keane now. But Keane got rid of himself.

Even before he knew the Cardinals were going to win, Keane had promised himself he was going to quit. He was upset about Busch's discussions with Durocher, and he wasn't happy that his friend Bing Devine had been fired. He had written the letter of resignation out longhand on September 28, staying up late into the night while his wife typed it on a borrowed typewriter.

The letter read:

Dear Mr. Busch:

This is to submit my resignation as field manager of the St. Louis Cardinals, effective at the end of the last championship National League game, whether it be the end of the regular season or at the completion of the World Series.

I want you to know that I have enjoyed working for you since you owned the Cardinals, as well as the many years I spent within the organization prior to that time.

I regret very much the necessity of this decision, especially severing the close relations I have had with so many of the Cardinals personnel.

I wish also to express my gratitude to the City of St. Louis and to the St. Louis people for being so kind to me and my family for so many years, and to the Cardinals players who have been so loyal and to whom I am deeply indebted for a full effort 100 percent of the time.

I resign my position with the friendliest of feelings and wish nothing but success to you and to your fine Cardinals team.

Respectfully, Johnny Keane

One of the players who was sad to see Keane leave was White, but he wasn't surprised. It also did not come as a shock to him when four days after he left St. Louis, Keane was named manager of the Yankees, replacing the fired Yogi Berra.

"Keane was an ideal manager," White said. "He stayed in the background and let the players play. I really liked him. You knew something was going on, because toward the end of the season Mayo Smith, who was a scout for the Yankees, was riding on our bus from the hotel to the ball park and he sat up front with John. The Yankees didn't think they were going to win either, so there had to be some discussions with John about moving.

"He obviously was not a New York–type manager. He could have stayed in St. Louis for a long time."

Keane managed the Yankees in 1965 and was fired 20 games into the 1966 season. Less than a year later, at the age of 55, he suffered a fatal heart attack at his home in Houston.

The Cardinals had to find a new manager, and the public and press outcry about the Durocher agreement and Keane's resignation obviously meant Busch had to do something else. In a great public relations move, he decided to elevate one of the team's coaches to the top job, one of the Cardinals' most popular players during his career, Red Schoendienst.

In many ways, Schoendienst was exactly like Keane. He had been brought up in the old school, and he had many of the same philosophies as Keane.

"Red was an easy guy to play for," Shannon said. "He'd just wind you up and send you out there and let you play the game. That was how he had played. If you didn't do the job, he would go get somebody else who could."

Unfortunately for Schoendienst and the Cardinals, nobody did much right in 1965. Sadecki and Simmons had big drop-offs, as did Boyer. Gibson did win 20 games, and White and Brock turned in solid seasons, but it wasn't enough to keep the Cardinals from dropping all the way to seventh place, 16½ games behind the Dodgers.

Schoendienst should have known what kind of year it was going to be early in the season, when the Cardinals were playing at Cincinnati. The Cardinals already were in 10th place, and Schoendienst had to walk to church because of a strike by cab drivers. He already had a cold and then got caught in a cloudburst. He arrived at Crosley Field, then found himself standing under a leaky roof in the dugout. When the team left Cincinnati that evening on its way to Milwaukee, a sliding cup of coffee landed on Schoendienst's suit.

As is usually the case, someone had to pay the price for the Cardinals' disappointing performance, and the two biggest victims were Boyer and White. Boyer was traded to the Mets; White went in a package to Philadelphia.

Boyer, who had been the Cardinals team captain for five years, was shocked by the news that he had been traded for third baseman Charley Smith and pitcher Al Jackson. He had grown up with the organization and had spent 11 years in the major leagues.

Schoendienst defended the trade, saying, "We felt we couldn't pass it up. We had a chance to get a man in Smith who is a power hitter and is a good fielder, and a fine starting pitcher in Jackson."

Boyer's fans criticized the trade, remembering Boyer's World Series grand slam and all the other memories he had provided them over the years. Playing professional baseball had been the only thing Boyer wanted to do ever since he was a small boy, growing up one of 12 children near the tiny southwest Missouri town of Alba. Six of his brothers also went on to play baseball, at least at the minor-league level.

"There was a filling station, a grocery store, and a cafe," Boyer once said describing his hometown. "We lived about three miles outside of town. When the sun came up, we'd go out to the pasture and play ball. And we wouldn't come in until it got dark."

A week after the Boyer trade, general manager Howsam struck again, sending White, Groat, and Uecker to the Phillies for catcher Pat Corrales, pitcher Art Mahaffey, and outfielder Alex Johnson, a player with exceptional potential who never realized his ability.

Smith took over at third base and was not as good a player as the Cardinals expected, hitting just 10 homers, driving in 43 runs and hitting .266. The team performance improved only slightly, as the Cardinals moved up to sixth, 12 games behind the Dodgers, even though they finished last in the league in runs for the first time since 1919.

The two most important developments in the 1966 season occurred during one week in May—the opening of the new Busch Stadium, and another trade, this one with San Francisco, sending Ray Sadecki to the Giants for first baseman Orlando Cepeda.

Busch had decided several years earlier that he wanted to build a new stadium, and he convinced the city's business leaders to go along with him on the project by committing the first $5 million for construction. He wanted the stadium built downtown, near the riverfront, and as it turned out the stadium became the first key element to a boom in the construction and economy of the downtown riverfront area.

The closing of the old stadium, known first as Sportsman's Park and then as Busch Stadium, marked the closing of an era in baseball history. Since it was the home of the Cardinals from 1920 to 1966 and for the Browns from 1902 to 1953, more major league games were played at the park than at any other major league ballpark.

After the final game, Bill Stocksick, the groundskeeper who had installed the original home plate in 1909, dug up the last home plate. It was taken by helicopter to the new stadium and inserted in the ground.

The assignment of starting the first game in the new stadium went to Ray Washburn, on May 12, 1966, against Atlanta.

Washburn pitched well, allowing five hits and two runs as the Cardinals eventually won the game 4–3 in 12 innings.

The Cardinals had closed Sportsman's Park four days earlier, losing 10–5 to the Giants, but made that day memorable by completing the Sadecki-for-Cepeda trade.

Cepeda played well, hitting .303 with 17 homers and 58 RBIs after joining the Cardinals, taking over first base from the departed Bill White. Javier still was playing second, and

Dal Maxvill had taken over for Groat at shortstop. McCarver was the catcher, and the outfield of Brock, Flood, and Shannon was among the best in the game. The pitching was still solid, led by Gibson's 21 wins, and Larry Jaster shut out the Dodgers five times. But the Cardinals still had one hole, however, and that was at third base, where they had not been pleased with Smith's performance.

"What our lineup needed was a left-handed power hitter," Shannon said. "There weren't a lot of those who also played third base around, probably only Eddie Mathews, and he wasn't available. They got the idea that if I could make the switch to third base, then we could trade for an outfielder.

"There were some selfish motives involved, too, because I knew that I was a streaky player. Teams have a lot of outfielders, but they usually only have one third baseman. I thought if I could do that job, it would give me a little security. There was a gamble involved, because I knew I wasn't going back to the outfield."

The Cardinals found the outfielder they were looking for in New York—Roger Maris, the man who had broken Babe Ruth's single-season home-run record but who had withered under the pressure and intensity of the New York media. He had said he wouldn't play anymore in New York, and he meant it. But when the Cardinals were able to deal Smith for him, his spirit was renewed.

"Roger wasn't really a power hitter anymore, but the National League didn't know that," said Shannon, who would develop a close personal relationship with Maris. "The reputation of Maris was so great that a lot of times teams intentionally walked him to get to Cepeda.

"Roger was so skilled in what he did. He was about as good a ballplayer as I've ever seen in fielding, baserunning, getting guys in from third with less than two outs. He was a real student of the game."

While there was no denying Maris's ability, there were serious doubts about how well Shannon would do in making the move to third base. All through spring training, he worked, fielding ground ball after ground ball. One day, Schoendienst hit him balls for more than two hours. Another day, he bunted more than 200 balls to Shannon.

"It was awful," Shannon said of his spring training memories. "For three weeks I didn't do anything right. But Red stuck by me, and it got better."

Shannon, who had signed with the Cardinals after turning down a football scholarship to the University of Missouri—where he likely would have been a star quarterback—still wasn't too confident of his fielding ability.

Before the opening game, he had a little talk with Maxvill, who would be playing next to him at shortstop.

"Moon [Shannon's nickname was Moon Man] was great," Maxvill said. "He took hundreds and hundreds of ground balls and he was ready. Then before the first game, he comes up to me, sticks a finger in my chest and says, in his deep voice, 'Hey Maxie, I'm not too good at pop flies here in the infield. I'm all right in the outfield, but in here I have trouble with them. So anything hit to this side I want you to take, or I'm gonna kill you.'"

The first game was in Candlestick Park in San Francisco, where the wind can play havoc with even the most experienced infielders. In the first inning, there was a pop-up hit near the stands down the third-base line.

"I look at Shannon," Maxvill said, "and he's staring right at me. So I took off and finally caught the ball right at the stands—I really had to go a long way. And then Moon comes up to me and says, 'Maxie my friend, you just saved your life.'"

That was an early indication of how well things were going to go for the Cardinals in 1967. Given the nickname El Birdos by Cepeda, they rode an MVP season by Cepeda to 101 wins and the pennant, topping the second-place Giants by 10½ games.

The Cardinals even survived the loss of their pitching leader,

Gibson, who suffered a broken leg when he was hit by a line drive off the bat of the Pirates' Roberto Clemente.

Flood also was out with an injury when the Cardinals made a shambles of the pennant race by winning 21 of 25 games after they already had been tied for first in July.

Before that streak started, Schoendienst didn't like the way the club was playing, particularly after a tough 13-inning loss to Atlanta (formerly the Milwaukee Braves). He went to his suburban St. Louis home and walked out into his backyard to mow the grass. He twice pulled the rip cord on his lawn mower, and he pulled it so hard the cord broke.

Still mad, he came back inside and challenged his wife Mary's method of boiling potatoes that were to accompany the steak he was about to barbeque. He got the grill going but got it so hot and made so much smoke a police officer came to the door and asked if the family was all right. Mary told him to go around back and "ask the manager."

The next day, trainer Bob Bauman took it upon himself to do something to try to change the team's luck. He made a heaping pot of tomato rice soup, and the Cardinals proceeded to sweep a doubleheader from the Braves.

Because the Cardinals decided they didn't want to eat the same soup the rest of the season, the colors red and white would have to do, in some kind of tribute to the soup. A baseball was painted half red with a china marker and became the only ball the Cardinals used in infield practice before each inning.

The Cardinals won 13 of their next 15 games, and several rules sprang up about how and when the red-and-white baseball would be used. Only coach Dick Sisler was allowed to catch it from Cepeda at the end of the warm-up throws. There had to be a new ball for each series, and each time a ball was used in a losing game it had to be discarded and a new ball painted and put into use. When Cepeda accidentally threw a winning ball into the stands after one game, two balls had to be given to the fan who caught it to get the red-and-white ball back.

Things were going so well for the Cardinals that they even got away with a little criminal behavior one night in Atlanta, when they boarded their team bus for the ride from the ball park to the hotel, only to discover the driver was missing.

After waiting for a while, relief pitcher Joe Hoerner decided to take it upon himself to drive the bus back to the hotel. Perhaps it was an omen of things to come for Hoerner, because even though he had no experience with buses, he would go on to open a travel agency with teammate Maxvill after their playing careers were over.

The players fiddled with the switches to find out what each one did, and finally Hoerner got the bus started and took off. The first challenge was an entrance ramp onto the highway, which he finally manipulated after a few stops and starts. It was while he was driving the bus through the downtown streets of Atlanta that he realized he was in reality driving a stolen bus in the middle of the night.

The bus passed four police cars, but nobody stopped them. A squad car had pulled over another bus, prompting one of Hoerner's teammates to shout, "Look, Joe, some nut must have stolen a bus."

Hoerner's driving was not without incident as he smashed a street sign when he finally parked in front of the hotel. The bus company later apologized to the Cardinals for the absence of their driver.

Another pitcher, Jack Lamabe, joined the Cardinals in a trade from the Mets in July. A month later, he sat with his teammates in the clubhouse and watched his wife go on a quiz show and win a wine collection, a tape recorder, an electric range, a stereo set, a full-length fur coat, and a 1967 Pontiac Firebird sports car. "Hey Jack," Hoerner said, "she isn't really that smart is she?"

It was as fun-loving a team, and as talented a team, as the Cardinals had had in many years. The players were close on and off the field, and they developed friendships that existed more than 25 years later.

"It was not unusual to see a lot of players together in the same place after a game," Shannon said. "In baseball that was rather unusual. We would all just sit together for hours in the clubhouse after a game talking about baseball. We were on a mission. We just wanted to win."

Shannon thinks that there were reasons, other than their close relationships, why that Cardinals team was so successful.

"We never made many mistakes," he said. "We weren't the most talented team, but we were the most fluid. Everybody was coming together at about the same time, in their prime ages, and we had the same philosophy on how to play. Everybody was just very fundamentally sound. We all believed in playing the game one way, and we played it that way."

Maris, who had been on some very good teams with the Yankees, agreed.

"We have speed and power, and we have guys who know what they are doing," he said in an interview that year with *Sports Illustrated*. "One of the few things that sometimes bothers us is that people are in such a hurry to compare us with the Gashouse Gang. We're El Birdos because Cha Cha [Cepeda] named us that, and that is what we want to be called and remembered as."

Cepeda was the leader of the team, on and off the field. He was "our spiritual leader," McCarver said. Cepeda led the league with 111 RBIs, hit 25 homers and batted .325. Brock became the first player in history to hit at least 20 homers and steal at least 50 bases in the same season.

"Off the field we used to get together after the game," Cepeda said. "We were a unit. I've never seen a team like that. We were a team. No superstars."

Cepeda helped keep the team loose off the field by introducing a record player to the Cardinals clubhouse and took one on the road with him as well, also carrying a stack of record albums. On the field, he said his success was simply a matter of getting a regular chance to play.

"Red gave me confidence," Cepeda said, "by his confidence in me. He simply said, 'you'll play first base and you'll bat fourth.' The rest was up to me."

The pitching staff was able to withstand the loss of Gibson for six weeks because of the performance of young Nellie Briles, who went 14–5. Another youngster, Steve Carlton, also won 14 games. The leading winner on the team, however, was a 29-year-old rookie off an Arkansas farm, Dick Hughes, who went 16–6. He won only four other games in his career.

Hughes made the major leagues after spending 10 years in the minors, earning the *Sporting News*'s nod as the Rookie of the Year.

"I was never happier in my life," Hughes said. "All the years in the small towns, the bad bus rides were behind me. After the season, when I got back home on the farm, I took my World Series check, expanded things there, and just waited for the next season to start."

What Hughes didn't know at the time, of course, was that 1967 was going to be his one season of glory. He came down with a sore arm the following spring and was never an effective pitcher again.

While the Cardinals had rolled to the NL pennant, the Red Sox had to fight to the season's final day to win the American League title. That left the Cardinals with Gibson ready to pitch the opening game of the World Series, while the Red Sox had to go with Jose Santiago.

The two hooked up in a pitching duel, tied 1–1 until the seventh inning, when Brock got his fourth straight hit, stole second, went to third on a groundout, and scored on a groundout by Maris for a 2–1 St. Louis victory.

That was the start of a great series for Brock, but the Red Sox wouldn't go down without a fight. They came back to win the second game 5–0 behind a one-hitter by Jim Lonborg. Lonborg was only four outs away from pitching the second no-hitter in World Series play when Javier doubled with two outs in the eighth for the Cardinals' only hit.

The series shifted to St. Louis for Game 3, and Briles pitched the Cardinals to a 5–2 win behind a home run by Shannon. Gibson came back and pitched a methodical 6–0 victory for his second win in the Series in Game 4, putting the Cardinals in front three games to one.

The Red Sox were able to stave off elimination the following day, however, as Lonborg again pitched another gem, a three-hitter to lead Boston to a 3–1 victory that sent them back to Boston trailing three games to two.

The Cardinals again lost a chance to complete the Series victory in an 8–4 loss in Game 6 that evened the series at three games each. Gibson was ready to pitch the deciding game for the Cardinals, but the Red Sox had to go with Lonborg on just two days' rest. The Cardinals jumped to a 2–0 lead in the third, then put the game away with two more runs in the fifth and three in the sixth en route to a clinching 7–2 triumph.

The stars of the Series were Brock, who hit .414 and stole a record seven bases, and Gibson, with three complete-game victories.

Gibson, of course, was just warming up for the season that was to come in 1968, the Year of the Pitcher, when he helped the Cardinals win another pennant by posting a 22–9 season and remarkable 1.12 ERA.

Gibson pitched 28 complete games out of his 34 starts, allowing just 198 hits in 304 ⅔ innings, striking out 268, and hurling 13 shutouts. Between May 28 and August 24, Gibson won 15 straight games, 10 of them shutouts. He won the Cy Young and MVP awards and shrugged off the performance that many said would never be bettered. He missed breaking Don Drysdale's record of consecutive scoreless innings (58 ⅔) because of a wild pitch, denying him a sixth straight shutout.

He had pitched 47 ⅔ scoreless innings before the wild pitch, then reeled off another 23 more scoreless innings before he allowed another run.

"I am not proud of that ability," Gibson said of how well he could throw a baseball. "It was a gift."

He earned a reputation for being a fierce competitor, probably stemming from his early childhood days in Omaha, Nebraska, where he grew up in a ghetto, without his father. He once had his ear bitten by a rat when he was a baby. Gibson suffered from asthma but went on to play basketball at Creighton University, then joined the touring Harlem Globetrotters before beginning his baseball career.

The biggest break he may have gotten in his career came when Keane replaced Solly Hemus as manager in 1961. Gibson had not done anything to impress Hemus, and the feeling was mutual.

Gibson recalled that one day early in his career, Hemus walked through the clubhouse, called him Julio (Gotay), patted him on the back, and said, "You did a good job out there at shortstop."

Gibson nearly destroyed his locker. "How can a player make this ball club when the manager doesn't even know who you are?" Gibson said.

It wasn't long before everyone knew all about Gibson and his ability.

"He was such a great competitor," Shannon said. "I don't think it was because he wanted to win so badly, I think it was because he despised losing. He didn't want to lose, and I think that went back to his childhood. He was small and sickly, and he grew up to be a hell of an athlete and a hell of a man.

"He was pushed around as a kid, and he vowed to himself that he wouldn't be pushed around again."

Gibson lived by his own rules, and if he wanted to do something, he did it. If he didn't, there wasn't anybody who could make him do it.

"I owe the fans 100 percent on the field and I give them exactly that," he said in an interview with Ed Wilks of the *Post-Dispatch* in 1975. "Anything else I give is completely up to me.

"If I felt like giving an autograph, I would. If I didn't, I wouldn't. Nothing was going to change my mind. I've never felt that I had to be an image for fathers to give their sons.

"A kid shouldn't have to be told to be like Bob Gibson. A kid shouldn't want to meet Bob Gibson because Bob Gibson is a professional athlete. Bob Gibson off the field could be an alcoholic, a dope user. Isn't it a lot better if the kid says, 'I dig my dad.'"

Said Shannon, "The two days after he pitched, Gibson was great. The day before he pitched and the day he pitched he was all business. If I had one game I wanted to win, I would pick Gibson. He could beat you in so many ways. There wasn't anything he couldn't do."

One thing Gibson—who won nine Gold Gloves for fielding excellence—did do was make sure that his opponents knew who they were dealing with. After White was traded to the Phillies, he remembers the first time he came up to face Gibson. White leaned across the plate and fouled off a fastball. The next pitch drilled White in the elbow. White screamed "You're crazy," and Gibson just stared back at him. His former teammate and friend was now the enemy.

Gibson didn't like interruptions from his catchers almost as much as he hated the opposing batters. McCarver remembered going to the mound in a tight situation, only to have Gibson storm off the mound toward him, yelling, "The only thing you know about pitching is that it's hard to hit. Now get out of here."

Early in his career, when Gibson would be working quickly, Johnny Keane would tell McCarver to go out and slow him down. "He doesn't want me out there," McCarver would tell Keane, who answered, "Well, I'm running this club and I don't give a damn what he wants."

So McCarver would go about halfway between home plate and the pitcher's mound and stand there, trying to please both parties. He was still too close for Gibson, however.

"Keep your ass away from me while I'm working," the

pitcher yelled. "I like to work fast, and I don't want any help from you. You just put those fingers down as fast as you can, and if I don't like it, I'll shake them off."

McCarver did offer a backhanded compliment to Gibson, however, in the form of a Yogi Berra–ism, saying, "That Bob Gibson is the luckiest pitcher ever. Whenever he pitches, the other team doesn't score."

Gibson also was not afraid to back up his teammates, such as the day in Chicago when Maxvill, after going 3 for 3, was hit by a pitch. "It stung, but I went to first base sort of exhilarated," Maxvill said. "It was the first time in my career that I was so honored by the opposition. In fact, I felt pretty chesty about it."

Gibson, however, wasn't pleased. He told Maxvill, "Pick out somebody on their team and we will retaliate." Maxvill had to stop and think for a minute, finally deciding that Billy Williams had always bothered him and Javier because of hard slides into second base. Gibson nodded and said, "Watch, you're going to enjoy this."

"I knew what was going to happen and Billy didn't . . . until the last second when it dawned on him that Gibby was going for the equalizer," Maxvill said. "He did the Dance of the Swans trying to get out of the way, but the ball nailed him in the small of the back. He realized it was retaliation, he knew the code of the baseball jungle and he walked to first base without rubbing and without a word."

That might have been the end of it, except Gibson wanted Williams to know he had hit him at Maxvill's behest. He turned to Maxvill at shortstop and pointed. Maxvill, quickly thinking that the Cubs would realize what had happened, turned to Lou Brock in left field, as if Gibson was telling them where he wanted them to play.

"If anything happened, Lou was a big boy, he'd been thrown at before, he could handle it," Maxvill said.

When Brock came up the next inning, he too was hit by a pitch.

"I figured enough was enough," Maxvill said. "Three hit batsman added up to quite a price. So I solved it the easy way. I promised myself I would never go 3 for 3 again."

Maxvill, like Shannon, almost wasn't a part of those exciting clubs in 1967 and 1968. Back in 1964, he had batted just 26 times in the first half of the season and finally was demoted to Jacksonville. An engineering graduate of Washington University, he had a waiting offer to leave baseball and go into private business. He thought about it but was persuaded by several persons, including his wife, to report to the minors. It wasn't long before he was back in the majors to stay.

Shannon had spent five years in the minors when he found out he would be starting the 1964 season at Jacksonville. He gave himself a deadline. If he wasn't up in the majors by the self-imposed date, he was going to quit and take another job.

He and his wife were the only ones aware of the date, which drew closer. Near the All-Star Game, Shannon got the call to report to the Cardinals. "I just beat the mark," he said. "By about a week or 10 days, I beat it."

Gibson wasn't the Cardinals' only star in 1968, however. After the Cardinals' clinched the pennant in Houston, they flew to San Francisco, only to get no-hit by the Giants' Gaylord Perry. The next afternoon, Ray Washburn came back and pitched a no-hitter for the Cardinals.

Washburn said he had left the previous night's game early to go back to the hotel and he wasn't aware of Perry's no-hitter until the following morning.

"It was the traditional game where nobody said anything to me the whole day," Washburn said. "As a pitcher, the worst part of a game like that is when you're sitting on the bench. You want to get back out there. The other players were more excited than I was at first."

Washburn's no-hitter wasn't easy. The last three outs in the ninth inning were Ron Hunt, Willie Mays, and Willie McCovey.

Bob Bauman said he actually hypnotized Washburn before the game and told him he was going to pitch a no-hitter.

Washburn may have been surprised by the no-hitter, but he wasn't surprised by the success of the Cardinals in 1967 and 1968.

"It was a self-motivating, self-disciplined club," Washburn said. "If somebody wasn't doing his job, other guys would let him know about it. Red kept everybody on their toes everyday."

The season was another successful one for center fielder Curt Flood, who hit .301. Just a few years earlier, Hemus had made another mistake in judging talent when he told Flood, "You'll never make it." One of the first moves Keane made as manager was to put Flood in center field and tell him he was going to be there everyday. Flood would go on to win seven Gold Gloves in his career.

Part of the reason Flood got a chance to play came because of Busch, who rarely interfered with his manager when it came to personnel decisions. But he had remembered a conversation he had had with Willie Mays, wondering how he could get a player who was even close to Mays's ability. Mays replied that the Cardinals had one already—Curt Flood.

"When Hemus told me that I wouldn't make it, I was as low as I could get, but I'd been told that before," Flood said in a 1968 interview with *Sports Illustrated*. "Stan Musial was one of the guys who helped pick me up, helped keep me going. I always admired Musial because of what he had done and his easygoing attitude. Nothing seemed to bother him on the surface, but one day Hemus took him out, and Stan went into the clubhouse where there was a big container that held the dirty towels. It was right in the middle of the room and he stood there and kicked it as hard as he could about 30 times. That's how much he wants to play ball."

Flood and the rest of the Cardinals wanted to play just as much, and they also liked to have fun, too. The team's favorite gag that year was a postgame quiz in the locker room following each game.

"It comes from the new scoreboards in the league," Flood explained at the time. "Most of them put up a question and then it is answered later. Ours is different. Everybody watches every mistake we make during a game. When the game ends, we get back in the clubhouse and somebody says, 'I've got a baseball quiz.' Everybody hollers, 'Yeah,' then the guy who says he has the quiz must act out what he saw somebody do poorly.

"And the guy who made the mistake knows it's him right away, and he dies second by second. The thing to do is keep the questioning going with silly answers: 'Who failed to slide into second base? Was it the immortal Ty Cobb? Nooo. George Herman What'shisname? Noooo. Max Patkin? Nooo.' Then you give the guy's name, and sometimes you boo him and sometimes you cheer him for looking so foolish. The thing about the quiz is that the guy will probably never make the same mistake again, and that's what it is really for. To be honest, if we find a guy who can't take it, we really don't want him around."

That didn't happen very often, especially that season. Flood said the players all had the same understanding of and approach to the game, and that was why they formed such a successful team on the field and why they were such close friends off the field.

"You must help one another on the Cardinals, because it is the team's winning that matters, not what the batting average is," Flood said that season. "There is something about being a Cardinal. The sense of the team's history is one thing, and the number of great players is another. Right now there is a feeling of unity all the way through the organization. You get the feeling when you are playing that everyone in the organization senses your problems and tries to help you.

"Most of us have been together a long time for ballplayers, and we truly like one another. We can say things to each other that only true friends dare say."

The Cardinals also were successful because teams could not figure out a way to stop Lou Brock.

"Brock would always get on base, steal second, a ground ball would move him to third, and we would get him in," Shannon said. "We didn't have a superstar. Brock and Gibson were stars and Cepeda had a superstar year. All teams ever thought was that if they could keep Brock off base they would have a better chance of beating us. They should have been concentrating on something else. Here was a guy who was going to get 3,000 hits and go into the Hall of Fame.

"It was like us saying that if we lost the pennant by four games and [Sandy] Koufax beat us five times, all we had to do was cut that total down. I think we probably should pick on somebody else.

"Brock was a guy who was on a mission. He made up his mind after a couple of years about what he was going to do, and he went out every day and did it."

Another member of the Cardinals family that year was Devine, reunited with the team after several years with the Mets. He resumed his former post as the team's general manager after Stan Musial had resigned, citing the death of his business partner as a reason he needed to devote more time to his private business activities.

Even though Busch had fired Devine four years earlier, he wasn't above bringing Devine back when he thought it was the right thing to do. Devine remembered Busch as a tough boss and a tough businessman, but he also was the kind of boss you liked having working for your side.

"I remember once we were discussing the installation of artificial turf at Busch Stadium in a board meeting," Devine said. "We had done a lot of research and gotten a lot of bids, and finally it came time to vote. He said to me, 'Bing, you're recommending it, right?' I said yes, and he said, 'It better work or off comes your head.' That's the kind of person he was. He said it in a cutting way, but he didn't really mean it.

"I was fortunate to have Dick Meyer as my liaison with the brewery and Mr. Busch. He was a businessman, but he also knew baseball. Whenever I couldn't get to Mr. Busch, I would get ahold of him and he said he would get me an answer."

The biggest problem Devine had in 1968 was defending the salaries the Cardinals were paying their players. In one of the more famous *Sports Illustrated* covers, the starting lineup plus Schoendienst was pictured sitting in front of their lockers. All of the players' salaries also were listed, under the heading, "The Highest Paid Team in Baseball History." The total of the 10 salaries was $607,000.

"Almost everyplace I go someone will ask me how Dal Maxvill can be making $37,500," Devine said then. "It really seems to bother people, but if you have seen the way he has played shortstop this year and how he gets himself involved in the good things we do, his salary wouldn't arouse you."

By August 1, the Cardinals had opened a 15-game lead. They coasted to the pennant, eventually winning by nine games, and were prepared to meet the Detroit Tigers in the World Series.

Like the Cardinals, the Tigers had won the AL pennant behind a big pitching performance, Denny McLain's 31 victories, the first pitcher to win 30 or more games since Dizzy Dean. McLain also was headed for the MVP and Cy Young awards like Gibson, and the two aces met in what promised to be a great duel in the opening game of the series in St. Louis.

Gibson rose to the challenge. He fired a five-hit shutout as the Cardinals won 4–0, and even more impressive he set a World Series record with 17 strikeouts. It also was Gibson's sixth straight World Series victory dating back to 1964.

Gibson struck out Al Kaline to lead off the ninth for his 15th strikeout, tying Sandy Koufax's record. With Gibson eager to get on with the game, McCarver just stood and held the ball.

"There were 50,000 people on their feet applauding and Gibby is yelling at me to throw him the ball, but I wouldn't,"

McCarver said. "I held it. He was embarrassed, standing out there with all that cheering pouring over him. And I wouldn't give him the ball so he could get on with it."

Finally, the game continued. Gibson struck out Norm Cash for the third time to break the mark. He ended the game by throwing a called third strike past Willie Horton.

The Cardinals had made sure Gibson's effort wasn't in vain by jumping on McLain for three runs in the fourth inning. Only once in the game was Gibson in any trouble, in the sixth, when the Tigers put runners on second and third with two outs.

McCarver went to the mound as Cash walked to the plate. "Who follows Cash?" Gibson asked. "What difference does it make?" McCarver said. "Let's get him."

Gibson struck him out. He would go on to record 35 strikeouts in the Series, a World Series record.

The Tigers came back to win the second game 8–1 behind Mickey Lolich, but Washburn and Hoerner pitched the Cardinals to a 7–3 win in Game 3 in Detroit, putting the Cardinals back in front two games to one. When Gibson was strong again, even hitting a home run, in a 10–1 win in the fourth game, it looked as if the Cardinals were on the verge of their second straight world championship.

The Tigers weren't ready to quit, however, and came back with a 5–3 victory behind Lolich to cut the lead to three games to two as the Series moved back to St. Louis.

Detroit exploded for 10 runs in the third inning of the next game, highlighted by a grand slam by Jim Northrup, and rolled to a 13–1 victory that once again put the Cardinals into a seventh game. Gibson was ready to pitch, and Tigers manager Mayo Smith elected to bring Lolich back on two days' rest to pitch for his ball club.

The game was scoreless into the seventh, when Cash and Horton singled with two outs. Northrup was the batter, and he hit a line drive to center, a ball the usually reliable Flood should have caught. Instead, he broke wrong and couldn't recover in time as the ball bounced over his head and went for a triple. Northrup also scored that inning, and the Tigers were ahead 3–0.

They added another run in the ninth, and the closest the Cardinals could come was 4–1, on a solo homer by Shannon in the bottom of the ninth. When McCarver fouled out to catcher Bill Freehan, the Tigers had won the World Series.

Nobody sensed any panic in the losing clubhouse, however, because the Cardinals knew virtually their entire lineup was coming back again in 1969. Maris was retiring, but outfielder Vada Pinson had been acquired from the Reds to take his place. The National League was expanding again, adding teams in Montreal and San Diego, and splitting into two divisions for the first time.

Because the Cardinals were the most successful team in the league and the best financial draw, the Mets had been able to persuade the other owners to leave the Cardinals and the Cubs in the Eastern Division, although geographically they should have been placed in the West. The owners thought it would make both divisions more balanced if the Cardinals were in the East, but it didn't make any difference in 1969 as the Mets overtook everybody else in an August-September drive for the division title.

The Cardinals fell off to fourth place, 13 games behind the Mets, and there were signs of more trouble ahead. Despite making another successful trade—sending Cepeda to the Braves for Joe Torre—Flood got involved in his first heated contract dispute with Busch. He wanted a raise, from $70,000 to $100,000 after the 1968 season, and he irritated the Cardinals boss by adding, "I don't mean $99,999.99 either."

Busch remembered how he had helped Flood break into the Cardinals lineup, how he had helped him out of personal and financial problems, and now he felt Flood was trying to take advantage of him. It was one of the first lessons Busch received in the changing face of baseball as a business, and he didn't like it.

Busch went to spring training in St. Petersburg and told his players he didn't think the fans appreciated what was going on, especially coming off their back-to-back pennants.

"If you don't already know it," Busch said, "I can tell you now . . . fans no longer are as sure as they were before about their high regard for the game and the players. Too many fans are saying our players are getting fat—that they only think of money, and less of the game itself. And it's the game the fans love and have enjoyed and paid for all these years.

"The fans will be looking at you this year more critically than ever before to watch how you perform and see whether you really are giving everything you have. If we don't have the right attitudes, if we don't give everything we have to those who pay their way into the park, then you can be sure they'll know it, and we'll know it."

Only two years earlier, Flood, an accomplished artist, had painted a portrait of Busch that so impressed the Cardinals owner he commissioned Flood to do portraits of the rest of his family members as well.

"The best damned centerfielder in baseball, and he paints, too," Busch said.

Busch's opinion also was about to change about a young left-handed pitcher, Steve Carlton, who had proved to be an excellent compliment to Gibson, who once again won 20 games. Carlton went 17–11 with a 2.17 ERA, but he was on the verge of a contract dispute with Busch as well that would not end amicably for the Cardinals.

The Cardinals had signed Carlton for a $5,000 bonus on the recommendation of then pitching coach Howie Pollet. After Pollet found out the team had let Carlton return home to Florida after a tryout without signing him, he said he thought so much of Carlton's ability that he offered to put up the bonus money himself.

Carlton's first major-league exposure came when he was pitching for Tulsa and manager Charlie Metro told him, "You're going to Cooperstown." Carlton said, "Me? The Hall of Fame already?"

Carlton was only joining the Cardinals for the exhibition game as part of the Hall of Fame ceremonies, but his excellent performance there played a factor in the team's decision to promote him to the major leagues a few weeks later. But tension that was building between Busch, Flood, and Carlton was an indication that some more dark days were ahead for the Cardinals in the 1970s.

7
Gibby and Lou
THE 1970s

◆

When Flood's performance fell off in 1969, Busch had the opening for which he was looking. After the season, Flood was traded to Philadelphia as part of a seven-player deal. Also going to the Phillies were Tim McCarver, Joe Hoerner, and Byron Browne. The Cardinals received Richie Allen, Cookie Rojas and Jerry Johnson.

The only problem with the trade was that Flood refused to go to Philadelphia. He said that when he had been traded before, from the Reds to the Cardinals as a 19-year-old kid playing winter ball in Venezuela, he made a vow to never again allow himself to be traded.

At a time when the term *reserve clause* had virtually no meaning in baseball and all sports, Flood was about to take a revolutionary stance. He was going to take his case to court, arguing that he ought to have the right to choose which team he played for and not have that decision dictated by somebody else. On December 24, 1969, Flood wrote a letter to Commissioner Bowie Kuhn:

Dear Mr. Kuhn:
After 12 years in the major leagues, I do not feel that I am a piece of property to be bought and sold irrespective of my wishes. I believe that any system that produces

that result violates my basic rights as a citizen and is inconsistent with the laws of the United States and the several states.

It is my desire to play baseball in 1970 and I am capable of playing. I have received a contract from the Philadelphia club, but I believe I have the right to consider offers from other clubs before making any decisions. I, therefore, request that you make known to all the major league clubs my feelings in this matter, and advise them of my availability for the 1970 season.

Kuhn, citing the reserve clause included in all players contracts, said he couldn't do that. The Cardinals had the right, under the contract, to trade Flood to the Phillies, and if he wanted to play in the major leagues in 1970, he was obligated to play for them. Flood's next stop was the courtroom.

In a 1970 article written for *Sport* magazine, Flood presented his side of why he was challenging the reserve clause. He said it was degrading and cited an incident that occurred during his career with the Cardinals.

"I never had to look beyond the Cardinal clubhouse, or my own locker, to see how the reserve clause degraded us all," Flood wrote. "One Sunday afternoon in a game against New York, I tried to break up a double play. The Mets' little shortstop, Bud Harrelson, tried to get out of my way, but he landed on my leg with his spikes. He cut a ten-inch wound from my knee to my thigh. They patched me up and I finished the game.

"After the game, they put stitches on the wound and gave me an antitetanus shot. The shot knocked me loopy and all night long I was nauseous and dizzy, the leg stiff and painful. I finally got to sleep at six in the morning.

"I knew that the Cardinals had scheduled a banquet for noon the next day and all the players were supposed to be there. But since the Cardinals knew how sick I'd been in the clubhouse, I was sure I wasn't expected to attend.

"I got up about two in the afternoon and arrived at the park at around 3:30 or so. I found a note in my locker to see the general manager. When I walked into his office, he said, 'Missing that banquet will cost you $250.' 'You don't understand,' I said. I had already undressed to my shorts, and I showed him the stitched-up leg. 'No excuses,' he said. I paid the $250.''

Flood thought any chance the Cardinals had of winning in 1969 ended that day in spring training when Busch made his address to the team. "Mr. Busch destroyed the intangible this team had—its unity and its feeling of pride in being a part of the Cardinals organization. We never got over that," Flood said.

Some people thought that what Flood was doing was going to ruin baseball. He received one letter that said, "Once you were compared with Willie Mays. Now you will be compared with Benedict Arnold."

Flood said at the time, "Some of the owners contend it will end baseball. The 600 players say we'll have a chance to make more money. . . . I'm not trying to create chaos or end baseball. I just want to stand up like a human being. I want something we can live with."

On January 16, 1970, Flood filed suit against baseball challenging the reserve clause. Because of his refusal to go to the Phillies, the Cardinals had to send another player, outfielder Willie Montañez, to Philadelphia in order to complete the trade. The lower courts ruled against Flood, and he eventually took his case to the U.S. Supreme Court, which ruled against him by a 5–3 margin in 1972.

"I remember meeting him on the steps of the courthouse after the trial each day and both of us wondering how it had gotten to this point," Devine said. "He was an independent thinker. He began to set the stage for the changes in the game, even though he never received much money or credit for it."

After sitting out the 1970 season, Flood attempted to come back with the Washington Senators the next season. He played just 13 games before retiring at the age of 33.

Flood moved to a small town in northern Denmark, where he said they knew nothing about reserve clauses, baseball, or Lou Brock. Even though the Supreme Court had ruled against him, Flood felt as if he had won. His case certainly was the foundation for when baseball did change a few years later and created free agency.

Flood also had no hard feelings toward the Cardinals or Busch.

"Mr. Busch treated us like sons," Flood said in a 1978 interview. "There is absolutely nothing negative I can say about being here, about playing here all those years.

"We were a family, and I was not really angry, but I was a little unhappy. We had won three pennants and two World Series, and it hurt me that they thought so little of what we did together. I guess there is a nice way to tell a guy they don't need him any more, but . . ."

Flood said he also was aware that some future players likely knew what he had contributed to their cause, and there were others who probably couldn't care less.

"I hope they appreciate it," Flood said. "I don't care though. It doesn't matter. But I hope so. I was happy I was able to do a little something to correct a situation."

Unfortunately for the Cardinals, the trouble with Flood was not their only problem in the early 1970s. Busch was also in the midst of a contract dispute with Carlton, saying at one point in spring training in 1970, "I don't care if he doesn't pitch another ball for us."

Busch was upset by Carlton's demand that his salary be increased from $25,000 to $40,000 while the club was offering $31,000. He took a stand that the team would not pay him any more money.

"I can't understand what's happening to our country," Busch said. "My hope is that some other owners will have the guts to do what I'm doing, help people reverse this thing and get back to normalcy."

Finally, a week after Carlton's contract was renewed, the

two sides agreed on a two-year deal that seemed like a perfect compromise: a salary of the Cardinals' offer of $31,000 for the first year and $40,000, Carlton's request, for the second year.

The deal did temporarily cool the problems between Busch and Carlton, but they were to heat up again two years later.

At the same time, Busch was involved in contract discussions with Richie Allen, the slugger acquired in the Flood trade. The problem again was money.

"I'm not mad, I'm disappointed," Busch said at the time.

"Instead of being a sport it has become a headache. I can't understand Curt Flood or the Allen case. Some of us have to take a stand for the good of baseball one way or the other. I hate to be the sucker who does it, but I am perfectly willing to do it. I think we can still work this thing out, but we are going through a hell of a turmoil right now.

"I'm fed up and I think the fans are, too. The players have a great pension plan and we've been pretty fair with salaries. Now they talk strike. They must think we're a bunch of soft-heads. I hope to God this is not a majority view."

As Busch was to find out, however, there were a lot of players who thought they were being treated unfairly. Allen did sign and reported to spring training, but there were problems on the field as well.

Mike Shannon, then just 30 years old, had come down with a mysterious kidney disease that threatened not only his career but his life. It had been discovered during a routine physical that Shannon was suffering from glomerulonephritis, a defect of the filtering function of the kidney.

"I wasn't worried about myself, but I had a young wife and five kids," Shannon said. "I was worried about what they'd do for the next 50 years. That was my prime concern. I spent about 30 days in the hospital while they were doing tests to find out what was wrong with me. They found out, and prescribed medication. Basically they said, 'Either this works or banzai, good-bye.'

"Fortunately, I was healthy enough and young enough to make it. The good Lord looked down and said, 'I'll get you next time.' I was a fortunate man."

But Shannon's baseball career was over. He played just 52 games that year and hit .213 as the Cardinals again finished fourth. Their best player in 1970 was Allen, who hit 34 homers but proved to be—as many had expected—a difficult player to have on the club.

He started out well in spring training, getting along with Schoendienst and his teammates, but the relationship soured when Allen was left alone to live by his rules while the rest of the team had other guidelines.

When he first reported to the Cardinals, his friend Joe Torre was walking to the shower when Allen asked him what he had done to get in such great shape, and he asked him how many pounds he had lost.

Torre replied that he had lost 13 pounds—waiting for Allen to show up.

"I'm not the big man here," Allen said then. "I'm just a part of this team and I feel welcome already. Everything here won't center around me like it did in Philadelphia. I'd forgotten how to win there and I know they won't let me forget that here. I want to get that winning feeling again."

By September, when he could use the excuse of an injured leg, Allen was out of the lineup except for one game in Philadelphia, where he left a message in the clubhouse saying, "I'll play tonight." A week after the season ended, he was traded to the Dodgers for second baseman Ted Sizemore and catching prospect Bob Stinson.

"The players didn't really care if Richie followed all the rules," Torre said. "We were more concerned about winning. Richie wanted to play. He didn't enjoy a whole lot of the pre-game activities, but nobody was jealous of him. If he got special treatment at that point, it was from the players. We protected him.

"Red wasn't anxious to get him but he really wasn't anxious to trade him, either. He just didn't present the image that you want to have."

There was one brief interlude in the Cardinals' troubles, and Busch's deepening disillusionment, and that came in 1971 with the marvelous season of Joe Torre.

"Even now, I'm pretty impressed with the numbers," Torre said 20 years later. "I think the consistency is the thing I'm most proud of. From month to month I hit pretty much the same. I was just so tuned in to what I was doing. I'd have to say it was my most enjoyable season."

Torre won the league MVP award after leading the league with a .363 average, 137 RBIs, 230 hits, and 352 total bases. No player had led the league in four offensive categories since Stan Musial in 1948. Torre also was the first third baseman to win the batting title since Heinie Zimmerman did in 1912.

Torre's best month of the season was June, when he hit .393. The worst was July, when he hit .324. He hit .363 against right-handers, .362 against left-handers.

"I was pretty much in a trance," Torre said. "I would go from one day to the next, know who was pitching and know exactly what pitches he was going to throw me. I can remember predicting one day that, because John Strohmayer was pitching the next day for Montreal, I would see a high slider and I'd hit it for a home run. And I did it."

Torre also remembered one night in Philadelphia when he already had two hits as he came up to bat for the third time.

"I popped up a pitch I really should have done something with," Torre said. "I normally don't show any emotion unless I get mad at an umpire. I don't bust watercoolers or throw bats. But I was mad and sat down next to Gibson and told him I should have had that third hit. He said, 'You really think you can get a hit every time up?' I told him that I did. 'Shhh,' he said, 'even I can't do that.'"

Torre credited the season partially to going on a water diet, which helped him lose 15 pounds, and also to the trade that sent Allen to Los Angeles.

"I had come to St. Louis when they had Brock, Flood, McCarver—players like that—so true pressure was never on me," Torre said. "When I played in Atlanta the real pressure was on Henry Aaron. When he didn't get a hit in a big situation, the whole bench would deflate. When Allen left the Cardinals, the pressure shifted to me. Actually, it isn't pressure as much as it is responsibility. Now I know that the guys are looking to me and I can't get down on myself because they are watching. I never rooted and hollered as much on a bench as I did last year because I didn't want anyone to get down on themselves or the team."

It was after that season that Torre was taught a lesson in humility. He was out running, preparing himself for the next season, when a youngster on a bicycle came up to him.

"I had on a red jacket, sweat pants and sneakers," Torre said. "He said, 'You a ballplayer?' I told him I was. 'Who'd you play for last year?' he asked. I told him the Cardinals. 'What's your name?' Torre. 'What position did you play?' 'Third base.' He said, 'I met a player named Russ Snyder once,' and pedaled off. I sure earned some kind of fame."

Torre had come a long way since the days in high school when he was primarily a first baseman and third baseman. Nobody wanted to sign him. On the advice of his older brother Frank, also a major-league player, Torre became a catcher. That was the break he needed for someone to discover him, and by the time he got to the major leagues, it was OK to become a first and third baseman again.

When Torre was traded to the Mets in 1974 to make room for a young first baseman named Keith Hernandez, his one regret was that he had not helped the Cardinals win a World Series.

One of those observers who was impressed by Torre's ability, on and off the field, was Bob Burnes, who wrote in the *Globe-Democrat* after Torre was traded, "He was quite an influence. He was the team leader. In a quiet way, which sadly was not obvious to the man in the stands, Joe was a team sparkplug. He helped the youngsters on the team, he was the leader of the veterans.

"He never ducked an issue. If he messed up on something, he was the first to tell you. He also was acutely aware of the fact that as a high-salaried player, he was expected to shoulder a major part of winning games. 'I don't blame fans for booing me,' he said. 'When you make the money I do, you have to expect it.'

"His buoyant spirits, his terrible intensity was masked beneath an outer phlegmatic veneer. If there is one thing we will remember most about Joe Torre, it was his almost schoolboyish determination to win. After his superb 1971 season, when he led the league in hitting and RBIs, Joe said, 'I'd trade it all right now for a World Series ring on my third finger, left hand.'"

Torre said most of his baseball knowledge, which he would later use a manager, came from his years in St. Louis.

"When I first joined the Cardinals and reported to spring training, the first player who came up and said hello was Gibson," Torre said. "He was the most intimidating pitcher I've ever faced, and when I caught him in the All-Star Game he didn't even acknowledge that I was in the game.

"It was in St. Louis where I really learned to have fun playing the game. We had the attitude that we would do the best we could and try to win the game, but if we lost it wasn't the end of the world. I was maturing as a player, and it was a good marriage for me."

The Cardinals did win 90 games in 1971, but that was good only for second place behind Pittsburgh's 97 wins. Carlton had another good year, winning 20 games, but those were to be the final games he would win for the Cardinals.

Carlton and the Cardinals once again got into a sticky contract dispute, and this time Busch would not be bullied. Even though the two sides were less than $10,000 apart, Busch ordered Bing Devine to make the best deal he could. Devine already had had some preliminary discussions with John Quinn, the general manager of the Phillies, and on February 25, he made an early-morning phone call to see if they could finalize a trade.

"He said, 'Get rid of him,'" Devine said of Busch. "He said, 'I don't want to talk about him again.'"

In the ensuing phone call, the deal was made, a straight swap of starting pitchers, Carlton for Rick Wise.

"Both are capable, winning and productive pitchers," Devine said at the time. "One is left-handed, one is right-handed."

As history has recorded, of course, there was a great deal of difference in the performance of the two pitchers after the trade, but at the time it was not viewed as such an outrageous deal.

"I thought we were getting a good pitcher who could help us," Torre said. "We knew Carlton was a good pitcher, too, but he and Mr. Busch had reached an impasse. It happened at a bad time because it was right before the strike, and Mr. Busch took it very personal. We were probably treated better than any other club, and it hurt him very deeply and he reacted to it. He made up his mind and that was that."

That same spring, because of another holdout that upset Busch, Devine traded young pitcher Jerry Reuss to Houston for Scipio Spinks.

Busch would say later that making those two trades, under his orders, were the biggest mistakes he had made as owner of the Cardinals.

"But remember, the tempers were short at that time," he said in 1978. "I guess the 'paternalism' they said some of us club owners practiced was true. All I can say is that both Dick Meyer and I thought Steve was grossly unfair in his salary demands. I sat with the bullheaded buzzard for seven hours and Dick, a great negotiator, tried for four hours. We couldn't budge him."

Busch also developed a stubborn attitude about the threatened strike by players upset with their fringe benefits. "Let 'em strike," Busch said. And they did, creating a delay in the opening of the 1972 season.

Busch was particularly upset that his two player representatives—Torre and Maxvill—voted to strike. The vote was 23–1.

"God that Torre," Busch said. "How can any man I pay $280,000 over two years vote to go on strike?"

Busch said he was concerned about the future of the game.

"I'm not disenchanted with baseball," he said in an interview in 1972 with the *Los Angeles Times*. "I've loved this game all my life. It's the greatest game in the world. I'll fight to the last to keep baseball going. Hell, we have budgeted $1.5 million just to make $6,000 this year. How do you think that sits with my stockholders?

"It worries me sick. If the reserve clause is ever kicked out, a club owner with all the money in the world would have all of the best ballplayers in the world. Now how the hell could anybody else run a club? Who would pay to see a team that had no stars?"

The Cardinals, of course, had stars. Gibson was nearing the end of his career, but Brock was still getting hits and running wild on the bases. A catcher named Ted Simmons was emerging, and a relief pitcher named Al Hrabosky was keeping fans amused.

Busch made sure his players, even his stars, knew he wasn't pleased with their decision to strike. He had the club switch to smaller planes for road trips. He ordered all players to have a roommate on the road instead of staying in separate rooms. The free case of beer given to each player at the start of each homestand was discontinued. All these actions were said to be an "economy" move.

After he was traded, Torre wrote a letter to Busch in which he said basically two things.

"The most unfortunate thing was the strike," Torre said he said in his letter. "I told him if everybody had treated their players like he had treated us, there probably wouldn't have been a strike. The other big disappointment was not getting to the World Series."

The strike wiped out six games and 13 days of the season, but it didn't really impact the Cardinals, who finished in fourth place, 21 ½ games behind the Pirates. Gibson won 19 games, the last big season of his career.

Gibson had won the 200th game of his career in 1971 and also did something he never thought he would accomplish, pitching a no-hitter against Pittsburgh. The usually unflappable Gibson said, "Just for an instant, my legs began shaking in the ninth inning."

He recovered in time to throw a called third strike past Willie Stargell to end the game, won by the Cardinals 11–0.

One of his teammates who appreciated what Gibson did and what he meant to the Cardinals was McCarver, his longtime catcher.

"He is by far the best athlete I've ever seen," McCarver said.

"He has a vicious competitiveness, he has desire and fantastic ability. That's a nasty combination to oppose. But it's a hell of a thing to have on your side.

"Major-league batters will never admit they are awed by anyone, so I've never seen or heard a batter express awe of Gibby. But I know I've been awed by his pitches, by his velocity . . . especially when one of them left a pain in my hand for three days."

In 1972, Gibson won his 211th victory, passing Jesse Haines for the most victories by a pitcher in Cardinals history. In 1974 he recorded the 3,000th strikeout of his career, at the time becoming the only pitcher other than Walter Johnson to record that many strikeouts.

One teammate who could only marvel at Gibson's accomplishments was Ted Simmons.

"Hitters almost always knew what was coming and they still couldn't hit him," Simmons said. "He really only had two pitches, a fastball and slider, which he threw at almost the same speed. Most pitchers need three pitches, but all he needed was two. It's very difficult to pitch that way on the major-league level and have success. But he had pretty remarkable, consistent success."

How intense was Gibson? In one spring training game, Pirates rookie Frank Taveras beat out a two-strike bunt. The next time Taveras came to the plate, Gibson drilled him in the back. As he was rolling on the ground, with the trainer and others attending to him, Gibson walked in from the mound, leaned over, and said, "Try to bunt that one, busher," turned, and walked back to the mound.

When Pete LaCock of the Cubs homered off Gibson once, Gibson followed him around the bases, cursing him every step of the way. Gibson's desire to control and intimidate opposing batters was legend. The story is often told that Gibson said the outside of the plate belonged to him. If a guy was leaning over the plate and got hit with a pitch, that was his own fault.

Umpires who used to warn him he would be fined $50 if he hit a player said Gibson replied, "I got a bunch of 50 bucks."

Torre recalled the human side of Gibson as well from the first game he played for the Cardinals in 1969.

"Willie Stargell hit a screamer toward me at first base, and it hit off my shoulder and went into the outfield," Torre said. "Gibson called time and called me over and said, 'When Stargell hits a ball that hard, don't get in front of it.'"

Gibson's tenacity paid off in 251 victories, two Cy Young awards, one MVP selection, and virtually every Cardinals pitching record. His uniform number 45 was retired when he retired after the 1975 season, and after waiting the minimum five years, he was elected to the Hall of Fame in his first year of eligibility.

The other great Cardinals player whose career was in full stride in the middle of the decade was Brock, who like Gibson would finish his playing days with a retired jersey number and a trip to the Hall of Fame.

Brock was a player who revolutionized the game, specifically the art of stealing bases. His big year came in 1974, when he broke Maury Wills's record of 104 stolen bases and finished the year with 118.

To most people, the distance from first base to second was 90 feet. To Brock, it was 13 steps.

"When I came up with the Cubs in 1961 my manager, Lou Klein, told me that, and I didn't believe him," Brock said. "I was a math major in college, and I was positive he was wrong. But it was 13 steps that day, and it has been 13 steps every day since.

"It doesn't bother me when writers call me the thief, but in my own mind I don't steal bases, I take them," Brock said that season. "If you steal, there's an element of surprise. I'm not trying to surprise anyone. They know I'm going. I look at it as psychological warfare. They know I'm going . . . but they don't know when."

Much like Gibson, a major ingredient of Brock's success was his desire and attitude to be the best. He didn't want anyone to beat him; he knew there were going to be times when he would be thrown out, but that wasn't going to get him to stop running.

"I don't mind being thrown out," Brock said. "It's not embarrassing to me. Even though I have pride in my reputation, I put fear of failure out of my mind at the moment of challenge. I know I can't make it every time. Nobody can. It's a matchup of skill against skill and I know that I'll make it four of five times . . . but I never think, 'This is the fifth time.'

"Pressure can create fear, doubt, and failure. You've got to want to be in the pressure situation. You have to have positive thoughts of why you want to be there. You can't be afraid to fail; rather, you have to have the attitude that the other guy has to beat you."

Brock said that was what impressed him about Gibson, and Gibson likewise appreciated Brock's attitude and approach to the game.

"You can talk about all the great ones since 1964, but he's been more exciting than any of them," Gibson said. "He does it all; he excites the fans. He upsets the mechanism of the other club. In spite of what he says, he's right there with the best. It's just too bad that people have waited until he got the record to really recognize his ability.

"In 10 years on this club, no one has been more of a factor."

The one disadvantage to Brock's great base stealing ability was that it caused people to overlook his ability at the plate. Not only did he break Ty Cobb's career record for stolen bases, he finished his career with more than 3,000 hits.

On more than one occasion, Brock said, "I look upon myself as a hitter. I know I gained the reputation of being a top base stealer . . . but that has to be secondary. If you can't hit, you don't get on base often enough to make a reputation as a base stealer. You have to hit. It's as simple as that.

"Once I reached base, I controlled my own destiny. I knew when I was going to steal. I knew in most cases when I could do it. I enjoyed base stealing . . . but I have always regarded myself as a team player, and it is more important to get on base than to steal."

Only one time in his career did Brock think something was stolen from him—the MVP award in 1974. In addition to breaking Wills's stolen base record, Brock hit .306 and scored 105 runs. He had kept the Cardinals in the pennant race until the final day of the season, finishing one and a half games behind the Pirates. Yet the MVP award went to the Dodgers' Steve Garvey.

Los Angeles Times columnist and eventual Hall of Famer Jim Murray wrote that the letters *MVP* had become *GYP*. "Lou must wonder what you have to do to win this award, cure cancer?" Murray wrote. Garvey received 13 first-place votes to eight for Brock in the voting by 24 members of the Baseball Writers Association of America. Garvey finished with 270 points, to 233 for Brock.

"If I steal a thousand bases next year and they offer me the

MVP, I wouldn't accept it," Brock said. "I was angry. I think I was entitled to be angry. I think anyone would be angry."

Schoendienst was convinced Brock would win.

"I don't mean to take anything away from Garvey, but I felt the Los Angeles performance was more of an all-around effort," Schoendienst said. "We had some fine contributions from other players, but really Lou was our big man and to me, he's the MVP."

Torre said that what stood out to him about Brock's performance was how he always seemed to come through in clutch situations.

"Every time there was a game in the balance Brock would hit a line drive somewhere," Torre said. "You can probably say that about only a handful of guys in the game. Those guys are born."

Torre remembered he got upset, in a friendly way, with Brock one time when Brock wasn't in the lineup on the final day of the 1970 season. Torre was trying to finish with 100 RBIs, and he thought his chances would be better of getting the last RBI he needed if Brock was in the lineup instead of Leron Lee.

"The reason he wasn't playing was because he had struck out 99 times and didn't want to make it 100," Torre said. "That was a lot bigger deal then than it is now. I just told him I would have to do it without you, and it turned out that Lee scored the run on my 100th RBI."

Simmons said he thinks most people were surprised when Brock began closing in on the 3,000 hit plateau, wondering how he got there.

"People just thought he was a base stealer, a speed guy," Simmons said. "But he got 3,000 hits. You can't fake that."

Brock proved he could both hit and steal bases. He broke Ty Cobb's career stolen base record in 1977, something he never thought he would be able to accomplish.

"One day I looked up at a scoreboard and saw the top 10 all-time base stealers," Brock said the night in San Diego he broke the record with his 893rd stolen base. "And then a couple of seasons later I looked up and saw my name on it. It was like making the honor roll. Still, I thought Ty Cobb's record was unattainable."

Brock had expressed some second thoughts about the record and whether he really wanted to pass Cobb.

"I feel sometimes like getting to 892 and stopping, so when somebody asks who was the best base stealer, people will say Brock and Cobb," Brock said. "Brock probably wouldn't mean very much, but Cobb would mean a lot."

Brock was wrong about that, as he found out when he got hit number 3,000 and later when he was selected for the Hall of Fame in his first season of eligibility.

Brock thought that the 3,000 hits was his greatest achievement. "It was by all odds the most trying ordeal, but it has given me the greatest satisfaction, because so many people thought I wouldn't do it."

When Brock was inducted into the Hall of Fame in 1985, he looked back on all the special moments in his career and how he had fallen in love with baseball as a youngster in Louisiana listening to the Cardinals games on KMOX.

"I sat in my room at night down in Louisiana listening to KMOX, a big city station carrying the word back to the sticks," Brock said on the steps outside the Hall of Fame in Cooperstown. "I knew what I wanted to do. I knew that Jim Crow was a foe I would have to combat and beat. Jim Crow was a barrier to society. I knew I had to overcome it.

"Those KMOX broadcasts made my spirits soar. They gave me the courage to react to my inner feelings, they fed me a fantasy. I was the one who had to take the step, to force myself to cross the railroad tracks and let me enjoy the fantasy I thrilled to in those broadcasts."

If Brock had any regrets in the closing seasons of his career, it likely was that the Cardinals came close to winning again and failed, both in 1973 and 1974. Each year, they went into the final weekend with a chance to win but lost. In 1973, after coming back from a woeful 5–25 start to the season, the Cardinals had completed play with a chance to tie the Mets if the Cubs could sweep a doubleheader from the Mets. New York won the first game, however, to clinch the title.

The following season, the Cardinals were ending the year in Montreal while the Pirates were playing Chicago. With Gibson pitching, the Cardinals were ahead of the Expos 2–1 in the eighth when Mike Jorgensen connected for a two-run homer that gave Montreal a 3–2 victory.

Still, the Cardinals had a chance heading into the season's final day. They were rained out in Montreal, but if the Pirates lost to the Cubs and the Cardinals could win a makeup game, the two teams would tie for the title and have to meet in a playoff.

With Busch watching on television with some friends at a St. Louis restaurant, the Cubs clung to a ninth-inning lead, only to have it wiped out by a passed ball that gave Pittsburgh the division title.

"Ben Kerner threw at a party at Bevo Mill so we could watch the Pirates," Busch said. "Then the third strike got past the catcher and Pittsburgh won. I told Ben to take me home, and for once, I didn't have a damned thing to say all the way down Gravois."

That was a frustrating moment for the Cardinals players as well. One player who never made it into postseason play wearing a St. Louis uniform was Simmons, and he believes that hurt him in terms of national exposure and attention at a time when Johnny Bench was being hailed as the greatest catcher ever.

"Bench and I were different people," Simmons said. "We were different kinds of hitters. He was a thumper who could stand up there and smash the ball, and he played in a ball park that was conducive to home runs. In St. Louis you had to pull the ball if you were going to hit home runs. Early in my career I wasn't strong enough physically and I was mostly a gap hitter. I also drove in runs, but we did it with different styles. If I had played in Cincinnati my approach might have been different."

Simmons had to live in Bench's shadow, because Bench always seemed to excel in the media-packed events, such as the All-Star Game and the World Series.

"The focus was definitely there, and he ended up making outstanding contributions in those games. But I think the players that I played with and against know what I can do," Simmons said.

Simmons, a first-round draft pick of the Cardinals in 1967 who signed after turning down a football scholarship to the University of Michigan, did not take much time to begin understanding how the game of baseball should be taught. His teacher was the same person who has taught almost every player to come up through the Cardinals farm system for 30 years, George Kissell.

"When I first signed and joined all of the kids in the rookie league, George was running it," Simmons said. "We had chalkboard sessions all the time, and I was bulletproof. I thought all I needed to do was go out and play. But George would stand there and draw cutoff and pickoff plays and present different dilemmas on the blackboard, and each time prior to explaining the situation he would turn to me and say, 'Mr. Simmons, I'm sure you must have some idea of what you should do here.' I would say no, and he would go ahead and explain it. By the time he did this over and over, it was plain that he was showing that a number one draft pick was no more in tune with what was going on than a guy who had been picked 50th. I learned humility very quickly. By day seven, I wasn't so smart.

"George is a fundamental person. He teaches A, B, C, and D. He won't give it to you any other way. And he won't go to B until he's convinced that you understand A. As far as teaching me fundamentals and an understanding of the way the game is played, George has had more impact on me than any person I've met or known."

Through all the changes in managers and general managers and all the changes in players, Kissell has remained, always out of the limelight working in St. Petersburg or in some other remote corner of the farm system, with his goal entirely focused on getting players ready for the major-league club.

"He's had his hand in every kid that's come through here in the last 35 or 40 years," Simmons said. "I'm sure Bing asked him if Carlton was ready. He was asked if Gibson was ready, or Boyer. Name anybody, Hernandez, [Bob] Forsch, all of them. He's been the guy around here that after everybody else has had their say, the general manager will turn to George and ask him what he thinks."

Another person who valued what Kissell taught him as a player was Torre.

"He basically taught me how to play the game," Torre said. "I had been with the Braves for eight years and in their organization for nine, but when I got to the Cardinals and met up with George Kissell was when I found out how the game should be played. The man is tireless. He cares, that's the biggest thing. He'll yell and scream at you, but it's like it's your mom or dad yelling. You don't like them for yelling at you, but you know they're doing it because they love you.

"His only satisfaction in the game is to watch kids progress. He's a very special person to me."

While the personal highlight of Simmons's career came against the Cardinals—playing for Milwaukee in the 1982 World Series—his most vivid memory of his playing career was the heat.

"In midsummer it is just blistering and unrelenting," Simmons said. "It was something every Cardinals player had to come to grips with very early in their careers or they had to go somewhere else. I saw people where it got to them and affected them. A pitcher would say I wish I was pitching Saturday night or Monday night instead of Sunday. You don't hear a player make those comments in Milwaukee."

Simmons, who made the All-Star team six times, enjoyed

his greatest season in 1975, when he hit 18 homers, drove in at least 100 runs for the second straight season, and finished with a .332 average despite catching 154 games.

"To me, Ted was the best pure hitter in the National League during that period," said pitcher Al Hrabosky. "I'll never forget his 1975 season. He was catching every day and was totally worn down. His arms were so weary and he got no leg hits. Everything he hit was hard. A lot of people criticized his defense and said he allowed a lot of passed balls, but when I was pitching and the game was on the line, he was the only guy I wanted to throw to."

Pitching, or specifically the lack of consistent pitching, was the biggest reason the Cardinals were unable to win in the 1970s, Simmons said.

"Our best games in the 1970s were with Pittsburgh and Philadelphia, and we could slug with anybody but we couldn't hold the other club down," Simmons said. "We just didn't have a dominant pitcher at that time."

That pitcher could have been either Carlton or Reuss had they not been traded away, but the players never thought that those trades cost them a couple of pennants, Torre said.

"In both 1973 and 1974, when we went down to the last day with a chance to win, you were more searching for what you could have done to help win one more game," Torre said. "You never questioned the fact they were traded."

One of the stars on the 1974 team was a rookie outfielder named Bake McBride, who won the Rookie of the Year award by hitting .309 while stealing 30 bases. Perhaps his biggest moment of the year came on September 11 in New York, when he scored from first base on a wild pickoff throw—in the 25th inning, the longest game in Cardinals history, which had been sent into extra innings on a ninth-inning homer by Ken Reitz.

It was McBride's speed that had first attracted the Cardinals' attention when he was attending Westminster College in Fulton, Missouri. Without ever seeing him play baseball, the Cardinals selected McBride in the 37th round of the 1970 draft.

"We drafted him on his speed recommendation alone," said George Silvey, at the time the Cardinals director of player procurement.

"Nobody in the Cardinals organization had ever seen him play baseball, had even seen him swing a bat when we selected him. As far as I know, he's the first player we ever signed without seeing him play."

McBride, who once refused to move up a level in the minor-league system because he did not think he was ready for the promotion, played with the Cardinals until 1977, when he was traded to the Phillies.

Another player who lasted fewer than three years in St. Louis was Reggie Smith, obtained from Boston in 1974 for Rick Wise and Bernie Carbo. He hit 23 homers and drove in 100 runs while hitting .309 in the Cardinals' futile pennant drive. He came back the next year with 19 homers, 76 RBIs, and a .302 average. But he and the Cardinals could not agree on a contract in 1976, and on the June 15 trading deadline he was sent to Los Angeles for catcher Joe Ferguson.

While the Cardinals' offense was producing with players such as Simmons, Brock, McBride, and Smith, the pitching, both starting and relieving, was struggling. The team did not have a consistent stopper in the bullpen until Hrabosky and his "Mad Hungarian" act came along.

Hrabosky said there was a simple reason for his transformation into the Mad Hungarian role, and it started out of necessity and not as an act.

"Early in the 1974 season I wasn't pitching well and the Cardinals were getting ready to send me back to the minors," Hrabosky said. "I was out of options, so I would have been frozen there. I was just kind of going through the motions, and I found out by stepping off the mound, relaxing myself, and trying to focus my concentration, it seemed to make me pitch better. It was a last-ditch effort to keep from going to the minor leagues."

The nickname "the Mad Hungarian" was the idea of Jerry

Lovelace, at the time a public relations official with the Cardinals, and was inspired not only by Hrabosky's actions of stalking off the mound, turning his back to the hitter, and pounding the ball into his glove when he was ready to pitch but also because of his physical appearance, which included a big bushy mustache.

"What surprised me at the time was the fan reaction," Hrabosky said. "You couldn't assume that just because you were doing something to help yourself, you would get a big fan reaction. I guess what it showed was that as great as the game of baseball is, we're still starved for color."

Hrabosky, who had been cut from his Little League team three years in a row and from his junior high team two straight years, finished the 1974 season with a team-leading nine saves and an 8–1 record. He was on the mound for a key game late in the season in Pittsburgh when Torre saw how intense Hrabosky had become.

"I dropped a pop-up," Torre said. "Hrabosky just walked over to me and said, 'Give me the ball so I can get this guy out.' And he did.

"What turned into a show for Al really started out just as a means to clearing his mind and getting his concentration. Then the fans got into it."

The fans really got into it in 1975, when in a major snub, Los Angeles manager Walter Alston failed to pick Hrabosky for the All-Star team even though he was leading the league in saves, had a winning record, and an ERA of less than 2.00.

Even worse, Alston picked relievers Mike Marshall and Tug McGraw for the team, both of whom were having subpar years. Alston likely overlooked Hrabosky primarily because he had not pitched enough innings to be listed among the league leaders, and the game still was not receiving the abundance of publicity, especially on television, that exists 20 years later.

"When somebody asked him why he didn't pick me, Alston replied that what kind of year could I be having if I wasn't listed in the stats in the Sunday newspaper," Hrabosky said.

"At that time, people just were not as aware of what was going on as they are today. We never even saw the stats in the locker room."

Inspired by the snub and the fact that the Cardinals were hosting the Dodgers in the series prior to the All-Star break, the team staged a "We Hlove Hrabosky" banner day. One of the signs that greeted Alston was a banner which read, "The Smog Is not the Densest Thing in LA."

"As it turned out, I beat them two straight games that weekend, then beat them again the next time we played in Los Angeles a week later," Hrabosky said. "He kind of found out who I was."

Another team that found out all about Hrabosky one day was the Cincinnati Reds, when he walked the bases loaded with nobody out in the 10th inning.

"I knew the game was about to be over," said Simmons, catching at the time. "I just knew he was going to walk at least one more. But he came right back and struck out Johnny Bench, George Foster, and Tony Perez on 11 pitches, all fastballs. There was one foul. The rest were swinging strikes. He was always getting into and out of jams like that."

Hrabosky finished 1975 with a league-leading 22 saves, a 13–3 record, and a 1.67 ERA, but that wasn't enough to help the Cardinals to more than a tie for third, 10 ½ games behind Pittsburgh. Both the team and Hrabosky fell off in 1976, with the Cardinals losing 90 games for the first time since 1916, and the team's management decided they needed more of a disciplinarian as manager. Schoendienst's record tenure as the Cardinals manager was over, and Vern Rapp came in to succeed him.

Hrabosky and Rapp immediately became the focal point of a battle that lasted for all of 1977, when the Cardinals still managed to somehow win 83 games and finish third.

"We had a lot of young guys coming up at that time whose initial thought was, 'Let's go party, and if we have time let's play the game, '" Hrabosky said. "We had a group of guys who had really kind of lost focus about what their primary job was.

"The decisions by Vern to not allow facial hair and to be more of a disciplinarian were not done to penalize me. But when problems continued to come up, that was the one thing the press always pointed to. The issue never died.

"Vern was the most insecure person I've ever been around. He thought the media was out to get him, after he came in right at the start and said that he was the manager and nobody had a right to second-guess what he did. We had a personality clash. There were always idle threats over stupid things. I can say now I wish I would have handled things differently."

On one occasion, Rapp suspended Hrabosky for "insubordination" because he wouldn't talk to him. They also feuded because of Hrabosky's personal request that he be allowed to hand the ball to the new pitcher when he was replaced by a reliever. Busch finally agreed to let Hrabosky grow his beard but warned him, "Boy are you going to look like a fool if you don't get batters out."

As it turned out, Hrabosky was gone before Rapp was. He was traded to Kansas City after the 1977 season for reliever Mark Littell. Rapp lasted until 15 games into the 1978 season, when he was fired and replaced by Ken Boyer.

"Vern was a disciplinarian, and in a major-league clubhouse it's difficult to be one," Simmons said. "He didn't have the longstanding credentials of a Whitey Herzog or Sparky Anderson or Earl Weaver. Without that kind of background and pattern of success, it's very difficult to be a strict disciplinarian.

"It also was hard for guys who had been used to playing under Red, which was very easy to do, to make the adjustment to a 180-degree different type of manager."

Rapp, who had been a catcher in the Cardinals farm system before managing for several years in the Reds minor-league system, never apologized for being a strict boss. He knew Busch and Devine had wanted him to change the image of the team, and that was all he tried to do.

"All I ask is they look and dress neatly," Rapp said in the middle of the 1977 season. "This is the type of image we ought to project to the youth of today. Have we lost that respect and dignity? Have we gone so far the other way?"

Rapp's biggest problem was that he was managing during a period when the players were in complete control, not only on the Cardinals, but throughout baseball. It also was a rebellious time in society in general, and that made his task of remodeling the Cardinals almost impossible.

"I'm not trying to treat them like little kids," Rapp said. "It's just they haven't been accustomed to discipline. Today, it's do your own thing, be a free soul, live today because tomorrow may never come. But reality has got to come some time."

Busch knew the club was suffering some of the same ills that were occurring in other businesses and that the players were in total command.

After the new basic agreement was reached between the players and the owners in 1976, Busch said, "In my opinion, we have lost this war and the only question is can we live with the surrender terms."

In defense of Rapp, any manager would likely have had trouble winning with the group of players on the roster in 1977. Simmons had a good season, and two of the best players were youngsters, 23-year-old Keith Hernandez and 21-year-old Garry Templeton, who were just beginning to show how good they could become. Bob Forsch won 20 games, but nobody else won more than 11.

In turning to Boyer, the Cardinals were hoping the respect the players had for what he had done as a player himself would be enough to cool the rebellious attitude that existed under Rapp. Many of the players had in fact played under Boyer in the minor leagues. The Cardinals' brain trust was partially right—there were fewer controversies, but there also were fewer wins.

The Cardinals lost 93 games in 1978, avoiding a last-place

finish only because the Mets lost 96. The only highlight of the year was a no-hitter by Forsch, but even that was somewhat tainted because of a belief by some observers that a ball that was ruled an error on Ken Reitz should have been scored a hit.

Busch again turned his anger on the players in a statement issued to them in June, warning everyone down to the batboys that the team had better start making fewer excuses and producing more victories.

"Management does not pay salaries to supposedly quality players for constant mental errors, for a loose and carefree attitude of 'Well, I know I am a better player and we are a better team, and tomorrow it's all going to work out,'" Busch said. "The only way it is going to work out is with actions, and not words: with desire and dedication, not careless play and lackadaisical attitudes, and with some old-fashioned Cardinals Gashouse Gang spirit and guts.

"I did not recommend the purchase of the Cardinals to the Anheuser-Busch board so that 25 years later the Cardinals would have the worst record in their history. I personally have not seen too many headfirst slides, the opposition's second baseman being kicked into left field on double plays, and people banging into the walls to make catches."

The disappointing performance again cost Devine his job, and he was replaced as general manager by John Claiborne.

Two trades that had been made by Devine brought the Cardinals two 15-game winners in 1979, Pete Vuckovich and Silvio Martinez, and they helped improve the team's record to 86–76, good for a third-place finish. Brock also rebounded to play well in his final season, but the biggest improvement came from Hernandez, who shared the league's MVP award with Willie Stargell after winning the batting title with a .344 average. He drove in 105 runs and scored 116.

With Templeton already in place, and George Hendrick and Bobby Bonds having been picked up in other trades, it appeared the Cardinals were building a team that could contend as the decade of the 1980s began. Some more changes had to be made, however, before the Cardinals could return to the top of the National League.

Three months into the 1980 season, the biggest change had been completed. The era of Whiteyball was about to begin.

8
Whiteyball
THE 1980s

Whitey Herzog, who had grown up in New Athens, Illinois, oftentimes hitchhiking across the Mississippi River to come see the Cardinals play, had managed the Kansas City Royals to three straight division titles between 1976 and 1978. His relationship with the team owner was always a little strained, however, and as soon as the Royals finished second in 1979, Herzog was fired.

With his record of success, Herzog knew he would not be out of work long. So he spent the first half of 1980 enjoying himself, fishing and skiing, playing golf. He was golfing at a course at the Lake of the Ozarks when on June 7 he got a call from Lou Susman, an attorney for Mr. Busch and a member of the Cardinals executive committee, asking him to come to St. Louis for a meeting with Gussie Busch.

Herzog said he knew that when he was called off the golf course it meant only one of two things—bad news or a job offer. It was the offer, and after initially turning down a one-year contract, Herzog and Busch agreed on a three-year deal to make him the manager of the Cardinals.

On June 8, 1980, between games of a doubleheader in Montreal, Ken Boyer was fired and Herzog was announced as the Cardinals' new manager. The team was 18–33 under Boyer, who was stunned when GM John Claiborne appeared in the clubhouse and delivered the news.

"I had no inkling," Boyer said. "I thought he was here to discuss a deal. There was no internal problem."

When Herzog had a chance to spend a few weeks observing the Cardinals, however, he found a myriad of problems. The team had talent, including three of the 10 highest-paid players in the game—Keith Hernandez, Garry Templeton, and Ted Simmons—but was not constructed to take advantage of playing in Busch Stadium, where Herzog believed a team needed to rely on speed and defense. The Cardinals didn't have much of either and also had no reliable relievers, another must in Herzog's theory of how to win.

Herzog had always established just two rules as a manager, to be at the ball park on time and to bust your tail when you were in uniform. After just a few weeks, he knew there were some players on the Cardinals who likely would have trouble with at least one of those rules.

Busch called Herzog out to Grant's Farm one day to ask his opinion about the team, and Herzog did not mince words.

"You've got a bunch of prima donnas, overpaid SOBs who ain't ever going to win a goddamned thing," Herzog told Busch. "You've got a bunch of mean people, some sorry human beings. It's the first time I've ever been scared to walk through my own clubhouse. We've got drug problems, we've got ego problems, and we ain't ever going anywhere."

Busch asked Herzog if he was sure the problem was really that bad.

"We ain't going to win with this sorry bunch," Herzog replied. "We've got to do some housecleaning."

It didn't take long for Busch and Herzog to form a bond. Both came from the school of laying things on the line, no matter what the consequences might be. They spoke the same harsh language, and both wanted to see the Cardinals win. A trust and understanding quickly developed between them—Busch knew that Herzog understood what moves the Cardinals had to make to become a winner, and Herzog knew that Busch would give him the authority to make those moves.

Still, Herzog was a little surprised in August when he got a call to see Mr. Busch at Grant's Farm one morning. Busch had fired John Claiborne a week earlier, and while Susman was in New York interviewing candidates, Busch was begging Herzog to take the GM job.

Finally, after getting Busch to promise he could run the job his way and could give it up anytime he wanted, Herzog agreed.

"I didn't want it," Herzog said. "All I want to do is manage, that's what I think I do best.

"I took the job for two reasons. One is that Gussie is a hell of a guy. I don't know anybody I've ever liked any better than I like him. He talks my language. We understand each other. He deserves a pennant. It's the one thing he wants. And I want to get it for him."

Herzog said the second reason was the ball club. He was concerned that if somebody else was named general manager, they might have conflicting ideas on what needed to be done to tear the team apart and rebuild it again.

"I miscalculated when I took over managing this team," Herzog said. "I was shocked at what I saw ... guys not running out ground balls, guys not hustling. For the money they're making, they oughta be tearing the place apart, but they're not.

"The Cardinals need major surgery. One or two changes won't do it. I told Gussie what I had in mind and he told me to go ahead."

Herzog turned over the managing duties to Schoendienst for the rest of the 1980 season and hit the road, checking out the talent in the Cardinals farm system. He found out there wasn't enough talent there to help the team. The Cardinals finished the year in fourth place with a 74–88 record, showing Herzog just how much work was ahead of him.

Herzog made up a checklist of what he thought needed to be done to improve the team. The first thing was to build a team that was better suited to playing in Busch Stadium, meaning he needed to improve the speed and the defense. The second was to get a better defensive catcher. The third step was to find a reliable reliever.

He considered only one player untouchable—Templeton. "He is a great player and that's not the only reason," Herzog said. "We have nobody in sight to replace him."

After thinking about the managing situation as well, Herzog decided there was only person he wanted for that job—himself. With Busch's backing, he announced that he would serve as both manager and general manager for the 1981 season.

So the job of Herzog the general manager that winter was to give Herzog the manager a more talented team with which to work. Aided by Joe McDonald, his loyal assistant who constantly worked the phones, Herzog laid the groundwork for some major moves before flying to Dallas for the winter meetings.

Two other moves by Herzog that paid huge dividends over the years were naming Lee Thomas director of player development and Fred McAlister scouting director. The Cardinals were able to pick and develop much of the talent of the 1980s teams.

One of the first things Herzog did was sign the catcher he wanted, his old friend from Kansas City, Darrell Porter. Porter, a free agent, agreed to a five-year contract on a ship-to-shore radio while celebrating his honeymoon on a Caribbean cruise.

After arriving in Dallas, the final touches were put on an 11-player swap with the San Diego Padres, with the Cardinals getting Rollie Fingers, Bob Shirley, Gene Tenace and minor-league catcher Bob Geren in exchange for catchers Terry Kennedy and Steve Swisher, infielder Mike Phillips, and pitchers John Littlefield, John Urrea, Kim Seaman, and Al Olmsted.

"They wanted Kennedy and I wanted Fingers, because at the time we didn't know if we could get [Bruce] Sutter," Herzog said. "It was a good trade for both teams."

Herzog was feeling a little better about the makeup of his team, but he wasn't done. He and Bob Kennedy, the Cubs general manager (and Terry's father) had been talking for weeks about a package for Sutter. Kennedy wanted Leon Durham and young second baseman Tommy Herr, while Herzog kept trying to push Ken Reitz instead of Herr. Finally, he got his way. Twenty-four hours after swinging the Padres deal, Herzog was back in the conference room telling reporters about the Cardinals-Cubs trade. In exchange for Sutter, the Cardinals sent Durham, Reitz, and utilityman Ty Waller to the Cubs.

In two days, Herzog had gone from having not one reliever he could trust with the game on the line, to having two of the best in the history of the game in the same bullpen—Fingers and Sutter. He didn't know if that was a workable combination or not, but he was willing to give it a try. If it didn't work, Herzog knew he could always make another deal.

The team was shaping up nicely now. With Porter catching, Herzog planned to move Simmons to first base, where he would join Herr, Templeton, and Ken Oberkfell, moving from second to third, on the field. Hernandez would shift to left field, with George Hendrick in right and either Tony Scott or Tito Landrum in center. Herzog was prepared to leave Dallas with that team intact and see what he had when he got to Florida for spring training.

He had one surprise waiting for him, however. LaRue Harcourt, Simmons's agent, found Herzog and told him that Simmons had had some second thoughts about moving to first base. He had a no-trade clause but would be willing to waive it for the right price and to the right team. That was a snag on which Herzog had not counted, but he went back out in the lobby and went to work.

He found two teams with interest in Simmons—Oakland and Milwaukee. He knew that Simmons would never approve a deal to the A's, because Oakland was too far from St. Louis. That left Milwaukee. After much haggling and debate, especially over who was going to pay Simmons to waive his no-trade clause, the deal was made—Simmons, Fingers, and Pete Vuckovich went to the Brewers and outfielders Sixto Lezcano and David Green and pitchers Lary Sorensen and Dave La-Point came to the Cardinals. The Brewers paid to buy out the no-trade agreement.

Finally, Herzog's wild week in Dallas was done. He had added nine players, traded away 13, and improved the areas he thought needed the biggest improvement. It was up to manager Herzog to see if the new-look Cardinals could produce better results on the field.

There was considerable public outcry in St. Louis, as in earlier years when Hornsby and then Slaughter and Schoendienst were traded. The fans especially were upset that Simmons was leaving, but Herzog had a ready response for anybody upset by the deals.

"You haven't won anything in 12 years, anyway," Herzog said. "Why not let me try to do things my way."

Herzog the general manager also was confident in the ability of Herzog the manager.

"The general manager has done his job," Herzog said. "If the manager doesn't mess it up we'll be all right."

Herzog liked at least one thing about his dual role—he didn't have to consult with many people before deciding what he was going to do about any particular situation.

"We don't have to have a lot of meetings," Herzog acknowledged. "I can go to sleep and have a meeting."

If not for a 59-day players strike in the middle of the season and the idea of Commissioner Bowie Kuhn to split the season and have the winners of the first half play the winners of the second half in an extra round of playoffs, the revamped Cardinals would have been in the playoffs in 1981. They had the best overall record in the Eastern Division, finishing with a 59–43 record, but they were second in the standings for each separate half, finishing one and one-half games behind the Phillies in the first half, when nobody knew they were playing for anything, and one-half game behind Montreal in the second half. The Reds were afforded the same treatment in the Western Division, losing out on a division title for the same reason.

Herzog's performance wasn't unrecognized, however, as he was named executive of the year by United Press International.

"It's always nice to get an honor when you're a bleep-bleep players," Herzog joked. "The only other trophies I got this year were in Mike Schmidt's golf tournament and my dog won a field trial."

Herzog wasn't all smiles, however. He had a new major dilemma on his hands, and that was what to do with his shortstop, Garry Templeton.

Herzog had never been as mad at a player as he was at Templeton on August 26, 1981, when Templeton made a series of obscene gestures to the Ladies' Day crowd at Busch Stadium. He already had been ejected from the game and was headed toward the dugout when Herzog reached up the steps and pulled him into the dugout. The only reason Herzog did not continue to attack him was that he and Templeton were separated by coaches and other players.

Templeton was fined $5,000 and suspended indefinitely. He was admitted to a hospital, where he was found to be suffering from a chemical imbalance and depression. Templeton, who had had run-ins with management and fans before, was an enigma for Herzog. Here was an extremely talented player, perhaps one of the best he had ever managed, and Herzog didn't think he could win with him as his shortstop.

The problem was to find a taker for Templeton and then to find somebody else to play shortstop.

There were only a few shortstops in the major leagues whom Herzog considered in Templeton's class, including Alan Trammell of the Tigers, Rick Burleson of the Angels, Ivan DeJesus of the Cubs and Ozzie Smith of the Padres. He knew that

Smith wasn't as good offensively as the others, but he thought Smith's defensive skills would offset any offensive short-comings.

Herzog quickly found out that Trammell and Burleson weren't available. DeJesus was and, in fact, would be traded to the Phillies for Larry Bowa and a minor-league infielder named Ryne Sandberg. That left Smith. When Herzog arrived at the winter meetings, he knew that his old buddy, San Diego general manager Jack McKeon, already had told him he would not trade Smith.

So Herzog was a little surprised when he ran into McKeon at the meetings, and found out he still didn't want to trade him, but he had run into some problems with Smith's agent in a contract dispute. The two agreed on a deal, Smith for Templeton.

It was more than two months later when the trade was finally completed, however. Smith had a no-trade clause in his contract, and he didn't want to leave San Diego. It took a personal visit from Herzog to Smith's home in San Diego and an impassioned letter for Smith to finally agree to waive the no-trade clause and approve the trade to the Cardinals.

While he was waiting for that deal to be finalized, Herzog had completed his remaking of the Cardinals with a few other deals. In June, a week before the strike began, he had traded Tony Scott to Houston for pitcher Joaquin Andujar. During the World Series, he had sent pitcher Bob Sykes to the Yankees for minor-league outfielder Willie McGee. McGee had been taken off the Yankees' 40-man roster when they signed Dave Winfield, and the Cardinals wanted to take McGee in the minor-league draft. They knew that other teams would likely be interested as well, however, and they didn't want to take the chance he would not be available when their turn came in the draft.

Another deal fell into their laps when Cleveland obtained outfielder Lonnie Smith from the Phillies for catcher Bo Diaz. The Indians needed pitching and immediately offered Smith to the Cardinals for Sorensen and Silvio Martinez. Herzog made that deal so quickly he didn't even have time to tell Mr. Busch until after the trade was completed.

Smith, who had been a Little League teammate of Ozzie Smith's in Los Angeles, turned out to be the leadoff hitter and offensive catalyst the Cardinals needed. Ozzie Smith also didn't turn out to be as poor an offensive player as had been expected, especially after he made a spring training bet with Herzog that netted him a dollar every time he hit a ground ball, or a line drive, or got a base hit. When he hit a fly ball or struck out, he had to pay Herzog a dollar.

The Cardinals had become a team that could take advantage of Busch Stadium, playing what the media was quick to call Whiteyball. What that basically boiled down to was a team that could run, using speed to manufacture runs without a lot of power. A 12-game winning streak in April got the team started in the right direction, and another break came in May, when David Green pulled a hamstring muscle. That forced the Cardinals to recall McGee from Triple A Louisville, and he was the last piece missing from the puzzle. He was supposed to be in the majors temporarily but simply played too well to be sent back down.

Taken under Smith's guidance and tutelage, McGee blossomed, hitting .296 with 56 RBIs and 24 stolen bases while also playing excellent defense in center field.

If the Cardinals had any doubts that 1982 was going to be their year, they were erased on a Sunday afternoon in August when third-string catcher Glenn Brummer, with one career stolen base to his credit, pulled off the play of the season. The Cardinals had loaded the bases with two outs in the 12th inning of a game against the Giants, with Brummer running at third.

With two strikes on the hitter, David Green, Brummer took off—and stole home to win the game for the Cardinals 5–4. The Giants protested that the pitch should have been an inning-ending strike three, but umpire Dave Pallone ruled otherwise.

"It was one of those 'oh no, oh . . . what a play, what a great play' type of plays," Ozzie Smith said.

Brummer said he noticed as soon as he reached third base that the pitcher, Gary Lavelle, was paying no attention to him and that the third baseman, Darrell Evans, was playing well away from the base. Because Lavelle is left-handed, his pitching motion meant his back was to Brummer.

"I went up to Chuck [Hiller, the third-base coach] and said, 'I can go,'" Brummer said. "He said, 'Yeah I know, but you better not.'"

For two more pitches, Brummer did wait. Then he could wait no more.

"When he got his sign he would look first to first then to second, but he never looked to third," Brummer said. "Then he threw. That all takes time. He never saw me."

Brummer said he never thought about the possibility that Green would swing at the pitch, putting him in a potentially dangerous position. But as the pitch and Brummer both headed for home, Green heard him coming and stepped away from the plate.

The only question was if the pitch was strike three, but Brummer said Pallone could not call it a strike because it never crossed the plate, as the Giants tried to make a play on him.

"He called me safe, and then I just wanted to get off the field," Brummer said. "Everybody was in disbelief. It felt like we had won the World Series. Hernandez started calling his father [in San Francisco] and everybody else he knew because he was so much in disbelief."

Nearly 10 years later, Brummer said he still sees people who mention the play to him and recall where they were and what they were doing at that precise moment.

"People still talk about it," he said. "A guy told me he was listening on the radio and drove off the highway. Another guy told me he was barbequeing and knocked his grill over. I guess it shocked them so much, they haven't forgotten what they were doing."

The one win didn't immediately guarantee the Cardinals the pennant, however. They still had some obstacles to overcome, including a leg injury to Ozzie Smith that forced him to miss a key two-week period in September. Mike Ramsey filled in admirably in his absence as the team continued to battle for the pennant.

A loss to Steve Carlton and the Phillies dropped them a half-game out of first with three weeks to go in the season, but rookie John Stuper and Sutter combined for a 2–0 shutout the following night that put the Cardinals back in first to stay.

Sutter, who saved the game by getting Mike Schmidt to hit into a pitcher-to-home-to-first double play with the bases loaded, helped the Cardinals reel off eight consecutive wins that built the lead to five and a half games and allowed the team to clinch its first division title since 1968.

Herzog had made sure all the changes he had engineered had paid off, not only with a division title, but also in terms of the type of players the Cardinals put on the field.

"This is the only ball club I've ever had that I didn't have to chew out as a group at least once during the season," Herzog said. "I had to get on some guys individually, but I did that in the privacy of my office. Only they and I know what was said."

That was the season when Ozzie Smith proved the value of defense was just as important as the value of offense, giving fans a glimpse of the type of plays they could expect for years to come.

"I've been in baseball 32 years and I've never seen his equal," Herzog said. "When a guy takes two hits away from the opposition, why isn't he as important as a guy who drives in runs?"

The defensive performance of Smith, who had grown up working on his defense by bouncing balls off walls and concrete steps and trying to catch them, did not surprise his old Little League teammate.

"I saw him play for the first time in Little League and I played against him a few times in high school," Lonnie Smith said. "You could see he had ability. You can go back and ask anybody and they will tell you the same thing. They were already calling him the Wizard of Oz. He was amazing. He was no different than he is now, balls couldn't go through."

The team's defense, and the way it manufactured runs, made up for the lack of power hitters. The starting pitching, led by Bob Forsch, Andujar, and the rookies Stuper and LaPoint, was just good enough to get the ball to Sutter with a lead. It was a combination the Cardinals would use successfully in the future as well.

The Cardinals had to wait until the final day of the season to find out who their opponent would be in the playoffs. It turned out to the Braves, who edged out the Dodgers by one game.

The Braves, managed by former Cardinal Joe Torre, were ahead 1–0 behind Phil Niekro in the opening game and were two outs away from an official game when rain moved in and washed out the game. Forsch got the start for the Cardinals the next night, and he pitched a three-hit shutout en route to a 7–0 victory.

A rainout the next night again caused a one-day delay in the series, but the Cardinals came back a night later and won again, this time 4–3. They trailed 3–1 after five innings, but tied the game with one run in the sixth and another in the eighth, and then won it in the ninth on an RBI single by Ken Oberkfell.

The series was then a best-of-five, and the Cardinals went for the sweep the following night in Atlanta behind Andujar. McGee was the star of the night, ripping a two-run triple to highlight a four-run second inning and adding a solo homer in the ninth that ensured a 6–2 victory that put the Cardinals back in the World Series for the first time since 1968.

Their opponent this time was the Milwaukee Brewers, the team Herzog had made a winner by the trade that sent them

Fingers, Vuckovich, and Simmons. Herzog joked that the deal had made him the General Manager of the Year . . . in Milwaukee.

For Herzog, getting to the World Series also allowed him to achieve a personal goal. He had never made it as a player, then had come close the three times he led the Royals to division titles, only to lose to the Yankees each year in the playoffs. Just as his relationship with Busch had been an important reason why he was able to make the moves to bring the Cardinals the players he wanted, he had nurtured those players and had developed a good rapport with them that was important to the team's success.

"Your players have to respect your knowledge," Herzog said. "Be honest, be fair. But first, they have to know that you know what the hell to do."

There was no doubt of that as the Cardinals prepared to open the Series. There might have been some doubt, however, after they were wiped out by the Brewers 10–0 in the opening game. One of the runs came on a home run by Simmons, who would homer again in Game 2.

Before the second game, Herzog was discussing his team's chances when he said, "Their guy has won 280 games, our guy has won nine. Their guy makes $900,000 a year, our guy makes $35,000. It doesn't look too good for us on paper."

As he has been known to do on occasion, Herzog was exaggerating slightly. The Milwaukee starter in Game 2, Don Sutton, actually had 264 career victories, including postseason games, and was earning just $700,000. Still, the matchup did seem to favor the Brewers, but rookie John Stuper, with some help from Porter, was able to even the Series at one game each.

The Brewers had led 4–2 in the sixth when Porter, a dead pull hitter, sliced a shot into the left-field corner to drive in two runs and tie the game. "He'll hit that ball down there about as often as Halley's comet comes around, but he did it," Sutton said. The Cardinals then pulled out the 5–4 victory on a bases-loaded walk to Steve Braun.

The Series shifted to Milwaukee, and Game 3 turned out to be the game for which Willie McGee will always be remembered. The rookie not only hit two home runs and drove in four runs in the 6–2 Cardinals win, he also made home-run saving catches on Paul Molitor and Gorman Thomas.

"I don't know of anybody who ever played any better than McGee," Herzog said. McGee was overwhelmed as usual by the accomplishment, saying only, "I can't believe I'm here."

McGee had hit only four homers during the regular season, and one of those was inside the park. No doubt the Yankees officials were a little shaken by his performance, recalling the fateful trade the previous October.

"The first I heard of the trade was when I read it under the transactions in the newspaper," McGee said. "Nobody called me. I had to call the Yankees two weeks later to find out where I was supposed to go."

The Cardinals' momentum appeared to be continuing in Game 4, when they built a 5–1 lead after six innings. A fielding error by LaPoint on a play at first base, however, opened the way for the Brewers to score six runs in the bottom of the seventh and take a 7–5 victory that evened the Series at two wins each. A 6–4 Milwaukee win in Game 5 let the Brewers return to St. Louis needing just one win for the world championship.

Herzog showed some observers how calm he appeared to be at that moment, when everybody expected him to be nervous and worried about the outcome. He told reporters his plans for the off day included fishing and maybe playing golf. Asked why he would do such a thing, Herzog had an answer. "Weatherman says it will be a nice day," Herzog said.

Herzog has never been the type of manager who will take a game home with him from the ball park. When some managers drink themselves to sleep after a tough loss, Herzog knows a surefire method for putting himself to sleep when all else fails—get out a copy of the rule book.

"One paragraph on 'obstruction' and I'm asleep," he said.

No doubt partially inspired by the confidence and attitude of their manager, the Cardinals proved they would not go down easily. They withstood a long rain delay to pound the Brewers 13–1 behind Stuper's complete game in Game 6, setting up the decisive seventh game.

In Game 7 the Cardinals trailed 3–1 in the sixth but tied the game when Keith Hernandez, celebrating his 29th birthday, lined a two-run single. George Hendrick's single that inning put the Cardinals ahead to stay, and they added two runs in the eighth to increase the lead to 6–3.

With Sutter on the mound, Gorman Thomas was the Brewers' last hope. When Sutter threw strike three past him, Porter threw his mask high into the air and the Cardinals could celebrate a world championship.

"It was without a doubt the biggest thrill of my career," Sutter said. "We had a three-run lead, it was a three–two count. He had fouled off about six pitches. I thought to myself, 'I'm not walking him and have to face another guy.' That team was the most special team to me. There were a lot of good guys as well as a lot of good ballplayers."

Sutter's feelings were shared by his teammates.

"Being on the World Series team was the biggest thing that ever happened to me," said Ramsey. "That whole season, from start to finish, was the most exciting season I ever had."

Stuper, who started two games in the Series and had to win Game 6 for there to be a Game 7, said his highlight was watching Sutter strike out Thomas.

"My most vivid memory was Porter throwing his mask up in the air," Stuper said. "You'd think it would be the games I pitched, but it wasn't. It was that third strike."

The series also was exciting for NBC-TV sportscaster Bob Costas, who had worked Cardinals games for KMOX Radio but who was making his World Series debut by doing the pregame and postgame shows.

"I was nervous anyway but in a way I was more nervous because St. Louis was in it," Costas said. "I just remember the crowds, and how everybody was into every game. There was a lot of positive energy, and people yelling to me in the stands. It was a great atmosphere."

One of the highlights for Herzog was when Porter, the first piece in his puzzle to rebuild the Cardinals, was named the Series MVP. He also had been the MVP in the playoffs and followed that performance by hitting .286 with five RBIs in the Series.

For at least a little while, the fans were on Porter's side and were able to forgive Herzog for trading Simmons.

"He was a leader for me in Kansas City, he is a leader here," Herzog said of Porter. "He is a sensitive man, and I know the criticism has hurt him. But he has kept his chin up."

In addition to surviving the comparisons to Simmons, Porter had to put up with fans aware of his past history of drug and alcohol abuse, even though those problems occurred when he was playing in Kansas City.

"In a correlation of my lows and highs, this has to be the highest high," said Porter the day he received the MVP trophy. "For me, baseball has been more agonies than ecstasies, but I think it's true generally. Baseball is a game of failures. You fail more than you succeed. My personal case happens to be more dramatic."

The MVP award could almost have easily been awarded to Hernandez, who led all players in the Series with eight RBIs; he had a lot of clutch hits included in his .259 average.

While Hernandez was celebrating with the rest of his teammates that night, he didn't know that just eight months later he would become a former Cardinal.

With the Cardinals hovering near the .500 level in their attempt to repeat in 1983 and with an apparent pitching shortage as well as questions about whether Hernandez could be re-signed if he became a free agent at the end of the season, Herzog traded Hernandez to the Mets for pitchers Neil Allen and Rick Ownbey.

Hernandez was stunned by the deal, which he learned about

from Herzog after he was called back into the clubhouse from the field, where he had been taking batting practice. The first thing he did was call his wife. The second call he made was to his agent, to see if he had enough money to allow him to quit.

What wasn't known at the time—but later was re-vealed—were accusations about drug use directed at Hernan-dez and some of his teammates. During a trial in Pittsburgh, Hernandez was granted immunity from prosecution in ex-change for his testimony, detailing drug use among some Cardinals players.

Shortly before he was traded, Hernandez said the Cardinals had had a team meeting in which FBI agents said they had information about drug use among some unidentified players.

"Whitey said there are a couple of players [the FBI] have hard evidence against, and he gave the players a week to turn themselves in, he said, or they weren't going to play for him," Hernandez said. "A week went by and no one turned them-selves in. The bluff was called and nothing happened. There must have been no hard evidence."

A week later, Lonnie Smith went to Herzog and admitted he had a drug problem and needed help. Four days later, Hernan-dez was traded. Shortly thereafter, relief pitcher Doug Bair also was traded.

None of this was known by the fans, however, and when the news of the Hernandez trade appeared on the Busch Stadium scoreboard before a game against the Phillies, it was greeted by a loud chorus of boos.

Hernandez, who learned a lot of his hitting skills from his father, a San Francisco fireman, found out he couldn't retire and had to report to the Mets. No one ever questioned his playing ability, and despite whatever personal problems he might have had, the trade turned out to be one of the worst in recent Cardinals history.

The Cardinals gave Allen a big contract, in part to justify the trade in the minds of their fans, but he compiled only a 20–16 record with five saves in a little more than two years in St. Louis before he was unceremoniously traded back to New York, to the Yankees, during the All-Star break in 1985. The trade was supposed to be for a player to be named later, but it was never completed. Even though Allen was a member of the 1985 NL champion team for more than three months, he was not even voted a partial share of the team's postseason money.

Ownbey had even less of an impact in St. Louis. He was gone after the 1986 season, a 1–6 career record as his legacy.

Allen did pitch decently in his first year with the Cardinals, winning 10 games, and they were just a half-game out of first place on Labor Day before they fell into a September slump and wound up fourth, 11 games behind the Phillies and four games under .500.

The only highlight of the season came with a week to play, when Forsch pitched his second career no-hitter, beating the Montreal Expos 3–0.

"I think what made the second one better was there were no questionable calls," Forsch said. "I remember I had pitched against them the week before and hadn't done well, so it was just nice to come back and pitch well."

Forsch pitched well for the Cardinals for a long time, finishing his career as the third-winningest pitcher in team history, with 163 career wins, trailing only Gibson and Jesse Haines.

Forsch said he learned a lot from being around Gene Tenace in 1982 and also from watching Sutter and how he approached the game.

"In 1982 we had Jim Kaat and Tenace and Porter who knew how to win," Forsch said. "The rest of us had never been on a team that had won. We learned from them. I learned a lot from Tenace. He was kind of the policeman on the team. When you messed up he told you what you did wrong. He explained that if you wanted to be successful and wanted to win, this was the approach you had to take.

"I liked the approach Sutter took to the game. He had good

days and bad days, but when the game was over you couldn't tell. He approached both the same way. He showed me you always have to be on an even keel, that you can't play the game on emotion."

Forsch and Sutter spent many quiet hours away from the ball park, sitting in the middle of a lake fishing. He thinks part of the reason why the Cardinals were successful was because they were able to relax and have fun moments like that.

"We would be out in the lake by the crack of dawn and back home by 11 A.M. and ready to play that night," Forsch said. "That was our release, to go out and do that. I never did it on the day I was going to pitch, but Bruce had to or he couldn't go. Fortunately, we had an understanding manager. If we were running a little late, he cleaned the fish for us. I think he did it so Bruce wouldn't cut his hand."

Sutter's performance was the only thing that made the 1984 season memorable for the Cardinals. In what turned out to be his farewell season in a St. Louis uniform, Sutter set a National League record by saving 45 games as the Cardinals won 84 games and finished third.

The Cardinals had gambled in spring training that they could save money by not signing Sutter, who was to be eligible for free agency after the season, until later in the year. It was obvious by the middle of the year that he was headed for a stellar season, meaning it would take more money to sign him.

It came down to a battle between the Cardinals and Ted Turner's Atlanta Braves, and when the Cardinals balked at giving Sutter a modified no-trade clause and an increased buy-out if he was traded, Sutter took his split-fingered fastball and signed with the Braves.

As it turned out, Sutter ended up hurting his shoulder and saved just 40 games over the next four seasons for Atlanta before retiring. But nobody could have predicted that would happen on the December day in 1984 when he signed with the Braves and Herzog lamented that he had just become a dumber manager by about 25 games.

Despite the success Sutter had with the split-finger pitch, he was not surprised that more pitchers did not ask him about it or try to learn to throw it.

"Major-league pitchers have got good stuff or they wouldn't get to the majors," Sutter said. "When you've got good stuff, you shouldn't fool around with trick pitches or you will end up hurting your arm and end up with nothing."

Sutter said he started to throw the split-finger, taught to him by Cubs minor-league pitching coach Fred Martin, because he didn't think his ability was good enough otherwise to get him to the majors.

"The whole secret to the pitch is arm speed," Sutter said. "Even if I hang one, I can get away with it if I've got good speed. When it's slow and I hang one, it's usually hit a long way. It's a unique pitch. Even though I've been around the league a long time, I might not pitch to Mike Schmidt or Dale Murphy but three or four times a year. They don't really get used to seeing it."

One sight Herzog had got used to seeing was Sutter warming up in the Cardinals bullpen. The one advantage to having a stopper of Sutter's ability, Herzog often said, was that he would never get second-guessed if he decided to bring him in the game and got beat.

Herzog knew as the 1985 season began that he didn't have that luxury. As the season began, he was forced to juggle a bullpen that included Allen, Bill Campbell, Ken Dayley, Rick Horton, and Jeff Lahti, all of them effective pitchers but none a threat to break Sutter's record.

While he was disappointed by the loss of Sutter—which cost Joe McDonald his job as general manager—Herzog was encouraged that the Cardinals had been able to swing a couple of trades that figured to make other parts of the team stronger.

He had traded Hendrick to the Pirates for pitcher John Tudor and reserve Brian Harper, and for a package of David Green, Dave LaPoint, Jose Uribe, and Gary Rajsich, had pried Jack Clark away from the Giants.

Before the Clark trade, Herzog had predicted that the Cardinals could finish anywhere from first to last. After the deal, Herzog amended his prediction to say the team wouldn't finish last.

Clark brought with him a reputation as a negative influence on a team, but that didn't concern Herzog. He had managed guys like that before, including Andujar, and had been able to motivate them to good seasons. He didn't see any reason why Clark would be any different.

Clark, for his part, also didn't know how things were going to work out in St. Louis. He was a Californian who had been drafted and signed by the Giants out of high school, and since he had been a small boy he had never lived anywhere else.

It didn't take long for the love affair to blossom between Clark and the Cardinals fans, however. After having gotten used to an offensive attack centered around the stolen base, it was nice to finally have a hitter in the middle of the lineup who was a home-run threat on every pitch.

Clark enjoyed a banner 1985 season, beginning with a home run in his first Cardinals at bat, off the Mets' Dwight Gooden. He finished the year with 22 homers, 87 RBIs, and a .281 average despite missing 36 games because of injuries.

Clark said one of the biggest keys to his performance was the rapport he quickly developed with Herzog.

"Probably the most important thing for me was playing for a guy like Whitey," Clark said. "He knows the game so well, and he makes it easy. You want to win for the Cardinals, and you want to win for the fans, and you want to win for him.

"When he made a move, you never had second-guessers. He had reasons. When I played against the Cardinals, you knew that he would probably outmanage your manager somewhere in the game. You knew you had to beat the other team and him, too."

Clark was also an immediate hit with his teammates, except for making an early comment that he knew what it was like to win because he had played on winners in San Francisco.

"The best finish they ever had while he was there was third," Forsch said. "We cut out that little article and put it on his locker, just for fun. We always had fun. That was the big thing. If you can have fun, a lot of times that will pull you through the rough times."

The 1985 season wasn't one of those rough spots, thanks to Clark and the rest of the team's offensive attack. The lineup also featured the league MVP in McGee, who won the batting title with a .353 average, led the league with 18 triples, drove in 82 runs, and stole 56 bases.

Second baseman Tommy Herr became the first player in 35 years to drive in more than 100 runs (he finished with 110) while hitting fewer than 10 homers (he hit eight). The other offensive force was a rookie outfielder named Vince Coleman, who ran away with the league's stolen base title and became a unanimous selection as the Rookie of the Year.

Coleman, who admitted he didn't even know which league the Cardinals were in when he was drafted in 1982 out of Florida A & M, was promoted from Triple A Louisville nine days into the season when McGee and Tito Landrum were injured. He was supposed to be in the majors for 10 days at the most, but like McGee when he was a rookie in 1982, there was no way he was going back to the minors.

He finished the year with 110 stolen bases, the second highest total in NL history behind Brock's 118 in 1974, and put to rest any doubts that maybe he had chosen the wrong professional sport. He had been invited to a Washington Redskins tryout camp after a good football career at Florida A & M, where he had been a punter.

Coleman was upset, however, when the Redskins wanted him to try out as a wide receiver instead of as a punter. If they had let him punt, he said, he probably would have tried to make it in pro football, which was his favorite sport, instead of baseball.

Coleman played well enough in his first month in the majors

that the Cardinals traded Lonnie Smith to Kansas City, in order to make sure Coleman had a regular spot in left field and as the leadoff hitter.

Even though he was an immediate success, Coleman did not let his performance go to his head, as evidenced by what happened the first time he ever traveled to California and checked in with his teammates to a hotel in San Francisco.

"I walked into my room and I thought I was in the wrong room," Coleman said. "I couldn't believe that room was for me."

Touring the new cities and stadiums was an experience for Coleman, who admitted he was "trying to find the stuff I see on TV."

Led by Coleman, the Cardinals became the first National League team since the 1912 New York Giants to steal more than 300 bases in a season, finishing the year with 314. Five players stole more than 30—Coleman, McGee, Andy Van Slyke, Herr, and Ozzie Smith.

While all those players, plus others on a daily basis, were making the offense click, the Cardinals were also enjoying a three-man show from starting pitchers Tudor, Andujar, and Danny Cox.

Tudor recorded 10 shutouts en route to a 21–8 season and a 1.93 ERA. The most remarkable part of his performance was that on May 29, his record was 1–7. He won 20 of his next 21 decisions, losing only a start to the Dodgers' Fernando Valenzuela when the Cardinals were shut out.

Andujar also finished with 21 victories, and Cox wound up with 18 wins. The trio totaled more wins than any other group of Cardinals starters since 1935, a staff that featured the Dean brothers.

Despite the success of the offense and the pitching, the Cardinals were not able to put away the New York Mets. They were one and one-half games ahead at the end of June, two games up at the end of July, and two games in front at the end of August.

Clark was sidelined with a pulled rib-cage muscle, but the Cardinals were able to obtain Cesar Cedeno from Cincinnati to fill in, and he exceeded all expectations by hitting six homers and driving in 19 runs in 28 games after the trade.

The other September surprise came from rookie reliever Todd Worrell, called up from Louisville, who reeled off three wins and five saves in moving into the closer's role.

The Cardinals had increased the lead to three games by the end of September, with six games to play, with the Mets coming to Busch Stadium. The lead dropped to two games when Darryl Strawberry ended a scoreless duel in the 11th inning of the first game with a home run off Ken Dayley off the clock on the scoreboard in right center.

Gooden outdueled Andujar the next night, winning 5–2, and suddenly the Cardinals were only one game in front with four to play. Cox reversed the streak, however, pitching the Cardinals to a 4–3 win in the final game of the series, the team's 99th win of the year. The 100th win, by Forsch, against the Cubs one day later clinched at least a tie for the title.

On the next-to-last day of the season, Tudor turned in a 7–1 victory over Chicago, and for the second time in four seasons the Cardinals were the division champions.

"Whitey pushed all the buttons and when he pushed them the players responded," said outfielder Andy Van Slyke. "It makes a manager look awfully smart when players can respond and play to the level of talent that we had, and that's what we did.

"We had everything on that team—great defense, a great fourth-place hitter, great starting pitching, great relief pitching. We had all the ingredients."

Third baseman Terry Pendleton said that the other thing the team possessed was a deep desire to win.

"I think back in April we were just trying to get to .500 and once we got there we just took off," Terry Pendleton said. "Vince came up and had a great year. I had played with him the previous year in Triple A and I knew the biggest thing about him was how well he was going to hit. Once he got on base I knew there would be no stopping him."

The opponent in the playoffs was the Dodgers, who shut down the Cardinals offense behind Fernando Valenzuela and Orel Hershiser in the first two games in Los Angeles, winning 4–1 and 8–2.

As the scene shifted back to Busch Stadium, the Cardinals got a home run from Herr and good pitching from Cox and Dayley to win 4–2 and cut the Los Angeles lead to two games to one.

It was moments before the fourth game that one of the strangest injuries ever hit the Cardinals and Coleman. As Coleman and several other players were taking batting practice, a light drizzle began to fall. The grounds crew immediately began to cover the field, and Coleman and the other players tossed their gloves into the dugout as they prepared to head for the indoor batting cage behind the left-field wall.

As Coleman turned to give his glove to somebody to take inside, he slipped. His left leg became caught just as the automatic tarpaulin was beginning to unroll to cover the field. The driver, in a hole past first base, was unaware of what was happening until enough people yelled that it got his attention.

The tarpaulin had rolled past Coleman's knee, and then once it was stopped, had to roll over the leg again before he could be freed.

Initial reports were encouraging, saying he had suffered nothing more than cuts and bruises. Coleman said the following day that the leg was stiff but that he thought he could return to the lineup in a couple of days.

Coleman had been afraid it would be much worse.

"It was fright and pain," he said at the time. "As I was trying to sleep last night, I had a dream about what could have happened. I visualized the tarp coming over my head. I'm just thankful to the Lord that they heard me and stopped it.

"I didn't see it and I didn't hear it. Before I knew it it had caught my shoe, and before I could pull it loose it knocked me down."

Coleman said he lost feeling in the leg for about five minutes. As it turned out, the accident ended his season. When he still was unable to play after a few days, more X rays were taken, which revealed bone chips near the knee.

The injury forced Tito Landrum into the lineup, and he responded by going 4 for 5 with three RBIs and a run scored to lead the Cardinals to a 12–2 rout that evened the Series at two wins each.

The pivotal fifth game, which the Cardinals had to win if they wanted to avoid returning to Los Angeles having to win two straight games, was another game—like the one that featured Brummer's steal of home—that people still replay in their minds, remembering where they were when Jack Buck implored them to "go crazy."

The game was tied 2–2 with one out in the ninth, with Ozzie Smith at the plate, hitting left-handed against Tom Niedenfuer, when he did something he had never done before in his career. He homered, giving the Cardinals a spine-tingling 3–2 triumph.

Buck, broadcasting the game on KMOX, made the home-run call by telling listeners to "go crazy folks, go crazy. It's a home run for the Wizard." As motorists headed home from work on Highway 40 heard the news, car horns began to blare repeatedly. Those lucky enough to miss work for the Monday afternoon game stood in Busch Stadium and cheered, refusing to leave.

As Smith addressed the masses of reporters gathered around his locker, he said he had never doubted his offensive ability, even though he knew he would never hit a lot of home runs. He knew defense was the best part of his game, but he resented people who labeled him a one-dimensional player.

"I'm not supposed to be able to hit," Smith said. "But if I listened to all those things, I wouldn't be in the position I am now.

"You've got to believe in yourself. I've always been taught you only get out of something what you put into it. I'm always going to have skeptics. This isn't going to change anything. This is the way it's been my whole career."

Smith was not referring to the Cardinals fans, whose love affair with him only increased because of the home run, or his teammates, who were sharing another special moment.

"It was a great moment for all of us to spend together," Smith said. "We've been down in the trenches together, and it was a special moment for all of us."

While the Cardinals had one day to enjoy that home run, they had to put it out of their minds when they arrived back in Los Angeles for Game 6. They still had a game to win to reach the World Series, and even though they had Tudor waiting to start a potential Game 7, they didn't want the Series to get that far.

It looked as if that would happen, however, when Mike Marshall hit a solo homer off Worrell in the eighth inning to put the Dodgers in front 5–4.

What followed was an inning that prompted a lot of people to wonder about the logic of Dodgers manager Tom Lasorda. With one out, McGee singled and stole second. Smith walked. Herr grounded out, moving the runners to second and third and bringing up Clark to hit against Niedenfuer. With first base open, nobody expected anything more than an intentional walk to Clark.

Lasorda, however, had Niedenfuer pitch to Clark, and he deposited the first pitch into the left-field bleachers for a three-run homer that put the Cardinals ahead 7–5 and three outs away from the World Series.

As Clark jogged slowly toward first base, he stopped to point a finger into the Cardinals dugout.

"They had helped me a lot," Clark said of his teammates. "Now I had helped them out.

"It was the way I had always imagined the big leagues being like. That type of moment I had dreamed of my whole life.

You hear so many stories of great players not getting there, getting to the World Series. I can say I got the chance to play in the World Series. Win or lose, I got to play."

Clark said he wasn't surprised Lasorda had Niedenfuer pitch to him but that he was sure Niedenfuer did not intend to lay a fastball over the middle of the plate for him to hit.

"Niedenfuer had struck me out the at bat before," Clark said. "I might have walked me if the count had gone to 2 and 0 or 3 and 1. He just didn't get the ball where he wanted to."

Herr said the Cardinals comeback from the 2–0 Series deficit was a tribute to the quality, and depth, of the team.

"After we lost the first two games, so much was said about the Dodgers shutting down our running game," Herr said. "But we knew we had many more weapons than stealing bases. And later in the series it became evident that to beat us you have to do more than stop our base stealers.

"We felt coming in we had the better club, but we had to prove it on the field."

Smith was named the MVP of the series, in which he hit .435 with three RBIs. In addition to his game-winning homer in the fifth game, he had a key triple in a three-run seventh in the sixth game that helped the Cardinals wipe out a 4–1 Los Angeles lead.

"His triple, which will probably be forgotten, was a key to our win," Herzog said.

For Herzog, the victory not only put the Cardinals back into the World Series, it meant he was going to be able to sleep in his own bed during the road games—in Kansas City, the first all-Missouri series since the 1944 clash between the Cardinals and the Browns.

Tudor and Worrell combined to pitch the Cardinals to a 3–1 victory in the opening game, and it looked as if they were going to head home with a split when they trailed the Royals 2–0 going into the ninth inning of the second game.

But the Cardinals did something no team had accomplished in the World Series since the Yankees did it in 1939—rally from a two-run deficit in the ninth to win. They scored four times, capped by a bases-loaded, bases-clearing double by Pendleton.

Bret Saberhagen allowed just one run in beating the Cardinals 6–1 in Game 3, but the Cardinals moved to the brink of another world championship when Tudor turned in a 3–0, five-hit shutout in Game 4. Danny Jackson and the Royals made sure the series returned to Kansas City, however, by beating Forsch and the Cardinals 6–1 the next night.

The sixth game was a pitching duel between Cox and Charlie Liebrandt through seven innings, with neither team able to score. Finally in the eighth, pinch-hitter Brian Harper delivered an RBI single to center that put the Cardinals ahead 1–0.

If the Cardinals had won the game, Harper would have been a hero. As Herzog lamented later, however, some guys aren't meant to be heroes. The Cardinals carried that 1–0 lead into the bottom of the ninth, when Don Denkinger, an American League umpire probably nobody in St. Louis had ever heard of, suddenly became a four-letter household name.

Pinch-hitter Jorge Orta hit a routine grounder to Herr at second base. Denkinger admitted later that he missed the call at first base, calling Orta safe when he should have been out. He ruled that Worrell, taking the throw at first, had missed the bag, when replays clearly indicated he had touched it.

A botched foul pop-up, a single, and a passed ball later, the Royals had the tying and winning runs on second and third, and an intentional walk loaded the bases and brought former Cardinal Dane Iorg to the plate. He burned his old team with a two-run single to center, and the Royals had staved off elimination and forced a seventh game.

The record books show the Cardinals lost the last game 11–0, with Andujar and Herzog being ejected from the game by Denkinger, who was working home plate. They really lost the Series the night before; even Herzog knew that coming into the seventh game his team already was defeated.

The players lamented what could have been, with Pendleton

still saying years later, "We felt it was honestly taken from us." Clark acknowledged the bad call but said it should not be remembered as the sole reason the Royals became the world champions instead of the Cardinals.

"It was a bad call, but those things happen," Clark said. "You can't harp on that. They came back. They didn't have too much problem in the seventh game."

Clark said part of the reason the Cardinals struggled so much offensively in the Series, hitting a team-record-low .185, was that they were playing the Royals.

"We had a lot of friends on Kansas City and they had a lot of friends on our team," Clark said. "It just seemed like a spring training game. The importance of it wasn't there. We just weren't up for it. We were happy for the Royals, and they were happy for us.

"It wasn't like we had a killer-type attitude. Everybody was like back home. Whoever won was no big deal because it was like we won anyhow. It took a little bit away. The games kind of floated along instead of us really taking it to them."

Bob Costas said the fact the Cardinals lost the Series prevented them from being remembered as a truly great team.

"They were the best team of the three pennant winners in the 1980s," Costas said. "They could beat you in so many ways. Because of the strange way the season ended, for Cardinals fans to think of 1985 is a bittersweet feeling, when it should have been one of the greatest years in the history of the franchise."

The Cardinals had not been pleased by Andujar's actions in the last game or that he had not pitched very well the last six weeks of the regular season. He had the best record in baseball at the All-Star break, 15–4, but finished the year 21–12 and was a combined 0–2 in the playoffs and the World Series. When it was suggested by officials of the brewery that he be traded over the winter, it didn't exactly come as a surprise to Herzog or general manager Dal Maxvill.

The deal was made at the winter meetings, sending Andujar to Oakland for catcher Mike Heath and pitcher Tim Conroy. Both those players turned out to be busts, but the Cardinals were able to send Heath to Detroit midway through the 1986 season for a promising minor-league pitcher, Ken Hill.

The trade ended Andujar's exciting stay in St. Louis, a five-year period in which he established himself as one of the best right-handed pitchers in baseball and also as one of the most unique. He said everything in baseball could be summed up in one word—"Youneverknow."

Andujar was terribly afraid of snakes, which made it a standard clubhouse prank to stick a rubber one someplace in his locker or in his clothes, then wait for him to find it and go wild.

"They like me a lot," Andujar said of his teammates. "It don't make me mad if your teammates play around with you. That means they like you. If they don't like you, they not going to play around with you. They're not even going to mention your name."

The fans supported Andujar, even after his seventh-game explosion. One person sent a $10 check to the Cardinals, made payable to Andujar, to help him pay his fine. The check was returned.

The Cardinals thought Cox was ready to replace Andujar as the number two starter in the rotation, but he suffered a chip fracture in his right ankle when he jumped off a sea wall while fishing during spring training. He didn't win his first game of the year until June 1, and by then the Cardinals already knew that 1986 wasn't going to be their year.

Due primarily to an overall offensive slump, the Cardinals fell back to third, again dropping below .500.

Clark missed all but 65 games after tearing ligaments in his thumb in an ill-advised slide into third base in a game in early June. He hit just nine homers and drove in only 23 runs. Quipped Herzog after the play, "I knew he was going to be out, I just didn't know he was going to be out for the season."

Joe Garagiola, blocking the plate. (National Baseball Library, Cooperstown, N.Y.)

Garagiola, now a broadcaster, at left, with Harry Caray, Jack Buck, and Homer Thieleu, calling a summer 1958 game from the bleachers. (*The Sporting News*)

Stan Musial connecting for his last major league hit, number 3630, on September 29, 1963. (Bob Kurt, *The Sporting News*)

Bill White, manager Johnny Keane, and Julian Javier. White and Javier were the nucleus of the Cardinals infield during the 1960s.

Orlando Cepeda.

Ken Boyer (right) is congratulated after his grand slam home run in the 1964 World Series by, from left, Bill White, Carl Warwick, Dick Groat and Curt Flood. (St. Louis Mercantile Library)

Curt Flood. (St. Louis Mercantile Library)

Lou Brock, airborne.

Nelson Briles (center) is joined in the locker room by Mike Shannon (left) and Lou Brock after Briles won Game 3 of the 1967 World Series. (Associated Press)

Tim McCarver crosses the plate with a 3-run homer in Game 3 of the 1968 World Series. Greeting him are Mike Shannon (left), Roger Maris, and Curt Flood. (UPI/Bettmann)

Batter's eye view of Bob Gibson.

Gibson suffered a broken leg when hit by a line drive off the bat of Roberto Clemente in 1968. (UPI/Bettmann)

Lou Brock reached two milestones in the 1970s: in 1974 setting a new single season stolen base record with 105 (here sliding in on Larry Bowa), and in 1979 getting his 3000th hit. (both photos UPI/Bettmann)

Al Hrabosky, The Mad Hungarian. (Bill Knight/ *The Sporting News*)

Bob Forsch celebrates a no-hitter against the Philadelphia Phillies, April 16, 1978. (UPI/Bettmann)

Glenn Brummer jumps into the arms of Tom Herr after stealing home to win a game against the Giants in 1982. (Courtesy Glenn Brummer)

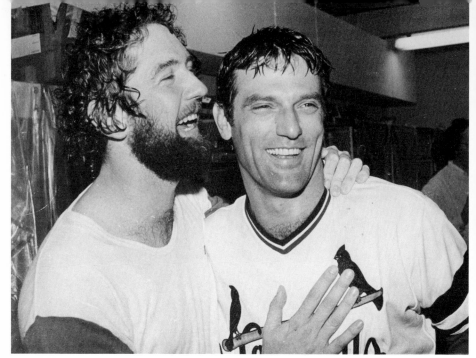

Bruce Sutter (left) and Darrell Porter celebrate after Cardinals win the World Series in 1982. Porter was named MVP of the series. (UPI/Bettmann)

Whitey Herzog and Gussie Busch after the 1982 series. (Courtesy Whitey Herzog)

The victory parade in 1982 brought all of St. Louis into the street. (St. Louis Mercantile Library)

Herzog in the dugout. (St. Louis Mercantile Library)

John Tudor. (Richard Pilling/ *The Sporting News*)

Joaquin Andujar. (Chuck Solomon/ *The Sporting News*)

Ted Simmons. (Jim Forbes/ *The Sporting News*)

Keith Hernandez. (St. Louis Mercantile Library)

Vince Coleman. (St. Louis Mercantile Library)

Willie McGee grabs one against the wall. (UPI/Bettmann)

Ozzie Smith, executing his pre-game backflip. (UPI/Bettmann)

Clark said the fact the Cardinals were able to win 79 games, with so many things having gone wrong, showed what type of manager Herzog was.

"The attitudes weren't good," Clark said. "I felt bad for Whitey. He probably did one of the best jobs of managing that I've seen in baseball. Because of injuries and because of problems and attitudes and different things going on, his ability to bring us in in third place was quite an accomplishment. Everybody got off upside down. It was kind of tough.

"We were kind of our own worst enemy. We couldn't get guys in from third. I don't know how many times we couldn't get a run in when we had guys at first and third and nobody out, myself included. All you've got to do is hit the ball, even if it's a double play. We couldn't even do that.

"We could only score three runs or less. The other teams had something else in mind. We were defending champs and all that, and they were wanting to take it to us. We weren't in the position to counter the attack."

It came out later that Herzog had even offered to resign if the upper management thought it would help, but nobody did.

The Cardinals had put that frustrating season out of their mind and were having a very good spring training in 1987, but Maxvill and Herzog thought there still was something missing.

Herzog especially had been a longtime admirer of Pittsburgh catcher Tony Peña, and with rookie Jim Lindeman enjoying a good spring after playing well in winter ball, he thought maybe the time was right to make a deal.

On April 1 the Cardinals traded Van Slyke, Mike LaValliere, and pitching prospect Mike Dunne to the Pirates for Peña.

Van Slyke, who had been hitting third almost every day in the spring, knew something was up when he looked at the lineup card before that day's game and the third spot was blank.

"I had had a sore hamstring early in the spring and it was coming along, but all of a sudden trainer Gene Gieselmann was real concerned about it, when for the previous week he had not been concerned at all," Van Slyke said. "The only thing I was thinking was please not Pittsburgh. At that time there were probably only two places on the planet that you didn't want to play, and that was Pittsburgh and Cleveland. I probably would have had an easier time adjusting to the Moscow Reds, because I wouldn't have had to change my shoes or undershirts."

When Van Slyke was informed that Herzog wanted to see him after the game, his first question was "Where to?" Herzog had already prepared his remarks and didn't answer the question, just telling Van Slyke he had been traded. When Van Slyke asked again and Herzog replied the Pirates, Van Slyke knew he wasn't kidding.

While Van Slyke was at first devastated, the move turned out to be a positive one for him and his career. And in acquiring Peña, a former all-star, the Cardinals thought they had significantly strengthened their own club.

They probably would have had a different reaction had they known that Peña would suffer a broken thumb when he was hit by a pitch in just his third game as a member of the Cardinals. He was out of the lineup until May 22. By that time, Lindeman—the player the Cardinals had expected to replace Van Slyke—was on the disabled list, suffering from back spasms.

Neither one of those injuries were as bizarre as the mishap that sidelined Tudor on April 19. Sitting in the dugout for the Easter Sunday game against the Mets, Tudor stood up to try to help New York catcher Barry Lyons from falling into the dugout as he chased a foul pop-up. Lyons crashed into Tudor, pinning Tudor back against the dugout bench and breaking a bone in his right knee.

Despite all those injuries, the Cardinals were never more than two games out of first place all season and moved into first place to stay on May 22.

"We were a little more mature, and our lineup was healthier

than it had been the year before," Pendleton said. "We knew with the lineup we had if we stayed healthy we had a chance to win. We just did the things we needed to do to win."

Even though they never fell out of first place, the Cardinals were never able to pull away from the rest of the division. They were in danger of seeing their lead fall to one-half game over the Mets if they lost September 11, with Dwight Gooden to face the next day. But Pendleton ripped a ninth-inning homer off Roger McDowell to bring the Cardinals back from an almost certain defeat. They won the game in the 10th, then routed Gooden the next day.

Their lead over the Mets was two games with seven to play, when Joe Magrane and Greg Mathews pitched a doubleheader shutout over the Expos, 1–0 and 3–0, to erase any fears about New York catching the Cardinals.

As had been the case in 1985, the offense was more than just a one-man show, but the most damage was done by Clark, who bounced back from his disappointing 1986 season to hit a career-high 35 homers and drive in 106 runs.

Pendleton drove in 96 runs, and Smith—the guy most people said was only a defensive player—hit .303 and drove in 75 runs, while also winning another Gold Glove. His 75 RBIs were a major league record for a player with no home runs.

For Smith, the season was a reward for all the hard work he had put into improving the offensive part of his game.

"I enjoy the game and I try to get the most out of what I've been blessed with, which is not a lot of size but quickness and an ability to get to the ball," Smith said. "Everybody would like to be a .300 hitter, but it all goes back to the saying that you can't have it all.

"I've always worked hard at everything I've done. All you can try to do is work hard every day and get the maximum out of what it is you possess, and I think I've done that."

Smith wasn't alone with those thoughts.

"Every place we go, the public address announcer says his name and he gets a hand, no matter where we are," Herzog said. "Ted Williams drew people, Musial drew people, and I really do think people come to see him play shortstop.

"When I played with Brooks Robinson I always thought he took one or two hits away from you a game, and that's the way Ozzie is. Those things are hard to gauge in what it means to a club."

Smith played his way into the hearts of Cardinals fans, and his teammates, by performing with a certain flair. Started at the suggestion of Gene Tenace when they were both in San Diego, Smith's annual somersaults in the first and last games of the season, plus in any postseason appearances, became a highly anticipated event.

"Whatever minor criticisms he got early in his career were put to rest," Costas said. "He is an exciting player and to his credit he has made himself into an outstanding player. If you could field like he does, a team would carry you if you could hit .240, but he does much better than that. He also deserves a lot of admiration for being so much a part of the community. I've never seen a player as accommodating as Ozzie."

One player who got as close a look at Smith as anybody was his longtime double-play partner, Tommy Herr, who also marveled at some of the things he was able to accomplish.

"I may be his teammate, but I'm also his fan," Herr said. "So many times I'll see the ball leave the bat and say, 'OK, that's a base hit.' And then somehow Ozzie will come up with it. A lot of the time I feel like standing out there and applauding with the rest of the fans. He's head and shoulders above every other shortstop."

Herr's own play in 1987 was good as well, as he drove in 83 runs in helping lead the Cardinals back to the playoffs, where this time the San Francisco Giants were waiting for them.

Herr and Forsch were the only Cardinals still on the team from before Herzog took over, which came as something of a surprise to Herr.

"It doesn't really make sense," he said. "When I look back

and remember all the old guys, I never would have guessed that I'd be the only one still here. A lot better players than me have gone."

Herzog appreciated Herr's ability, however, and he often said he was one player he didn't think the Cardinals could afford to lose going down the stretch in a pennant race. Part of that was because of Herr's desire to win and to his own innate ability about how to play the game.

"That's the way I've always had to do it," Herr said. "I have good athletic ability, but I still needed to play the game properly to get here. I've never been a supertalented player, so I've always had to stress the fundamentals and the basics."

At no time are those two things more important than the postseason, and the Cardinals knew they would have to be on top of their game to beat the Giants.

The series opened in St. Louis, and the Cardinals jumped on top with a 5–3 win behind Greg Mathews, an emergency starter when Cox came up with a stiff neck, who pitched seven and one-third strong innings and also singled in two runs. The Giants came back to even the series a day later, 5–0, behind the two-hit pitching of Dave Dravecky.

Most of the time, hitting a batter is not a smart thing for a pitcher to do. But when Forsch hit Jeff Leonard with a pitch in the third game—the Giants were ahead 4–0, after Leonard had homered earlier, his third homer in as many games—it seemed to inspire the Cardinals, who got back into the game on a two-run homer by Lindeman and then pulled out a 6–5 win with a four-run seventh.

The Giants were the team that was inspired the next two days, however, winning 4–2 and 6–3 to put the Cardinals one loss away from elimination as they returned home.

That's when the pitching staff, led by Tudor and Cox, took matters into its own hands. Tudor, Worrell, and Dayley combined on a six-hit 1–0 victory in Game 6, and Cox went all the way in a 6–0 shutout in Game 7 that gave the Cardinals the victory.

It was on to the World Series again, this time against the Minnesota Twins. The Cardinals already were behind, even before the first pitch, because of the loss of Clark, who had suffered torn ligaments in his ankle on September 9. He had tried to play in the playoffs but struck out in his only pinch-hit appearance. He would not be able to play at all against the Twins.

Rookie Joe Magrane got the start in the opening game, but he was gone by the fourth inning of the Twins' 10–1 rout. The Minnesota offense was almost as effective against Cox in Game 2, winning 8–4 to put the Cardinals in a deep hole.

The tenor of the Series changed, however, when the scene shifted away from the Metrodome and to Busch Stadium, where the Cardinals—without Clark and Pendleton, out with a pulled rib-cage muscle—ripped off three straight victories. Tudor won 3–1, Forsch (in relief) won 7–2, and Cox came back with a 4–2 win that sent the Cardinals back to Minneapolis needing just one win to come away with the championship.

As had been the case in 1985, they came close. They were ahead 5–2 in the fifth inning of Game 6 when Kent Hrbek blasted a grand slam off Dayley to lead the Twins to an 11–5 win.

The Cardinals did not fall apart in the seventh game as they had in 1985 and were clinging to a 2–1 lead in the fifth. The Twins tied it, however, and went on to win 4–2 to become the first team in history to win a World Series simply by winning all four games at home and none on the road.

The loss left a bitter taste in the mouths of the Cardinals. "The Twins beat us with what we had, but we didn't have Jack and I wasn't healthy either," Pendleton said. "I would have liked to have played them with both of us healthy and see what would have happened."

It turned out to be the final World Series for Gussie Busch, and he still enjoyed it, riding across the artificial turf in his Clydesdale-driven beer wagon and sitting in Herzog's office soaking up all the atmosphere of the Series.

Herzog had promised when he was hired to bring him one more pennant, and he had won three. He had helped the Cardinals draw an almost unheard of 3 million fans to Busch Stadium, which brought a lot of smiles to Busch's face.

Unfortunately, there weren't many occasions for him or the Cardinals fans to smile the next two years. The team skidded to fifth in 1988, and although they rebounded to third in 1989 and again drew 3 million fans, they couldn't catch the division-champion Cubs.

On September 29, 1989, at the age of 90, Busch died.

One era in Cardinals history was over. Only a few months later, another one also would come to an end.

9

A New Beginning

THE 1990s

◆

The stars of the 1980s were fading from the St. Louis scene as the decade of the 1990s began. Tommy Herr had been traded in 1988, Clark had signed as a free agent with the Yankees, Peña as a free agent with the Red Sox. Forsch had been traded to Houston and then retired.

Herzog was not immune to all the changes. Some of them he had approved of, others he had opposed. When the 1990 team struggled, especially to put away games it should have won, the losses ate at Herzog more than at any other point in his managerial career.

It reached a breaking point in early July, a week before the All-Star break, when the Cardinals were on the West Coast. The team was embarrassed in a series in San Francisco, and Herzog made up his mind. When the team reached its next stop, San Diego, on July 6, Herzog quit as manager of the Cardinals.

The Cardinals had a record of 33–47 and were in last place in the NL East. The team had already been in last place for 56 days.

"I still enjoy managing," Herzog said at the news conference to announce his resignation. "But I just don't feel like I've done the job. I feel like I've underachieved. I can't get the guys to play."

Herzog was particularly frustrated by the performance of the 10 Cardinals players who were in the last year of their contracts: Tom Brunansky, Vince Coleman, Dave Collins, Ken Dayley, Frank DiPino, Greg Mathews, Willie McGee, Tom Niedenfuer, Terry Pendleton, and Denny Walling. He knew the status of their future bothered them, and he thought they were worrying too much about that and not enough about trying to win games.

"I didn't realize how fed up he was with his inability to make things happen like he used to," said Rick Hummel, covering the Cardinals for the *Post-Dispatch*. "He always wanted things to happen and moves to be made, but he was mad that what he had wouldn't play any better."

The only move he was able to make was trading Brunansky to Boston for reliever Lee Smith, in what turned out to be a great trade.

Herzog said the concept of Whiteyball and team-oriented baseball was missing because the players were too concerned about their own statistics so they could get a better contract for the next year.

"All of a sudden, team ball is gone," he said. "A guy might act like he's giving himself up, but it doesn't happen. I don't think you can go to a player in his free-agent year and get on him for not hitting the ball to the right side when he might hit .290 instead of .300."

Some of the players accepted the responsibility that they had caused Herzog to quit with two and a half years remaining on his contract.

"He shouldn't have to motivate this club," pitcher John Tudor told Hummel. "This club should motivate itself and it hasn't. We haven't played very well. We've messed up every aspect of the game. We've messed it up every way possible.

"It's really a sorry sight to watch. I can't blame him at all for leaving."

Said Herzog, "I've had some bad teams before. We were ter-

rible in '86 and terrible in '88 and last year we overachieved.
I can stand losing, if I think the club is playing up to its capa-
bilities. It just isn't happening."

Pitcher Joe Magrane said that the Cardinals lost a big part
of their arsenal when Herzog resigned.

"That's a weapon the Cardinals have always had and I think
clubs realized it," Magrane said. "He's forced every club to
make moves they wouldn't ordinarily have made. All of a sudden, you lose the big ace. It's really a big-time mental
hotfoot."

Hummel said having Herzog in the dugout was worth an
extra 5 to 10 wins a season for the Cardinals.

"He was as good a field technician as we've seen in baseball
in our lifetimes," Hummel said. "He was always two or three
steps ahead of the other guy. I think other managers were in-
timidated by him. They tried to manage him instead of worrying about their own team."

The search to find a successor to Herzog didn't take long.
On August 1 general manager Dal Maxvill announced that the
candidate who had been the favorite from the beginning, former Cardinal Joe Torre, had taken the job.

Torre had been working as a broadcaster for the California
Angels, a job he had taken after he had been fired by the
Braves in 1984. Maxvill had been a teammate of Torre's in St.
Louis and also had served as a coach when Torre was the man-
ager in New York and Atlanta.

"You couldn't find anybody better anywhere on earth,"
Maxvill said. "This man is going to do a great job for us. We're
very happy to have Joe Torre as our manager to lead us into
the 1990s."

Partially because of his past relationship with the St. Louis
fans, Torre's transition as the manager replacing Herzog was
a little easier than it might have been for some other managers. He was also able to win over doubting fans because of his
straightforward, no-nonsense approach to the situation.

"I'm not coming here to try to replace Whitey," Torre said. "I have a lot of respect for Whitey, as does everyone. If I tried to copy him, I'd come out on the losing end."

What Torre wanted to do for the last two months of the 1990 season was watch, and learn, about his players and the league and what changes the team needed to make to become competitive in 1991 and beyond.

He likely sacrificed a few wins that way, especially when he benched free-agent-to-be Terry Pendleton and had rookie Todd Zeile move from catcher to third base. But he learned Zeile could in fact play third, and that made it easier to decide not to re-sign Pendleton.

The Cardinals also decided they would not re-sign Willie McGee, and when Oakland's Dave Henderson was injured with a month to go in the season, they seized the opportunity to trade McGee to the A's for two young players, outfielder Felix Jose and third baseman Stan Royer.

For the first time since 1918, the Cardinals finished last. Tudor retired. Vince Coleman was another of the great players from the 1980s who said his good-byes after the season, signing as a free agent with the New York Mets. Pendleton signed with the Braves.

Ozzie Smith was the only player remaining who had been on all three pennant-winning teams in the 1980s, but he could tell that the Cardinals were in an era of transition toward younger players and that those players had some ability.

"One of the things I talked to the team about in the spring was pride," Torre said. "You need pride to be able to play this game. The Cardinals are one of only 26 clubs. There are 650 or so players who can say they are major leaguers. Be proud of that uniform you're wearing.

"I remember talking about Boyer, and Gibson, and Brock, and Musial. Guys like that are responsible for the banners that are hanging over your heads. Ozzie was sitting right behind me, and I said that he was a big part of the three teams that had gone to the World Series in the 1980s.

"Sometimes you have to get away from the fact that this is just a business. The players are not just going to an office and putting in time. There's more to it than that. It takes more than that to be a winning team."

Picked by most observers to finish last again, the Cardinals instead mounted the biggest challenge to the Pirates. They eventually finished second, winning more games than anybody could have expected.

"You know what's good about this year?" Torre said. "We've been legitimate. A lot of times, teams will gain ground and pull to within four or five games after the race already has been decided. But we won games when he had to.

"We had a lot of untried people, rather than bad players playing well. It was a matter of trying to approach the year without any pressure. Have fun."

Rookie Ray Lankford showed the potential to become a star. Zeile made the transition to third base better than most people expected. Even though Magrane missed the entire season after undergoing elbow surgery, the pitching was better than expected. Lee Smith broke Bruce Sutter's club and NL record for saves, finishing with 47. After the depressing, sullen season of 1990, it was fun to come to Busch Stadium again.

"Joe [Torre] seemed to handle the young players real well, and that had been a concern when he was in Atlanta," Hummel said. "That the team was able to come from behind so well indicated what kind of attitude it had about trying to win. They were an exciting team. They're on the right track."

In 1992 season will mark the Cardinals' 100th anniversary. The team that has won the most World Series—nine—of any National League team has getting there again as its goal in its centennial season.

The history of the team will be stressed even more this season, and it's a lesson from which the players can learn and become a part of. Smith has been around longer than any of his current teammates, and maybe that's why he understands just a little better what it has meant to him to be a member of the St. Louis Cardinals.

"This town has such a rich baseball history, you can't help but be caught up in it," Smith told *Sports Illustrated* in 1987. "They're all here, all the great ones, Musial, Marion, Schoendienst, Gibson. They're people you see all the time, people you can reach out and touch. And the memories of others, like the Deans, are still here, too.

"I'm proud to be a part of this. I'm complimented to be compared with players like Marty Marion. Everything here seems to come full circle back to the ball park. I feel as if I'm part of, well, a common cause."

Appendix

ALL-TIME ST. LOUIS CARDINALS

RECORDS

CARDINALS' ALL-TIME COACHES LIST

Tony Auferio	1973	Darold Knowles	1983
Joe Becker	1965-66	Fred Koenig	1976
Vern Benson	1961-64 1970-75	Jack Krol	1977-80
Ray Blades	1930-32, 1951	Hal Lanier	1981-85
Ken Boyer	1971-72	Johnny Lewis	1973-76, 1984-89
Steve Braun	1990	Nick Leyva	1984-88
Joe Coleman	1991	Marty Marion	1950
Dave Collins	1991	Dal Maxvill	1979-80
Walker Cooper	1957	Bill McKechnie	1927
Joe Cunningham	1982	Bob Milliken	1965-70, 1976
Bucky Dent	1991	Terry Moore	1949-52, 1956-58
Preston Gomez	1976	Mo Mozzali	1977-78
Mike Gonzalez	1934-46	Billy Muffett	1967-70
Stan Hack	1957-58	Greasy Neale	1929
Rich Hacker	1986-90	Charley O'Leary	1913-17
Chuck Hiller	1981-1983	Jack Onslow	1928
Al Hollingsworth	1957-58	Claude Osteen	1977-80
Johnny Hopp	1956	Heinie Peitz	1913
Darrell Johnson	1960-61	Gaylen Pitts	1991
Lou Kahn	1954-55	Howie Pollet	1959-64
Ray Katt	1959-61	Bill Posedel	1954-57
Tony Kaufmann	1947-50	Jamie Quirk	1984
Johnny Keane	1959-61	Dave Ricketts	1974-75, 1978-1991
Bill Killefer	1926	John Riddle	1952-55
George Kissell	1969-75	Jim Riggleman	1989-90
Hub Kittle	1981-83	Mike Roarke	1984-90

Sonny Ruberto 1977-78
Mike Ryba 1951-54
Red Schoendienst 1962-64, 1979-
Barney Schultz 1971-75
Joe Schultz 1963-68
Burt Shotton 1923-25
Dick Sisler 1966-70
Hal Smith 1962
Al Sothoron 1927-28
Joe Sugden 1921-25
Lee Thomas 1972, 1983

Ray Thomas 1922
Tim Thompson 1981
Tink Turner 1924
Mickey Vernon 1965
Dixie Walker 1953, 1955
Harry Walker 1959-62
Buzzy Wares 1930-35, 51
Otto Williams 1926
Bart Zeller 1970
Tom Zimmer 1976

CARDINALS' ALL-TIME ROSTER

Includes all players who have participated in one or more official National League games with the Cardinals starting with the 1892 season and including the 1991 season.

A

Ody Abbott 1910
Ted Abernathy 1970
Babe Adams 1906
Buster Adams 1939, 43, 45-46
Joe Adams 1902
Sparky Adams 1930-33
Jim Adduci 1983
Henry Adkinson 1895
Tommie Agee 1973
Juan Agosto 1991
Eddie Ainsmith 1921-23
Gibson Alba 1988
Cy Alberts 1910
Grover Alexander 1926-29
Luis Alicea 1988-
Ethan Allen 1933
Neil Allen 1983-85
Richie Allen 1970
Ron Allen 1972
Matty Alou 1971-73
Tom Alston 1954-57
Walter Alston 1936
George Altman 1963
Luis Alvarado 1974, 76
Brant Alyea 1972
Ruben Amaro 1958
Red Ames 1915-19

Craig Anderson 1961
Dwain Anderson 1972-73
Ferrell Anderson 1953
George Anderson 1918
John Anderson 1962
Mike Anderson 1976-78
John Andrews 1973
Nate Andrews 1937
Joaquin Andujar 1981-85
Pat Ankenman 1936
John Antonelli 1944-45
Harry Arndt 1905-07
Scott Arnold 1988-
Luis Arroyo 1955
Rudy Arroyo 1971
Dennis Aust 1965-66
Benny Ayala 1977

B

Les Backman 1909-10
Bill Bailey 1921-22
Doug Bair 1981-83, 85
Doug Baird 1917-19
Dave Bakenhaster 1964
Bill Baker 1948-49
Steve Baker 1983
O.F. Baldwin 1908
Art Ball 1894

Jimmy Bannon 1893
Jap Barbeau 1909-10
George Barclay 1902-04
Ray Bare 1972, 74
Clyde Barfoot 1922-23
Greg Bargar 1986
Mike Barlow 1975
Frank Barnes 1957-58, 60
Skeeter Barnes 1987
Frank Barrett 1939
Red Barrett 1945-46
Shad Barry 1906-08
Dave Bartosch 1945
Frank Bates 1899
Ed Bauta 1960-63
John Baxter 1907
Johnny Beall 1918
Ralph Beard 1954
Jim Beauchamp 1963, 70-71
Johnny Beazley, 1941-42, 46
Zinn Beck 1913-16
Jake Beckley 1904-07
Bill Beckmann 1942
Fred Beebe 1906-09
Ed Beecher 1897
Clarence Beers 1948

CARDINALS' ALL-TIME ROSTER

(Continued)

Hi Bell 1924, 26-27, 29-30
Les Bell 1923-27
Joe Benes 1931
Pug Bennett 1906-07
Vern Benson 1951-53
Sid Benton 1922
Augie Bergamo 1944-45
Jack Berly 1924
Joe Bernard 1909
Frank Bertaina 1970
Harry Berte 1903
Bob Boescher 1915-17
Frank Betcher 1910
Hal Betts 1903
Bruno Betzel 1914-18
Jim Bibby 1972-73
Lou Bierbauer 1897-98
Steve Bilko 1949-54
Dick Billings 1974-75
Frank Bird 1892
Ray Blades 1922-28, 30-32
Harry Blake 1899
Sheriff Blake 1937
Coonie Blank 1909
Don Blasingame 1955-59
Johnny Blatnik 1950
Buddy Blattner 1942
Bob Blaylock 1956
Gary Blaylock 1959
John Bliss 1908-12
Clyde Bloomfield 1963
Charlie Boardman 1915
Joe Boever 1985-86
Sammy Bohne 1916
Dick Bokelmann 1951-53
Bill Bolden 1919
Don Bollweg 1950-51
Bobby Bonds 1980
Frank Bonner 1895
Rod Booker 1987-89
Pedro Borbon 1980
Frenchy Bordagaray 1937-38
Rick Bosetti 1977

Jim Bottomley 1922-32
Bob Bowman 1939-40
Cloyd Boyer 1949-52
Ken Boyer 1955-65
Buddy Bradford 1975
Dave Brain 1903-05
Harvey Branch 1962
Jackie Brandt 1956
Kitty Brashear 1902
Joe Bratcher 1924
Steve Braun 1981-85
Al Brazie 1943, 46-54
Harry Brecheen 1940, 43-52
Ted Breitenstein 1892-96, 1901
Herb Bremer 1937-39
Roger Bresnahan 1909-12
Rube Bressler 1932
Ed Bressoud 1967
Rod Brewer 1990-
Marshall Bridges 1959-60
Rocky Bridges 1960
Grant Briggs 1892
Nellie Briles 1965-70
Ed Brinkman 1975
John Brock 1917-18
Lou Brock 1964-79
Steve Brodie 1892-93
Ernie Broglio 1959-64
Herman Bronkie 1918
Jim Brosnan 1958-59
Tony Brottem 1916
Buster Brown 1905-07
Jim Brown 1915
Jimmy Brown 1937-43
Three Finger Brown 1903
Tom Brown 1895
Willard Brown 1894
Byron Browne 1969
Cal Browning 1960
Pete Browning 1894
Glenn Brummer 1981-84
Tom Brunansky 1988-90
George Brunet 1971

Tom Bruno 1978-79
Ron Bryant 1975
Johnny Bucha 1948
Jerry Buchek 1961, 63-66
Jim Bucher 1938
Dick Buckley 1892-94
Fritz Buelow 1899-1900
Nels Burbrink 1955
Al Burch 1906-07
Bob Burda 1962, 71
Lew Burdette 1963-64
Tom Burgess 1954
Sandy Burk 1912-13
Jimmy Burke 1903-05
John Burke 1899
Leo Burke 1963
Jesse Burkett 1899-1901
Ken Burkhardt 1945-48
John Burnett 1907
Ed Burns 1912
Farmer Burns 1901
Ray Burris 1986
Ellis Burton 1958
Guy Bush 1938
Ray Busse 1973
Art Butler 1914-16
John Butler 1904
Johnny Butler 1929
Bud Byerly 1943-45
Bill Byers 1904
Bobby Byrne 1907-09

C

Al Cabrera 1913
John Calhoun 1902
Jim Callahan 1898
Wes Callahan 1913
Ernie Camacho 1990
Harry Camnitz 1911
Llewellyn Camp 1892
Bill Campbell 1985
Billy Campbell 1905
Dave Campbell 1973
Jim Campbell 1970

Sal Campisi 1969-70
Chris Cannizzaro 1960-61
Doug Capilla 1976-77
Bernie Carbo 1972-73, 79-80
Jose Cardenal 1970-71
Tex Carleton 1932-34
Steve Carlton 1965-71
Duke Carmel 1959-60, 63
Cris Carpenter 1988-
Hick Carpenter 1892
Clay Carroll 1977
Cliff Carroll 1892
Kid Carsey 1897-98
Bob Caruthers 1892
Pete Castiglione 1953-54
Danny Cater 1975
Ted Cather 1912-14
Cesar Cedeno 1985
Orlando Cepeda 1966-68
Bill Chambers 1910
Cliff Chambers 1951-53
John Chambers 1937
Charlie Chant 1976
Chappy Charles 1908-09
Tom Cheney 1957
Cupid Childs 1899
Pete Childs 1901
Nels Chittum 1958
Bob Chlupsa 1970-71
Larry Ciaffone 1951
Al Cicotte 1961
Gino Cimoli 1959
Ralph Citarella 1983-84
Doug Clarey 1976
Danny Clark 1927
Jack Clark 1985-87
Jim Clark 1911-12
Mark Clark 1991
Mike Clark 1952-53
Phil Clark 1958-59
Josh Clarke 1905
Stan Clarke 1990
Dad Clarkson 1893-95
Doug Clemens 1960-64
Jack Clements 1898
Lance Clemons 1972

Verne Clemons 1919-24
Donn Clendenon 1972
Reggie Cleveland 1969-73
Tony Cloninger 1972
Ed Clough 1924-26
Dick Cole 1951
John Coleman 1895
Percy Coleman 1897
Vince Coleman 1985-90
Bill Collins 1892
Dave Collins 1990
Phil Collins 1935
Ripper Collins 1931-36
Jackie Collum 1951-53, 56
Bob Coluccio 1978
Joe Connor 1895
Roger Connor 1894-97
Tim Conroy 1986
Ed Conwell 1911
Duff Cooley 1893-96
Jimmy Cooney 1924-25
Mort Cooper 1938-45
Walker Cooper 1940-45, 56-57
Mays Copeland 1935
Joe Corbett 1904
Roy Corhan 1916
Rheal Cormier 1991
Pat Corrales 1966
Frank Corridon 1910
Jim Cosman 1966-67
John Costello 1988-90
Tom Coulter 1969
John Coveney 1903
Bill Cox 1936
Danny Cox 1983-90
Estel Crabtree 1933, 41-42
Roger Craig 1964
Doc Crandall 1913
Forrest Crawford 1906-07
Glenn Crawford 1945
Pat Crawford 1933-34
Willie Crawford 1976
Jack Creel 1945
Bernie Creger 1947
Creepy Crespi 1938-42
Lou Criger 1899-1900

Jack Crimian 1951-52
John Crooks 1892-93, 98
Ed Crosby 1970, 72-73
Jeff Cross 1942, 46-48
Dave Cross 1898-1900
Monte Cross 1896-97
Bill Crouch 1941
George Crowe 1959-61
Walton Cruise 1914, 16-19
Gene Crumling 1945
Cirilio Cruz 1973
Hector Cruz 1973, 1975-77
Jose Cruz 1970-74
Mike Cuellar 1964
George Culver 1970
John Cumberland 1972
Joe Cunningham 1954, 56-61
Ray Cunningham 1931-32
Nig Cuppy 1899
Clarence Currie 1902-03
Murphy Currie 1916
John Curtis 1974-76

D

John D'Acquisto 1977
Gene Dale 1911-12
Jack Damaska 1963
Pete Daniels 1898
Rolla Daringer 1914-15
Alvin Dark 1956-58
Vic Davalillo 1969-70
Jerry Davanon 1969-70, 74, 77
Curt Davis 1938-40
Jim Davis 1957
Kiddo Davis 1934
Ron Davis 1968
Spud Davis 1928, 34-36
Willie Davis 1975
Bill Dawley 1987
Boots Day 1969
Pea Ridge Day 1924-25
Ken Dayley 1984-90
Cot Deal 1950
Dizzy Dean 1930, 32-37
Paul Dean 1934-39

CARDINALS' ALL-TIME ROSTER

(Continued)

Doug DeCinces 1987
George Decker 1898
Tony DeFate 1917
Rube DeGroff 1905-06
Ivan DeJesus 1985
Joe Delahanty 1907-09
Bill DeLancey 1932, 34-35, 40
Art Delaney 1924
Jose DeLeon 1988-
Luis DeLeon 1981
Bobby Del Greco 1956
Eddie Delker 1929, 31-32
Wheezer Dell 1912
Frank Demaree 1943
Harry DeMiller 1892
Lee DeMontreville 1903
Don Dennis 1965-66
John Denny 1974-79
Paul Deringer 1931-33
Russ Derry 1949
Joe DeSa 1980
Leo Dickerman 1924-25
Murry Dickson 1939-40, 42-43, 46-48, 56-57
Chuck Diering 1947-51
Larry Dierker 1977
Pat Dillard 1900
Pickles Dillhoefer 1919-21
Mike Dimmel 1979
Frank DiPino 1989-
Dutch Distel 1918
Bill Doak 1913-24, 29
George Dockins 1945
Cozy Dolan 1914-15
John Dolan 1893
Red Donahue 1895-97
She Donahue 1904
Jim Donely 1898
Mike Donlin 1899-1900
Blix Donnelly 1944-46
Patsy Donovan 1900-03
Klondike Douglas 1896-97

Taylor Douthit 1923-31
Tommy Dowd 1893-98
Dave Dowling 1964
Carl Doyle 1940
Jeff Doyle 1983
Moe Drabowsky 1971-72
Lee Dressen 1914
Rob Dressler 1978
Dan Driessen 1987
Carl Druhot 1906-07
Bob Duliba 1959-60, 62
Taylor Duncan 1977
Wiley Dunham 1902
Grant Dunlap 1953
John Dunleavy 1903-05
Don Durham 1972
Joe Durham 1959
Leon Durham 1980, 89
Leo Durocher 1933-37
Erv Dusak 1941-42, 46-51
Frank Dwyer 1892
Jim Dwyer 1973-75, 77-78
Eddie Dyer 1922-27

E

Bill Earley 1986
George Earnshaw 1936
Jack Easton 1892
Rawly Eastwick 1977
Johnny Echols 1939
Al Eckert 1935
Joe Edelen 1981
Johnny Edwards 1968
Wish Egan 1905-06
Red Ehret 1895
Harry Elliott 1953
Jim Ellis 1969
Rube Ellis 1909-12
Bones Ely 1893-95
Bill Endicott 1946
Del Ennis 1957-58
Charlie Enwright 1909
Hal Epps 1938

Eddie Erautt 1953
Duke Esper 1897-98
Chuck Essegian 1959
LeRoy Evans 1897
Steve Evans 1909-13
Bob Ewing 1912
Reuben Ewing 1921

F

Fred Fagin 1895
Ron Fairly 1975-76
Pete Falcone 1976-78
George Fallon 1943-45
Harry Fanok 1963-64
Doc Farrell 1930
John Farrell 1902-05
Jack Faszholz 1953
Bobby Fenwick 1973
Joe Ferguson 1976
Don Ferrarese 1962
Neil Fiala 1981
Mike Fiore 1972
Sam Fisburn 1919
Bob Fisher 1918-19
Chauncey Fisher 1901
Eddie Fisher 1973
Showboat Fisher 1930
Mike Fitzgerald 1988
Max Flack 1922-25
Tom Flanigan 1958
Curt Flood 1958-69
Tim Flood 1899
Ben Flowers 1955-56
Jake Flowers 1923, 26, 31-32
Rich Folkers 1972-74
Curt Ford 1985-88
Hod Ford 1932
Bob Forsch 1974-88
Alan Foster 1973-74
Jack Fournier 1920-22
Jesse Fowler 1924
Earl Francis 1965

Tito Francona 1965-66
Charlie Frank 1893-94
Fred Frankhouse 1927-30
Herman Franks 1939
Willie Fraser 1991
George Frazier 1978-80
Joe Frazier 1954-1956
Roger Freed 1977-79
Gene Freese 1958
Howard Freigau 1922-25
Benny Frey 1932
Frankie Frisch 1927-37
Danny Frisella 1976
Art Fromme 1906-08
John Fulgham 1979-81
Chick Fullis 1934
Les Fusselman 1952-53

G

Phil Gagliano 1963-70
Del Gainor 1922
Fred Gaiser 1908
Bad News Galloway 1912
Pud Galvin 1892
Bill Gannon 1898
Joe Garagiola 1946-51
Danny Gardella 1950
Glenn Gardner 1945
Art Garibaldi 1936
Mike Garman 1974-75
Debs Garms 1943-45
Wayne Garrett 1978
Rich Gedman 1991
Charley Gelbert 1929-32, 35-36
Frank Genins 1892
Al Gettel 1955
Charlie Getzein 1892
Rube Geyer 1910-13
Bob Gibson 1959-75
Billy Gilbert 1908-09
George Gilham 1920-21
Frank Gilhooley 1911-12
Bernard Gilkey 1990-
Carden Gillenwater 1940
George Gilpatrick 1898
Hal Gilson 1968

Dave Giusti 1969
Jack Glasscock 1892-93
Tommy Glaviano 1949-52
Kid Gleason 1892-94
Bob Glenn 1920
Harry Glenn 1915
John Glenn 1960
Danny Godby 1974
Roy Golden 1910-11
Hal Goldsmith 1929
Jose Gonzalez 1984
Julio Gonzalez 1981-82
Mike Gonzalez 1915-18, 24-25, 31-32
Bill Goodenough 1893
Marv Goodwin 1917, 19-22
George Gore 1892
Herb Gorman 1952
Hank Gornicki 1941
Julio Gotay 1960-62
Al Grabowski 1929-30
Mike Grady 1897, 1904-06
Alex Grammas 1954-56, 59-62
Wayne Granger 1968, 73
Mudcat Grant 1969
Mark Grater 1991
Dick Gray 1959-60
Bill Greason 1954
David Green 1981-84, 87
Gene Green 1957-59
Bill Greif 1976
Tim Greisenbeck 1920
Tom Grieve 1979
Sandy Griffin 1893
Bob Grim 1960
Burleigh Grimes 1930-31, 33-34
John Grimes 1897
Charlie Grimm 1918
Dan Griner 1912-16
Marv Grissom 1959
Dick Groat 1963-65
Johnny Grodzicki 1941, 46-47
Joe Grzenda 1972
Mario Guerrero 1975

Pedro Guerrero 1988-
Harry Gumbert 1941-44
Joe Gunson 1893
Don Gutteridge 1936-40
Santiago Guzman 1969-72

H

Bob Habenicht 1951
Jim Hackett 1902-03
Harvey Haddix 1952-56
Chick Hafey 1924-31
Casey Hageman 1914
Kevin Hagen 1983-84
Joe Hague 1968-72
Don Hahn 1975
Fred Hahn 1952
Hal Haid 1928-30
Ed Haigh 1892
Jesse Haines 1920-37
Charley Hall 1916
Russ Hall 1898
Bill Hallahan 1925-26, 29-36
Bill Hallman 1897
Dave Hamilton 1978
Fred Haney 1929
Larry Haney 1973
Dick Harley 1897-98
Bob Harmon 1909-13
Chuck Harmon 1956-57
Brian Harper 1985
George Harper 1928
Jack Harper 1900-01
Ray Harrell 1935, 37-38
Vic Harris 1976
Bill Hart 1896-97
Chuck Hartenstein 1970
Fred Hartman 1897
Andy Hassler 1984-85
Grady Hatton 1956
Arnold Hauser 1910-13
Bill Hawke 1892-93
Pink Hawley 1892-94
Doc Hazleton 1901-02
Francis Healy 1934
Bunny Hearn 1910-11
Jim Hearn 1947-50

CARDINALS' ALL-TIME ROSTER

(Continued)

Mike Heath 1986
Cliff Heathcote 1918-22
Jack Heidemann 1974
John Heidrick 1899-1901
Don Heinkel 1989
Tom Heintzelman 1973-74
Bob Heise 1974
Clarence Heise 1934
Charlie Hemphill 1899
Solly Hemus 1949-56, 59
George Hendrick 1978-1984
Harvey Hendrick 1932
Roy Henshaw 1938
Keith Hernandez 1974-83
Larry Herndon 1974
Tom Herr 1979-88
Neal Hertweck 1952
Ed Heusser 1935-36
Mike Heydon 1901
Jim Hickman 1974
Jim Hicks 1969
Irv Higginbotham 1906, 08-09
Dennis Higgins 1971-72
Festus Higgins 1909-10
Andy High 1928-31
Palmer Hildebrand 1913
Tom Hilgendorf 1969-70
Carmen Hill 1929-30
Hugh Hill 1904
Ken Hill 1988-1991
Marc Hill 1973-74
John Himes 1905-06
Bruce Hitt 1917
Glen Hobbie 1964
Ed Hock 1920
Art Hoelskoetter 1905-08
Joe Hoerner 1966-69
Marty Hogan 1894-95
Mul Holland 1929
Ed Holly 1906-97
Wattie Holm 1924-29, 32
H. Ducky Holmes 1898
J. Ducky Holmes 1906

Don Hood 1980
Sis Hopkins 1907
Johnny Hopp 1939-45
Bill Hopper 1913-14
Bob Horner 1988
Rogers Hornsby 1915-26, 33
Oscar Horstmann 1917-19
Rick Horton 1984-87, 89- 90
Paul Householder 1984
John Houseman 1897
Doug Howard 1975
Earl Howard 1918
Art Howe 1984-85
Roland Howell 1912
Bill Howerton 1949-51
Al Hrabosky 1970-77
Jimmy Hudgens 1923
Rex Hudler 1990-
Charles Hudson 1972
Frank Huelsman 1897
Miller Huggins 1910-16
Dick Hughes 1966-68
Terry Hughes 1973
Tom Hughes 1959
Jim Hughey 1898
Rudy Hulswitt 1909-10
Bob Humphreys 1963-64
Ben Hunt 1913
Joel Hunt 1931-32
Randy Hunt 1985
Ron Hunt 1974
Herb Hunter 1921
Steve Huntz 1967
Walter Huntzinger 1926
Clint Hurdle 1986
Ira Hutchinson 1940-41
Bill Hutchison 1897
Ham Hyatt 1915
Pat Hynes 1903

I

Dane Iorg 1977-84
Walt Irwin 1921

J

Ray Jablonski 1953-54, 59
Al Jackson 1966-67
Larry Jackson 1955-62
Mike Jackson 1971
Elmer Jacobs 1919-20
Tony Jacobs 1955
Bob James 1909
Charlie James 1960-64
Hal Janvrin 1919-21
Hi Jasper 1916
Larry Jaster 1965-68
Julian Javier 1960-71
Hal Jeffcoat 1959
Adam Johnson 1918
Alex Johnson 1966-67
Billy Johnson 1951-53
Bob Johnson 1969
Darrell Johnson 1960
Jerry Johnson 1970
Ken Johnson 1947-50
Lance Johnson 1987
Si Johnson 1936-38
Syl Johnson 1926-33
Cowboy Jones 1899-1901
Gordon Jones 1954-56
Howie Jones 1921
Nippy Jones 1946-51
Red Jones 1940
Sam Jones 1957-58, 63
Tim Jones 1988-
Bubber Jonnard 1929
Mike Jorgensen 1984-85
Felix Jose 1990-
Lyle Judy 1935
Al Jurisich 1944-45
Skip Jutze 1972

K

Jim Kaat 1980-83
Ed Karger 1906-08
Eddie Kasko 1957-58
Ray Katt 1956, 58-59

Tony Kaufmann 1927-28,
30-31, 35
Marty Kavanagh 1918
Eddie Kazak 1948-52
Bob Keely 1944-45
Vic Keen 1926-27
Jeff Keener 1982-83
Bill Keister 1900
John Kelleher 1912
Mick Kelleher 1972-73, 75
Alex Kellner 1959
Win Kellum 1905
Bill Kelly 1910
John Kelly 1907
Jim Kennedy 1970
Terry Kennedy 1978-80
Matt Keough 1985
Kurt Kepshire 1984-86
George Kernek 1965-66
Don Kessinger 1976-77
Newt Kimball 1940
Hal Kime 1920
Wally Kimmick 1919
Ellis Kinder 1956
Charlie King 1959
Jim King 1957
Lynn King 1935-36, 39
Walt Kinlock 1895
Tom Kinslow 1898
Matt Kinzer 1989
Mike Kircher 1920-21
Bill Kissinger 1895-97
Lou Klein 1943, 45-46, 49
Nub Kleinke 1935
Ron Kline 1960
Rudy Kling 1902
Clyde Klutz 1946
Alan Knicely 1986
Jack Knight 1922
Mike Knode 1920
Darold Knowles 1979-80
Willis Koenigsmark 1919
Gary Kolb 1960, 62-63
Ed Konetchy 1907-13
Jim Konstanty 1956
George Kopshaw 1923

Ernie Koy 1940-41
Lew Krausse 1973
Kurt Krieger 1949
Howie Krist 1937-38, 41-
43, 46
Otto Krueger 1900-02
Ted Kubiak 1971
Willie Kuehne 1892
Ryan Kurosaki 1975
Whitey Kurowski 1941-49
Bob Kuzava 1957

L
Mike Laga 1986-88
Lerrin LaGrow 1976
Jeff Lahti 1982-86
Eddie Lake 1939-41
Steve Lake 1986-88
Bud Lally 1897
Jack Lamabe 1967
Fred Lamline 1915
Hobie Landrith 1957-58
Don Landrum 1960-62
Tito Landrum 1980-83, 84-
87
Don Lang 1948
Max Lanier 1938-46, 49-51
Ray Lankford 1990-
Paul LaPalme 1955-56
Dave LaPoint 1981-84, 87
Ralph LaPointe 1948
Bob Larmore 1918
Lyn Lary 1939
Don Lassetter 1957
Arlie Latham 1896
Mike LaValliere 1985-86
Doc Lavan 1919-24
Tom Lawless 1985-88
Brooks Lawrence 1954-55
Tom Leahy 1905
Leron Lee 1969-71
Jim Lentine 1978-80
Barry Lersch 1974
Roy Leslie 1919
Dan Lewandowski 1951
Bill Lewis 1933

Johnny Lewis 1964
Sixto Lezcano 1981
Don Liddle 1956
Gene Lillard 1940
Bob Lillis 1961
Johnny Lindell 1950
Jim Lindeman 1986-89
Jim Lindsey 1929-34
Royce Lint 1954
Larry Lintz 1975
Frank Linzy 1970-71
Mark Littell 1978-82
Jeff Little 1980
Dick Littlefield 1956
John Littlefield 1980
Carlisle Littlejohn 1927-28
Danny Litwhiler 1943-44,
46
Paddy Livingston 1917
Lary Locke 1962
Whitey Lockman 1956
Bill Lohrman 1942
Jeoff Long 1963-64
Tommy Long 1915-17
Art Lopatka 1945
Aurelio Lopez 1978
Joe Lotz 1916
Lynn Lovenguth 1957
John Lovett 1903
Grover Lowdermilk 1909
Lou Lowdermilk 1911-12
Peanuts Lowrey 1950-54
Con Lucid 1897
Bill Ludwig 1908
Memo Luna 1954
Ernie Lush 1910
Johnny Lush 1907-10
Bill Lyons 1983-84
Denny Lyons 1895
George Lyons 1920
Hersh Lyons 1941

M
Bob Mabe 1958
Ken MacKenzie 1963
Johnny Mackinson 1955

CARDINALS' ALL-TIME ROSTER

(Continued)

Max Macon 1938
Bill Magee 1901
Lee Magee 1911-14
Sal Maglie 1958
Joe Magrane 1987-
Art Mahaffey 1966
Mike Mahoney 1898
Duster Mails 1925-26
Jim Mallory 1945
Gus Mancuso 1928, 30-32, 41-42
Les Mann 1921-23
Fred Manrique 1986
Rabbit Maranville 1927-28
Walt Marbet 1913
Marty Marion 1940-50
Roger Maris 1967-68
Fred Marolewski 1953
Charlie Marshall 1941
Doc Marshall 1906-08
Joe Marshall 1906
Freddie Martin 1946, 49-50
John Martin 1980-83
Morrie Martin 1957-58
Pepper Martin 1928, 30-40, 44
Stu Martin 1936-40
Marty Martinez 1972
Silvio Martinez 1978-81
Teddy Martinez 1975
Ernie Mason 1894
Greg Mathews 1986-90
Wally Mattick 1918
Gene Mauch 1952
Harry Maupin 1898
Dal Maxvill 1962-72
Jakie May 1917-21
Jack McAdams 1911
Ike McAuley 1917
Bake McBride 1973-77
George McBride 1905-06
Pete McBride 1899
Joe McCarthy 1906
Lew McCarty 1920-21

Tim McCarver 1959-61, 63-69, 73-74
Pat McCauley 1893
Bob McClure 1991
Billy McCool 1970
Jim McCormick 1892
Harry McCurdy 1922-23
Lindy McDaniel 1955-62
Von McDaniel 1957-58
Mickey McDermott 1961
Mike McDermott 1897
John McCougal 1895-96
Sandy McDougal 1905
Will McEnaney 1979
Guy McFadden 1895
Chappie McFarland 1902-06
Ed McFarland 1896-97
Dan McGann 1900-01
Bill McGee 1935-41
Willie McGee 1982-90
Dan McGeehan 1911
Jim McGinley 1904-05
Lynn McGlothen 1974-76
Stoney McGlynn 1906-08
Bob McGraw 1927
John McGraw 1900
Mark McGrillis 1892
Austin McHenry 1918-22
Otto McIver 1911
Ed McKean 1899
Ralph McLaurin 1908
Larry McLean 1904
Jerry McNertney 1971-72
Larry McWilliams 1988
Lee Meadows 1915-19
Joe Medwick 1932-40, 47-48
Sam Mejias 1976
Luis Melendez 1970-76
Steve Melter 1909
Ted Menze 1918
John Mercer 1912
Lloyd Merritt 1957
Sam Mertes 1906

Steve Mesner 1941
Clarence Metzger 1977-78
Bert Meyers 1896
Ed Mickelson 1950
Ed Mierkowicz 1950
Larry Miggins 1948
Pete Mikkelsen 1968
Eddie Miksis 1957
Bob Miller 1957, 59-61
Charlie Miller 1913-14
Doggie Miller 1894-95
Dots Miller 1914-17, 19
Dusty Miller 1899
Eddie Miller 1950
Elmer Miller 1912
Stu Miller 1952-54, 56
Buster Mills 1934
Larry Milton 1903
Minnie Minoso 1962
Clarence Mitchell 1928-30
Johnny Mize 1936-41
Vinegar Bend Mizell 1952-53, 56-60
Herb Moford 1955
Fritz Mollwitz 1919
Wally Moon 1954-58
Jim Mooney 1933-34
Donnie Moore 1980
Gene Moore 1933-35
Randy Moore 1937
Terry Moore 1935-42, 46-48
Tommy Moore 1975
Whitey Moore 1942
Jerry Morales 1978
Bill Moran 1903
Charley Moran 1903
Forrest More 1909
Bobby Morgan 1956
Eddie Morgan 1936
Joe Morgan 1964
Gene Moriarity 1892
John Morris 1986-90
Walter Morris 1908
Hap Morse 1911

Walt Moryn 1960-61
Mike Mowrey 1909-13
Jamie Moyer 1991
Heinie Mueller 1920-26
Billy Muffett 1957-58
Jerry Mumphrey 1974-79
George Munger 1943-44, 46-52
Les Munns 1936
Steve Mura 1982
Simmy Murch 1904-05
Tim Murchison 1917
Wilbur Murdock 1908
Ed Murphy 1901-03
Howard Murphy 1909
Mike Murphy 1912
Morgan Murphy 1896-97
Soldier Boy Murphy 1902
Tom Murphy 1973
Red Murray 1906-08
Stan Musial 1941-44, 46-63
Hy Myers 1923-25
Lynn Myers 1938-39

N
Mike Nagy 1973
Sam Nahem 1941
Sam Narron 1935, 42-43
Ken Nash 1914
Mike Naymick 1944
Mel Nelson 1960, 68-69
Rocky Nelson 1949-51, 56
Art Nichols 1901-03
Kid Nichols 1904-05
Charlie Niebergall 1921, 23-24
Tom Niedenfuer 1990
Dick Niehaus 1913-15
Bert Niehoff 1918
Bob Nieman 1960-61
Tom Nieto 1984
Tom Niland 1896
Pete Noonan 1906-07
Irv Noren 1957-59
Fred Norman 1970-71
Lou North 1917, 20-24
Ron Northey 1947-49

Joe Nossek 1969-70
Howie Nunn 1959
Rich Nye 1970

O
Rebel Oakes 1910-13
Ken Oberkfell 1977-84
Dan O'Brien 1978-79
Johnny O'Brien 1958
Jack O'Connor 1899-1900
Paddy O'Connor 1914
Ken O'Dea 1942-46
Bob O'Farrell 1925-28, 33
Brusie Ogrodowski 1936-37
Bill O'Hara 1910
Tom O'Hara 1906-07
Charley O'Leary 1913
Ed Olivares 1960-61
Omar Olivares 1990-
Gene Oliver 1959, 61-63
Diomedes Olivo 1963
Al Olmsted 1980
Randy O'Neal 1987-
Dennie O'Neil 1893
Jack O'Neill 1902-03
Mike O'Neill 1901-04
Jose Oquendo 1986-
Joe Orengo 1939-40
Charlie O'Rourke 1959
Patsy O'Rourke 1908
Tim O'Rourke 1894
Ernie Orsatti 1927-35
Champ Osteen 1908-09
Claude Osteen 1974
Jim Otten 1980-81
Joe Otten 1895
Mickey Owen 1937-40
Rick Ownbey 1984, 86

P
Gene Packard 1917-18
Dick Padden 1901
Don Padgett 1937-41
Tom Pagnozzi 1987-
Phil Paine 1958
Lowell Palmer 1972

Al Papai 1948
Stan Papi 1974
Freddy Parent 1899
Kelly Paris 1982
Harry Parker 1969-71, 75
Roy Parker 1919
Roy Parmelee 1936
Tom Parrott 1896
Stan Partenheimer 1945
Mike Pasquriello 1919
Daryl Patterson 1971
Harry Patton 1910
Gene Paulette 1917-19
Gil Paulsen 1925
George Paynter 1894
George Pearce 1917
Frank Pears 1893
Alex Pearson 1902
Homer Peel 1927
Charlie Peete 1956
Heinie Peitz 1892-95, 1913
Joe Peitz 1892
Geronimo Pena 1990-
Orlando Pena 1973-74
Tony Pena 1987-89
Terry Pendleton 1984-90
Ray Pepper 1932-33
Hub Perdue 1914-15
Mike Perez 1990-
Pol Perritt 1912-14
Gerald Perry 1991
Pat Perry 1985-87
Bill Pertica 1921-23
Steve Peters 1987
Jeff Pfeffer 1921-24
Ed Phelps 1909-10
Ed Phillips 1953
Mike Phillips 1977-80
Bill Phyle 1906
Ron Piche 1966
Charlie Pickett 1910
George Pickney 1892
Vada Pinson 1969
Cotton Pippen 1936
Tim Plodinec 1972
Tom Poholsky 1950-51, 54-56

CARDINALS' ALL-TIME ROSTER

(Continued)

Howie Pollet 1941-43, 46-51
Bill Popp 1902
Darrell Porter 1981-85
J W Porter 1959
Mike Potter 1976-78
Nels Potter 1936
Jack Powell 1899-1901
Ted Power 1989
Joe Presko 1951-54
Mike Proly 1976
George Puccinelli 1930
Bob Purkey 1965
Ambrose Puttman 1906

Q
Finners Quinlan 1913
Joe Quinn 1893-96, 98
Jamie Quirk 1983
Dan Quisenberry 1988-89

R
Roy Radebaugh 1911
Dave Rader 1977
Ken Raffensberger 1939
Gary Rajsich 1984
John Raleigh 1909-10
Milt Ramirez 1970-71
Mike Ramsey 1978, 80-84
Dick Rand 1953
Vic Raschi 1954-55
Eric Rasmussen 1975-78, 82-83
Tommy Raub 1906
Floyd Rayford 1983
Bugs Raymond 1907-08
Art Rebel 1945
Phil Redding 1912-13
Milt Reed 1911
Ron Reed 1975
Bill Reeder 1949
Jimmy Reese 1932
Tom Reilly 1908-09
Art Reinhart 1919, 25-28

Jack Reis 1911
Ken Reitz 1972-75, 77-80
Bob Repass 1939
Rip Repulski 1953-56
Jerry Reuss 1969-71
Bob Reynolds 1971
Ken Reynolds 1975
Flint Rhem 1924-28, 30-32, 34
Bob Rhoads 1903
Charlie Rhodes 1906, 08-09
Dennis Ribant 1969
Del Rice 1945-55, 60
Hal Rice 1948-53
Lee Richard 1976
Bill Richardson 1901
Gordie Richardson 1964
Pete Richert 1974
Don Richmond 1951
Dave Ricketts 1963, 65, 67-60
Dick Ricketts 1959
John Ricks 1894
Elmer Rieger 1910
Joe Riggert 1914
Lew Riggs 1934
Andy Rincon 1980-82
Jimmy Ring 1927
Tink Riviere 1921
Skipper Roberts 1913
Hank Robinson 1914-15
Wilbert Robinson 1900
Jack Roche 1914-15, 17
Preacher Roe 1938
Wally Roettger 1927-29, 31
Cookie Rojas 1970
Stan Rojek 1951
Ray Rolling 1912
Johnny Romano 1967
John Romonosky 1953
Gene Roof 1981-83
Jorge Roque 1970-72
Jack Rothrock 1934-35

Stan Royer 1991
Dave Rucker 1983-84
Ken Rudolph 1975-76
Jack Russell 1940
Paul Russell 1894
J. Ryan 1895
John Ryan 1901-03
Mike Ryba 1935-38

S
Ray Sadecki 1960-66, 75
Bob Sadowski 1960
Mark Salas 1984
Slim Sallee 1908-16
Ike Samuels 1895
Orlando Sanchez 1981-83
Ray Sanders 1942-45
War Sanders 1903-04
Rafael Santana 1983
Al Santorini 1971-73
Bill Sarni 1951-52, 54-56
Ed Sauer 1949
Hank Sauer 1956
Ted Savage 1965-67
Carl Sawatski 1960-63
Jimmie Schaffer 1961-62
Bobby Schang 1927
Bob Scheffing 1951
Carl Scheib 1954
Richie Scheinblum 1974
Bill Schindler 1920
Freddy Schmidt 1944, 46-47
Walter Schmidt 1925
Willard Schmidt 1952-53, 55-57
Red Schoendienst 45-56, 61-63
Dick Schofield 1953-58, 68, 71
Ossee Schreckengost 1899
Pop Schriver 1901
Heinie Schuble 1927
Johnny Schulte 1927

Barney Schultz 1955, 63-65
Buddy Schultz 1977-79
Joe Schultz 1919-24
Walt Schulz 1920
Ferdie Schupp 1919-21
Lou Scoffic 1936
George Scott 1920
Tony Scott 1977-81
Kim Seaman 1979-80
Diego Segui 1972-73
Epp Sell 1922-23
Carey Selph 1929
Walter Sessi 1941, 46
Jimmy Sexton 1983
Mike Shannon 1962-70
Spike Shannon 1904-06
Wally Shannon 1959-60
Bobby Shantz 1962-64
Al Shaw 1907-09
Don Shaw 1971-72
Danny Shay 1904-05
Gerry Shea 1905
Jimmy Sheckard 1913
Biff Sheehan 1895-96
Ray Shepherdson 1924
Bill Sherdel 1918-30, 32
Tim Sherrill 1990
Charlie Shields 1907
Vince Shields 1924
Ralph Shinners 1925
Bob Shirley 1981
Burt Shotton 1919-23
Clyde Shoun 1938-42
Frank Shugart 1893-94
Dick Siebert 1937-38
Sonny Siebert 1974
Curt Simmons 1960-66
Ted Simmons 1968-80
Dick Simpson 1968
Dick Sisler 1946-47, 52-53
Ted Sizemore 1971-75
Bob Skinner 1964-66
Gordon Slade 1933
Jack Slattery 1906
Enos Slaughter 1938-42, 46-53

Bill Smith 1958-59
Bob Smith 1957
Bobby Gene Smith 1957-59, 62
Bryn Smith 1990-
Charley Smith 1966
Earl Smith 1928-30
Frank Smith 1955
Fred Smith 1917
Germany Smith 1898
Hal Smith 1956-61
Jack Smith 1915-26
Jud Smith 1893
Keith Smith 1979-80
Lee Smith 1990-
Lonnie Smith 1982-85
Ozzie Smith 1982-
Reggie Smith 1974-76
Tom Smith 1898
Wally Smith 1911-12
Homer Smoot 1902-06
Red Smyth 1917-18
Frank Snyder 1912-19, 27
Ray Soff 1986-87
Eddie Solomon 1976
Kid Sommers 1893
Lary Sorensen 1981
Elias Sosa 1975
Allen Sothoron 1924-26
Billy Southworth 1926-27, 29
Chris Speier 1984
Daryl Spencer 1960-61
Ed Spiezio 1964-68
Scipio Spinks 1972-73
Ed Sprague 1973
Jack Spring 1964
Joe Sprinz 1933
Tuck Stainback 1938
Gerry Staley 1947-54
Harry Staley 1895
Tracy Stallard 1965-66
Virgil Stallcup 1952-53
Pete Standridge 1911
Eddie Stanky 1952-53
Harry Stanton 1900
Ray Starr 1932

Bill Steele 1910-14
Bob Steele 1916-17
Bill Stein 1972-73
Jake Stenzel 1898-99
Ray Stephens 1990-1991
Bobby Stephenson 1955
Stuffy Stewart 1916-17
Bob Stinson 1971
Chuck Stobbs 1958
Milt Stock 1919-23
Dean Stone 1959
Tige Stone 1923
Alan Storke 1909
Allyn Stout 1931-33
Gabby Street 1931
Cub Stricker 1892
Joe Stripp 1938
Johnny Stuart 1922-25
John Stuper 1982-84
Willie Sudhoff 1897-1901
Joe Sugden 1898
Harry Sullivan 1909
Joe Sullivan 1896
Suter Sullivan 1898
Tom Sunkel 1937
Max Surkont 1956
Gary Sutherland 1978
Bruce Sutter 1981-84
Jack Sutthoff 1899
Johnny Sutton 1977
Charlie Swindell 1904
Steve Swisher 1978-80
Bob Sykes 1979-81

T

John Tamargo 1976-78
Lee Tate 1958-59
Don Taussig 1961
Carl Taylor 1970
Chuck Taylor 1969-71
Ed Taylor 1903
Jack Taylor 1898
Jack Taylor 1904-06
Joe Taylor 1958
Ron Taylor 1963-65
Bud Teachout 1932
Patsy Tebeau 1899-1900

CARDINALS' ALL-TIME ROSTER

(Continued)

Garry Templeton 1976-81
Gene Tenace 1981-82
Greg Terlecky 1975
Scott Terry 1987-
Dick Terwilliger 1932
Bob Tewksbury 1989-
Moe Thacker 1963
Tommy Thevenow 1924-28
Jake Thielman 1905-06
Roy Thomas 1978-80
Tom Thomas 1899-1900
Gus Thompson 1906
Mike Thompson 1973-74
Milt Thompson 1989-
John Thornton 1892
Bobby Tiefenauer 1952, 55
Bud Tinning 1935
Bobby Tolan 1965-68
Fred Toney 1923
Specs Toporcer 1921-28
Joe Torre 1969-74
Mike Torrez 1967-71
Paul Toth 1962
Harry Trekell 1913
Coaker Triplett 1941-43
Bill Trotter 1944
Tommy Tucker 1898
John Tudor 1985-88, 90
Oscar Tuero 1918-20
Lee Tunnell 1987-88
Tuck Turner 1896-98
Old Hoss Twineham 1893- 94
Mike Tyson 1972-79

U

Bob Uecker 1964-65
Tom Underwood 1977
Jack Urban 1959
John Urrea 1977-80
Lou Ury 1903

V

Benny Valenzuela 1958
Dazzy Vance 1933-34

Bill Van Dyke 1892
John Vann 1913
Jay Van Noy 1951
Andy Van Slyke 1983-86
Emil Verban 1944-46
Johnny Vergez 1936
Ernie Vick 1922, 24-26
Bob Vines 1924
Bill Virdon 1955-56
Dave Von Ohlen 1983-84
Bill Voss 1972
Pete Vuckovich 1978-80

W

Ben Wade 1954
Leon Wagner 1960
Bill Walker 1933-36
Duane Walker 1988
Harry Walker 1940-43, 46-
47, 50-51, 55
Joe Walker 1923
Roy Walker 1921-22
Tom Walker 1976
Bobby Wallace 1899-1901,
17-18
Mike Wallace 1975-76
Elliott Waller 1980
Denny Walling 1988-90
Dick Ward 1935
Cy Warmoth 1916
Lon Warneke 1937-42
John Warner 1905
Bill Warwick 1925-26
Carl Warwick 1961-62, 64-
65
Ray Washburn 1961-69
Gary Waslewski 1969
Steve Waterbury 1976
George Watkins 1930-33
Milt Watson 1916-17
Art Weaver 1902-03
Skeeter Webb 1932
Herm Wehmeier 1956-58
Bob Weiland 1937-40

Perry Werden 1892-93
Bill Werle 1952
Wally Westlake 1951-52
Gus Weyhing 1900
Dick Wheeler 1918
Jim Whelan 1913
Pete Whisenant 1955
Lew Whistler 1893
Abe White 1937
Bill White 1959-65, 69
Ernie White 1940-43
Hal White 1953-54
Jerry White 1986
Burgess Whitehead 1933-
35
Fred Whitfield 1962
Possum Whitted 1912-14
Bob Wicker 1901-03
Floyd Wicker 1968
Bill Wight 1958
Fred Wigington 1923
Del Wilber 1946-49
Hoyt Wilhelm 1957
Denney Wilie 1911-12
Ted Wilks 1944-51
Jim Williams 1966-67
Otto Williams 1902-03
Stan Williams 1971
Steamboat Williams 1914
Howie Williamson 1928
Joe Willis 1911-13
Ron Willis 1966-69
Vic Willis 1910
Charlie Wilson 1932-33, 35
Craig Wilson 1989-
Jimmie Wilson 1928-33
Owen Wilson 1914-16
Zeke Wilson 1899
Jim Winford 1932, 34-37
Ivy Wingo 1911-14
Tom Winsett 1935
Rick Wise 1972-73
Corky Withrow 1963
Chicken Wolf 1892

Harry Wolter 1907
John Wood 1896
Gene Woodburn 1911-12
Hal Woodeshick 1965-67
Frank Woodward 1919
Floyd Wooldridge 1955
Todd Worrell 1985-
Red Worthington 1934
Mel Wright 1954-55

Y
Stan Yerkes 1901-03

Ray Yochim 1948-49
Babe Young 1948
Bobby Young 1948
Cy Young 1899-1900
Dave Young 1895
J. D. Young 1892
Pep Young 1941
Joel Youngblood 1977
Eddie Yuhas 1952-53
Sal Yvars 1953-54

Z
Chris Zachary 1971
Elmer Zacher 1910
George Zackert 1911-12
Dave Zearfoss 1904-05
Todd Zeile 1989-
Bart Zeller 1970
Eddie Zimmerman 1906
Ed Zmich 1910-11

WHERE THEY FINISHED

Year	Position	Won	Lost	Pct.	Manager
1892	11	56	94	.373	Chris Von Der Ahe
1893	10	57	75	.432	Bill Watkins
1894	9	56	76	.424	George Miller
1895	11	39	92	.298	Al Buckenberger, Joe Quinn, Lew Phelan, Von der Ahe
1896	11	40	90	.308	Harry Diddlebock, Arlie Latham, Von der Ahe, Roger Connor, Tommy Dowd
1897	12	29	102	.221	Dowd, Hugh Nicol, Bill Hallman, Von der Ahe
1898	12	39	111	.260	Tim Hurst
1899	5	84	67	.556	Oliver Tebeau

WHERE THEY FINISHED—1892-1991

Year	Position	Won	Lost	Pct.	Attendance	Manager
1900	5†	65	75	.464		Oliver Tebeau & Louis Heilbroner
1901	4	76	64	.543	379,988	Patsy Donovan
1902	6	56	78	.418	226,417	Patsy Donovan
1903	8	43	94	.314	263,538	Patsy Donovan
1904	5	75	79	.487	386,750	Charles "Kid" Nichols
1905	6	58	96	.377	292,800	Nichols, Jimmy Burke, Matthew Robison
1906	7	52	98	.347	283,770	John J. McCloskey
1907	8	52	101	.340	185,377	John J. McCloskey
1908	8	49	105	.318	205,129	John J. McCloskey
1909	7	54	98	.355	299,982	Roger Bresnahan
1910	7	63	90	.412	363,624	Roger Bresnahan
1911	5	75	74	.503	447,768	Roger Bresnahan
1912	6	63	90	.412	241,759	Roger Bresnahan
1913	8	51	99	.340	203,531	Miller Huggins

WHERE THEY FINISHED—1892-1991
(Continued)

Year	Position	Won	Lost	Pct.	Attendance	Manager
1914	3	81	72	.529	346,025	Miller Huggins
1915	6	72	81	.471	252,657	Miller Huggins
1916	7†	60	93	.392	224,308	Miller Huggins
1917	3	82	70	.539	301,948	Miller Huggins
1918	8	51	78	.395	110,596	Jack Hendricks
1919	7	54	83	.394	173,604	Branch Rickey
1920	5	75	79	.487	325,845	Branch Rickey
1921	3	87	66	.569	384,790	Branch Rickey
1922	3†	85	69	.552	536,343	Branch Rickey
1923	5	79	74	.516	338,548	Branch Rickey
1924	6	65	89	.422	272,884	Branch Rickey
1925	4	77	76	.503	405,297	Rickey & Rogers Hornsby
1926	1*	89	65	.578	681,575	Rogers Hornsby
1927	2	92	61	.601	763,615	Bob O'Farrell
1928	1	95	59	.617	778,147	Bill McKechnie
1929	4	78	74	.513	410,921	McKechnie & Billy Southworth
1930	1	92	62	.597	519,647	Gabby Street
1931	1*	101	53	.656	623,960	Gabby Street
1932	6†	72	82	.468	290,370	Gabby Street
1933	5	82	71	.536	268,404	Street & Frank Frisch
1934	1*	95	58	.621	334,863	Frank Frisch
1935	2	96	58	.623	517,805	Frank Frisch
1936	2†	87	67	.565	457,925	Frank Frisch
1937	4	81	73	.526	443,039	Frank Frisch
1938	6	71	80	.470	295,229	Frisch & Mike Gonzales
1939	2	92	61	.601	410,778	Ray Blades
1940	3	84	69	.549	331,899	Blades, Gonzales & Billy Southworth
1941	2	97	56	.634	642,496	Billy Southworth
1942	1*	106	48	.688	571,626	Billy Southworth
1943	1	105	49	.682	535,014	Billy Southworth
1944	1*	105	49	.682	486,751	Billy Southworth
1945	2	95	59	.617	594,180	Billy Southworth
1946	1*	98	58	.628	1,062,553	Eddie Dyer
1947	2	89	65	.578	1,248,013	Eddie Dyer
1948	2	85	69	.552	1,111,454	Eddie Dyer
1949	2	96	58	.623	1,430,676	Eddie Dyer
1950	5	78	75	.519	1,093,199	Eddie Dyer
1951	3	81	73	.526	1,013,429	Marty Marion
1952	3	88	66	.571	913,113	Eddie Stanky
1953	3†	83	71	.539	880,242	Eddie Stanky
1954	6	72	82	.468	1,039,698	Eddie Stanky
1955	7	68	86	.442	849,130	Stanky & Harry Walker

1956	4	76	78	.494	1,029,773	Fred Hutchinson
1957	2	87	67	.565	1,183,575	Fred Hutchinson
1958	5†	72	82	.468	1,063,730	Hutchinson & Stan Hack
1959	7	71	83	.461	929,953	Solly Hemus
1960	3	86	68	.558	1,096,632	Solly Hemus
1961	5	80	74	.519	855,305	Hemus & Johnny Keane
1962	6	84	78	.519	953,895	Johnny Keane
1963	2	93	69	.574	1,170,546	Johnny Keane
1964	1*	93	69	.574	1,143,294	Johnny Keane
1965	7	80	81	.497	1,241,195	Albert Schoendienst
1966	6	83	79	.512	1,712,980	Albert Schoendienst
1967	1*	101	60	.627	2,090,145	Albert Schoendienst
1968	1	97	65	.598	2,011,177	Albert Schoendienst
1969	4+	87	75	.537	1,682,583	Albert Schoendienst
1970	4	76	86	.469	1,628,729	Albert Schoendienst
1971	2	90	72	.556	1,604,671	Albert Schoendienst
1972	4	75	81	.481	1,196,894	Albert Schoendienst
1973	2	81	81	.500	1,574,012	Albert Schoendienst
1974	2	86	75	.535	1,838,413	Albert Schoendienst
1975	3†	82	80	.506	1,695,394	Albert Schoendienst
1976	5	72	90	.445	1,207,036	Albert Schoendienst
1977	3	83	79	.512	1,659,287	Vernon Rapp
1978	5	69	93	.426	1,278,175	Rapp, Jack Krol, Ken Boyer
1979	3	86	76	.531	1,627,256	Ken Boyer
1980	4	74	88	.457	1,385,147	Boyer, Jack Krol, Whitey Herzog, Albert Schoendienst
1981‡	1	59	43	.578	1,010,247	Whitey Herzog
1982	1*	92	70	.568	2,111,906	Whitey Herzog
1983	4	79	83	.488	2,317,914	Whitey Herzog
1984	3	84	78	.519	2,037,448	Whitey Herzog
1985	1	101	61	.623	2,637,563	Whitey Herzog
1986	3	79	82	.491	2,471,817	Whitey Herzog
1987	1	95	67	.586	3,072,121	Whitey Herzog
1988	5	76	86	.469	2,892,629	Whitey Herzog
1989	3	86	76	.531	3,080,980	Whitey Herzog
1990	6	70	92	.432	2,573,225	Herzog, Albert Schoendienst, Joe Torre
1991	2	84	78	.518	2,449,537	Joe Torre

Totals		7,722	7,580	.505		

† - Tied for Position * - World Champions + - Start of Divisional Play
‡ - Split season due to players' strike. Cardinals finished second in each half, but had best over-all record in Eastern Division.

CARDINALS IN THE WORLD SERIES

Year	Opponent	Winner	Games
1926	New York	St. Louis	4-3
1928	New York	New York	4-0
1930	Philadelphia	Philadelphia	4-2
1931	Philadelphia	St. Louis	4-3
1934	Detroit	St. Louis	4-3
1942	New York	St. Louis	4-1
1943	New York	New York	4-1
1944	St. Louis Browns	Cardinals	4-2
1946	Boston	St. Louis	4-3
1964	New York	St. Louis	4-3
1967	Boston	St. Louis	4-3
1968	Detroit	Detroit	4-3
1982	Milwaukee	St. Louis	4-3
1985	Kansas City	Kansas City	4-3
1987	Minnesota	Minnesota	4-3

CARDINAL HALL OF FAMERS

Players	Year Inducted	Pos	Career Avg.	Years with Cardinals
Walter Alston	1983	1B	.000	1936
Jake Beckley	1971	1B	.309	1904-07
Jim Bottomley	1974	1B	.310	1922-32
Roger Bresnahan	1945	C	.279	1909-12
Lou Brock	1985	LF	.293	1964-79
Jesse Burkett	1948	LF	.342	1899-1901
Roger Connor	1976	1B	.325	1894-97
Frank Frisch	1947	2B	.316	1927-37
Chick Hafey	1971	LF	.317	1924-31
Rogers Hornsby	1942	2B	.358	1915-26, 33
Miller Huggins	1964	2B	.265	1910-16
Rabbitt Maranville	1954	SS	.258	1927-28
John McGraw	1937	3B	.334	1900
Joe "Ducky" Medwick	1968	LF	.324	1932-40, 47-48
John Mize	1981	1B	.312	1936-41
Stan Musial	1969	LF	.331	1941-44, 46-63
Wilbert Robinson	1945	C	.273	1900
Albert "Red" Schoendienst	1989	2B	.289	1945-56, 61-63
Enos Slaughter	1985	RF	.300	1938-42, 46-53
Bobby Wallace	1953	SS	.267	1899-1901, 17-18

Pitchers	Year Inducted	Career Wins	Career ERA	Years with Cardinals
Grover Cleveland Alexander	1938	373	2.56	1926-29
Mordecai Brown	1949	239	2.06	1903
Jerome "Dizzy" Dean	1953	150	3.04	1930, 32-37
James "Pud" Galvin	1965	361	2.87	1892
Bob Gibson	1981	251	2.91	1959-75
Burleigh Grimes	1964	270	3.52	1930-31, 33-34
Jesse Haines	1970	210	3.64	1920-37
Charles "Kid" Nichols	1949	361	2.94	1904-05
Arthur "Dazzy" Vance	1955	197	3.24	1933-34
Hoyt Wilhelm	1985	143	2.52	1957
Denton "Cy" Young	1937	511	2.63	1899-1900

Managers	Year Inducted	Cardinal Wins	Years with Cardinals
Roger Bresnahan	1945	255	1909-12
Frank Frisch	1947	457	1933-38
Rogers Hornsby	1942	153	1925-26
Miller Huggins	1964	346	1913-17
Bill McKechnie	1962	128	1928-29
Branch Rickey	1967	458	1919-25

CARDINALS' NATIONAL LEAGUE MVP WINNERS

1925 .... Rogers Hornsby	1946 .... Stan Musial
1926 .... Bob O'Farrell	1948 .... Stan Musial
1928 .... Jim Bottomley	1964 .... Ken Boyer
1931 .... Frank Frisch	1967 .... Orlando Cepeda
1934 .... Dizzy Dean	1968 .... Bob Gibson
1937 .... Joe Medwick	1971 .... Joe Torre
1942 .... Mort Cooper	1979 .... Keith Hernandez*
1943 .... Stan Musial	1985 .... Willie McGee
1944 .... Marty Marion	

*Co-Recipient with Pittsburgh's Willie Stargell

CARDINAL CY YOUNG AWARD WINNERS

1968 .... Bob Gibson
1970 .... Bob Gibson

CARDINALS SELECTED FOR
BBWAA ROOKIE AWARD

1954	...	Wally Moon, of	1985	...	Vince Coleman, of
1955	...	Bill Virdon, of	1986	...	Todd Worrell, rhp
1974	...	Bake McBride, of			

CARDINALS SELECTED ON
THE SPORTING NEWS'-RAWLINGS GOLD GLOVE
ALL-STAR FIELDING TEAM

Year	Player	Year	Player
1958	Ken Boyer, 3b	1970	Bob Gibson, p
1959	Ken Boyer, 3b	1971	Bob Gibson, p
1960	Bill White, 1b	1972	Bob Gibson, p
	Ken Boyer, 3b	1973	Bob Gibson, p
1961	Bill White, 1b	1975	Ken Reitz, 3b
	Ken Boyer, 3b	1978	Keith Hernandez, 1b
1962	Bobby Shantz, p	1979	Keith Hernandez, 1b
	Bill White, 1b	1980	Keith Hernandez, 1b
1963	Bobby Shantz, p	1981	Keith Hernandez, 1b
	Bill White, 1b	1982	Keith Hernandez, 1b
	Ken Boyer, 3b		Ozzie Smith, ss
	Curt Flood, of	1983	Ozzie Smith, ss
1964	Bill White, 1b		Willie McGee, of
	Curt Flood, of	1984	Ozzie Smith, ss
1965	Bob Gibson, p		Joaquin Andujar, p
	Bill White, 1b	1985	Ozzie Smith, ss
	Curt Flood, of		Willie McGee, of
1966	Bob Gibson, p	1986	Ozzie Smith, ss
	Curt Flood, of		Willie McGee, of
1967	Bob Gibson, p	1987	Ozzie Smith, ss
	Curt Flood, of		Terry Pendleton, 3b
1968	Bob Gibson, p	1988	Ozzie Smith, ss
	Dal Maxvill, ss	1989	Ozzie Smith, ss
	Curt Flood, of		Terry Pendleton, 3b
1969	Bob Gibson, p	1990	Ozzie Smith, ss
	Curt Flood, of	1991	Ozzie Smith, ss
			Tom Pagaozzi, c

CARDINAL SELECTED FOR THE ALL-STAR GAME

1933 Frank Frisch, 2b; Bill Hallahan, p; Pepper Martin, 3b; Jim Wilson, c.

1934 Dizzy Dean, p; Frank Frisch, 2b; Pepper Martin, 3b; Joe Medwick, of.

1935 Frank Frisch, manager and 2b; Rip Collins, 1b; Dizzy Dean, p; Pepper Martin, 3b; Joe Medwick, of; Bill Walker, p; Burgess Whitehead, 2b.

1936 Rip Collins, 1b; Dizzy Dean, p; Leo Durocher, ss; Stu Martin, 2b; Joe Medwick, of.

1937 Dizzy Dean, p; Pepper Martin, of; Joe Medwick, of; Johnny Mize, 1b.

1938 Joe Medwick, of.

1939 Curt Davis, p; Joe Medwick, of; Johnny Mize, 1b; Terry Moore, of; Lon Warneke, p.

1940 Johnny Mize, 1b; Terry Moore, of.

1941 Johnny Mize, 1b; Terry Moore, of; Enos Slaughter, of; Lon Warneke, p.

1942 Jim Brown, 2b; Mort Cooper, p; Walker Cooper, c; Terry Moore, of; Enos Slaughter, of.

1943 Billy Southworth, manager; Mort Cooper, p; Walker Cooper, c; Whitey Kurowski, 3b; Max Lanier, p; Marty Marion, ss; Stan Musial, of; Howie Pollet, p; Harry Walker, of.

1944 Billy Southworth, manager; Walker Cooper, c; Whitey Kurowski, 3b; Max Lanier, p; Marty Marion, ss; Red Munger, p; Stan Musial, of.

1945 No game.

1946 Whitey Kurowski, 3b; Marty Marion, ss; Stan Musial, of; Howie Pollet, p; Red Schoendienst, 2b; Enos Slaughter, of.

1947 Eddie Dyer, manager; Harry Brecheen, p; Whitey Kurowski, 3b; Marty Marion, ss; Red Munger, p; Stan Musial, 1b; Enos Slaughter, of.

1948 Harry Brecheen, p; Marty Marion, ss; Stan Musial, of; Red Schoendienst, 2b; Enos Slaughter, of.

1949 Eddie Kazak, 3b; Marty Marion, ss; Red Munger, p; Stan Musial, of; Howie Pollet, p; Red Schoendienst, 2b; Enos Slaughter, of.

1950 Marty Marion, ss; Stan Musial, 1b; Red Schoendienst, 2b; Enos Slaughter, of.

1951 Stan Musial, of; Red Schoendienst, 2b; Enos Slaughter, of; Wally Westlake, of.

1952 Stan Musial, of; Red Schoendienst, 2b; Enos Slaughter, of; Gerry Staley, p.

1953 Harvey Haddix, p; Stan Musial, of; Del Rice, c; Red Schoendienst, 2b; Enos Slaughter, of; Gerry Staley, p.

1954 Harvey Haddix, p; Ray Jablonski, 3b; Stan Musial, of; Red Schoendienst, 2b.

1955 Luis Arroyo, p; Harvey Haddix, p; Stan Musial, 1b; Red Schoendienst, 2b.

1956 Ken Boyer, 3b; Stan Musial, of; Rip Repulski, of.

1957 Larry Jackson, p; Wally Moon, of; Stan Musial, 1b; Hal Smith, c.

1958 Don Blasingame, 2b; Larry Jackson, p; Stan Musial, 1b.

1959 (1st Game) Ken Boyer, 3b; Joe Cunningham, of; Wilmer Mizell, p; Stan Musial, 1b; Hal Smith, c; Bill White, of.

1959 (2nd Game) Ken Boyer, 3b; Joe Cunningham, of; Wilmer Mizell, p; Stan Musial, 1b; Hal Smith, c.

1960 (Both Games) Ken Boyer, 3b; Larry Jackson, p; Lindy McDaniel, p; Stan Musial, of; Bill White, 1b.

CARDINAL SELECTED FOR THE ALL-STAR GAME

(Continued)

1961 (Both Games) Ken Boyer, 3b; Stan Musial, of; Bill White, 1b.

1962 (Both Games) Ken Boyer, 3b; Bob Gibson, p; Stan Musial, of.

1963 Ken Boyer, 3b; Dick Groat, ss; Julian Javier, 2b; Stan Musial, of; Bill White, 1b.

1964 Ken Boyer, 3b; Curt Flood, of; Dick Groat, ss; Bill White, 1b.

1965 Bob Gibson, p.

1966 Curt Flood, of; Bob Gibson, p; Tim McCarver, c.

1967 Lou Brock, of; Orlando Cepeda, 1b; Bob Gibson, p; Tim McCarver, c.

1968 Red Schoendienst, manager; Steve Carlton, p; Curt Flood, of; Bob Gibson, p; Julian Javier, 2b.

1969 Red Schoendienst, manager; Steve Carlton, p; Bob Gibson, p.

1970 Rich Allen, 1b; Bob Gibson, p; Joe Torre, c.

1971 Joe Torre, 3b; Steve Carlton, p; Lou Brock, of.

1972 Bob Gibson, p; Lou Brock, of; Joe Torre, 3b; Ted Simmons, c; Red Schoendienst, coach.

1973 Rick Wise, p; Joe Torre, 3b; Ted Simmons, c.

1974 Ted Simmons, c; Lou Brock, of; Reggie Smith, of; Lynn McGlothen, p; Red Schoendienst, coach.

1975 Lou Brock, of; Reggie Smith, of; Red Schoendienst, coach.

1976 Bake McBride, of.

1977 Ted Simmons, c; Garry Templeton, ss.

1978 Ted Simmons, c.

1979 Lou Brock, of; Keith Hernandez, 1b; Ted Simmons, c; Garry Templeton, ss; Dave Ricketts, coach.

1980 George Hendrick, of; Keith Hernandez, 1b; Ken Reitz, 3b.

1981 Bruce Sutter, p.

1982 Ozzie Smith, ss; Lonnie Smith, of; Gene Gieselmann, trainer.

1983 Ozzie Smith, ss; Willie McGee, of; George Hendrick, of; Whitey Herzog, manager; Chuck Hiller, coach; Dave Ricketts, coach.

1984 Joaquin Andujar, p; Ozzie Smith, ss; Bruce Sutter, p.

1985 Joaquin Andujar, p; Jack Clark, 1b; Tom Herr, 2b; Willie McGee, of; Ozzie Smith, ss.

1986 Ozzie Smith, ss; Whitey Herzog, manager; Mike Roarke, coach.

1987 Jack Clark, 1b; Willie McGee, of; Ozzie Smith, ss; Gene Gieselmann, trainer.

1988 Vince Coleman, of; Willie McGee, of; Ozzie Smith, ss; Todd Worrell, p; Whitey Herzog, manager; Rich Hacker, coach; Nick Leyva, coach; Johnny Lewis, coach.

1989 Vince Coleman, of; Pedro Guerrero, dh; Tony Pena, c; Ozzie Smith, ss.

1990 Ozzie Smith, ss.

1991 Ozzie Smith, ss; Lee Smith, c; Felix Jose, of.

NOTE: Whitey Kurowski replaced Bob Elliott of Boston on the 1947 squad, and Julian Javier replaced Bill Mazeroski of Pittsburgh on the 1963 squad.

CARDINAL PITCHING FEATS

20-Game Winners

Year	Pitcher	W	L	Year	Pitcher	W	L
1892	Kid Gleason	20	24	1942	Mort Cooper	22	7
1894	Ted Breitenstein	27	22		Johnny Beazley	21	6
1895	Ted Breitenstein	20	29	1943	Mort Cooper	21	8
1899	Cy Young	26	15	1944	Mort Cooper	22	7
	Jack Powell	23	21	1945	Red Barrett	23	12
1900	Cy Young	20	18		2-3 Boston		
1901	Jack Harper	20	12		21-9 St. Louis		
1904	Kid Nichols	21	13	1946	Howie Pollet	21	10
	Jack Taylor	20	19	1948	Harry Brecheen	20	7
1911	Bob Harmon	23	16	1949	Howie Pollet	20	9
1920	Bill Doak	20	12	1953	Harvey Haddix	20	9
1923	Jesse Haines	20	13	1960	Ernie Broglio	21	9
1926	Flint Rhem	20	7	1964	Ray Sadecki	20	11
1927	Jesse Haines	24	10	1965	Bob Gibson	20	12
	Grover Alexander	21	10	1966	Bob Gibson	21	12
1928	Bill Sherdel	21	10	1968	Bob Gibson	22	9
	Jesse Haines	20	8	1969	Bob Gibson	20	13
1933	Dizzy Dean	20	18	1970	Bob Gibson	23	7
1934	Dizzy Dean	30	7	1971	Steve Carlton	20	9
1935	Dizzy Dean	28	12	1977	Bob Forsch	20	7
1936	Dizzy Dean	24	13	1984	Joaquin Andujar	20	14
1939	Curt Davis	22	16	1985	Joaquin Andujar	21	12
					John Tudor	21	8

N.L. Strikeout Leaders

Year	Player	SO	Year	Player	SO
1906	Fred Beebe	171	1935	Dizzy Dean	182
1930	Bill Hallahan	177	1948	Harry Brecheen	149
1931	Bill Hallahan	159	1958	Sam Jones	225
1932	Dizzy Dean	191	1966	Bob Gibson	268
1933	Dizzy Dean	199	1989	Jose DeLeon	201
1934	Dizzy Dean	195			

N.L. Era Leaders

Year	Player	G	IP	ERA	Year	Player	G	IP	ERA
1914	Bill Doak	36	256	1.72	1948	Harry Brecheen	33	233	2.24
1921	Bill Doak	32	209	2.58	1968	Bob Gibson	34	305	1.12
1942	Mort Cooper	37	279	1.77	1976	John Denny	30	207	2.52
1943	Howie Pollet	16	118	1.75	1988	Joe Magrane	24	165	2.18
1946	Howie Pollet	40	226	2.10					

Cardinal No-Hitters

Jessie Haines—Boston	5-0	7-17-24
Paul Dean—Brooklyn	3-0	9-21-34
Lon Warneke—at Cincinnati	2-0	8-30-41
Ray Washburn—at San Francisco	2-0	9-18-68
Bob Gibson—at Pittsburgh	11-0	8-14-71
Bob Forsch—Philadelphia	5-0	4-16-78
Bob Forsch—Montreal	3-0	9-26-83

No-Hit Games vs. Cardinals

Christy Mathewson—New York Giants	5-0	7-15-01
Mal Eason—Brooklyn Dodgers	2-0	7-20-06
Hod Eller—Cincinnati Reds	6-0	5-11-19
Don Cardwell—Chicago Cubs at Chicago	4-0	5-16-60
Gaylord Perry—San Francisco Giants at San Francisco	1-0	9-17-68
Tom Seaver—Cincinnati Reds at Cincinnati	4-0	6-16-78
David Palmer—Montreal Expos (5 innings)	4-0	4-21-84
Fernando Valenzuela—Los Angeles Dodgers at Los Angeles	6-0	6-29-90

CARDINALS' ALL-TIME TOP TEN IN PITCHING DEPARTMENTS

Games

1. Jesse Haines 554
2. Bob Gibson 528
3. Bill Sherdel 465
4. Bob Forsch 455
5. Al Brazle 441
6. Bill Doak 376
7. Lindy McDaniel 336
8. Larry Jackson 330
9. Al Hrabosky 329
10. Slim Sallee 316

Shutouts

1. Bob Gibson 56
2. Bill Doak 32
3. Mort Cooper 28
4. Harry Brecheen 25
5. Jesse Haines 24
6. Dizzy Dean 23
7. Max Lanier 20
   Howie Pollet 20
9. Bob Forsch 19
10. Ernie Broglio 18

Innings Pitched

1. Bob Gibson 3885
2. Jesse Haines 3204
3. Bob Forsch 2658
4. Bill Sherdel 2450
5. Bill Doak 2387
6. Slim Sallee 1902

Earned Run Average

1. John Tudor 2.52
2. Slim Salee 2.67
   Jack Taylor 2.67
4. Johnny Lush 2.74
   Red Ames 2.74
6. Mort Cooper 2.77

7. Ted Breitenstein 1897
8. Harry Brecheen ....・ 1790
9. Dizzy Dean 1736
10. Larry Jackson 1672

7. Fred Beebe 2.79
8. Max Lanier 2.84
9. Harry Brecheen 2.91
    Bob Gibson 2.91

Wins

1. Bob Gibson 251
2. Jesse Haines 210
3. Bob Forsch 163
4. Bill Sherdel 153
5. Bill Doak 145
6. Dizzy Dean 134
7. Harry Brecheen 127
8. Mort Cooper 105
    Slim Sallee 105
10. Max Lanier 101
    Larry Jackson 101

Winning Percentage

1. John Tudor .... .705
2. Mort Cooper .... .677
3. Dizzy Dean .... .641
4. Lon Warneke .... .629
5. Grover Alexander .... .618
6. Harry Brecheen .... .617
7. Al Brazle .... .602
    George Munger .... .602
9. Howie Pollet .... .599
10. Max Lanier .... .594

Complete Games

1. Bob Gibson 255
2. Jesse Haines 209
3. Ted Breitenstein 196
4. Bill Sherdel 144
    Bill Doak 144
6. Dizzy Dean 141
7. Slim Sallee 122
    Harry Brecheen 122
9. Mort Cooper 105
10. Jack Powell 101

Strikeouts

1. Bob Gibson 3117
2. Dizzy Dean 1087
3. Bob Forsch 1079
4. Jesse Haines 979
5. Steve Carlton 951
6. Bill Doak 938
7. Larry Jackson 899
8. Harry Brecheen 857
9. Vinegar Bend Mizell 789
10. Bill Hallahan 784

Bases on Balls

1. Bob Gibson 1336
2. Jesse Haines 870
3. Ted Breitenstein 825
4. Bob Forsch 780
5. Bill Doak 740
6. Bill Hallahan 651
7. Bill Sherdel 595
8. Bob Harmon 594
9. Vinegar Bend Mizell 568
10. Max Lanier 524

Saves

1. Bruce Sutter 127
2. Todd Worrell 126
3. Lee Smith 74
4. Lindy McDaniel 64
5. Joe Hoerner 60
    Al Brazle 60
7. Al Hrabosky 59
8. Ken Dayley 39
9. Dizzy Dean 30
10. Ted Wilks 29

N.L. TOTAL BASE LEADERS

Year	Player	TB	Year	Player	TB
1901	Jesse Burkett	314	1937	Joe Medwick	406
1917	Rogers Hornsby	253	1938	Johnny Mize	326
1920	Rogers Hornsby	329	1939	Johnny Mize	353
1921	Rogers Hornsby	378	1940	Johnny Mize	368
1922	Rogers Hornsby	450	1942	Enos Slaughter	292
1924	Rogers Hornsby	373	1946	Stan Musial	366
1925	Rogers Hornsby	381	1948	Stan Musial	429
1926	Jim Bottomley	305	1949	Stan Musial	382
1928	Jim Bottomley	362	1951	Stan Musial	355
1934	Rip Collins	369	1952	Stan Musial	311
1935	Joe Medwick	365	1971	Joe Torre	352
1936	Joe Medwick	367			

N.L. RBI LEADERS

Year	Player	RBI	Year	Player	RBI
1920	Rogers Hornsby	94	1938	Joe Medwick	122
1921	Rogers Hornsby	126	1940	Johnny Mize	137
1922	Rogers Hornsby	152	1946	Enos Slaughter	130
1925	Rogers Hornsby	143	1948	Stan Musial	131
1926	Jim Bottomley	120	1956	Stan Musial	109
1928	Jim Bottomley	136	1964	Ken Boyer	119
1936	Joe Medwick	138	1967	Orlando Cepeda	111
1937	Joe Medwick	154	1971	Joe Torre	137

N.L. SLUGGING LEADERS

Year	Player	Slug Pct.	Year	Player	Slug Pct.
1917	Rogers Hornsby	.484	1938	Johnny Mize	.614
1920	Rogers Hornsby	.559	1939	Johnny Mize	.626
1921	Rogers Hornsby	.639	1943	Stan Musial	.562
1922	Rogers Hornsby	.722	1944	Stan Musial	.549
1923	Rogers Hornsby	.627	1946	Stan Musial	.587
1924	Rogers Hornsby	.696	1948	Stan Musial	.702
1925	Rogers Hornsby	.756	1950	Stan Musial	.596
1927	Chick Hafey	.590	1952	Stan Musial	.538
1934	Rip Collins	.615	1987	Jack Clark	.597
1937	Joe Medwick	.641			

HIT IN 25 OR MORE CONSECUTIVE GAMES

Year	Player	Games	Year	Player	Games
1922	Rogers Hornsby	33	1935	Joe Medwick	28
1950	Stan Musial	30	1954	Red Schoendienst	28
1943	Harry Walker	29	1971	Lou Brock	26
1959	Ken Boyer	29			

HOME RUN CHAMPIONS

Year	Player	HR	Year	Player	HR
1922	Rogers Hornsby	42	1937	Joe Medwick	31
1925	Rogers Hornsby	39	1939	Johnny Mize	28
1928	Jim Bottomley	31	1940	Johnny Mize	43
1934	Rip Collins	35			

BATTING CHAMPIONS

Year	Player	Avg	Year	Player	Avg
1901	Jesse Burkett	.382	1946	Stan Musial	.365
1920	Rogers Hornsby	.370	1948	Stan Musial	.376
1921	Rogers Hornsby	.397	1950	Stan Musial	.346
1922	Rogers Hornsby	.401	1951	Stan Musial	.355
1923	Rogers Hornsby	.384	1952	Stan Musial	.336
1924	Rogers Hornsby	.424	1957	Stan Musial	.351
1925	Rogers Hornsby	.403	1971	Joe Torre	.363
1931	Chick Hafey	.349	1979	Keith Hernandez	.344
1937	Joe Medwick	.374	1985	Willie McGee	.353
1939	Johnny Mize	.349	1990	Willie McGee	.335
1943	Stan Musial	.357			

CARDINALS' ALL-TIME TOP TEN IN BATTING DEPARTMENTS

Batting Avg.

1. Rogers Hornsby .359
2. Johnny Mize .336
3. Joe Medwick .335
4. Stan Musial .331
5. Chick Hafey .326
6. Jim Bottomley .325
7. Frankie Frisch .312
8. George Watkins .309
9. Joe Torre .308
10. Rip Collins .307

Games

1. Stan Musial 3026
2. Lou Brock 2289
3. Enos Slaughter 1820
4. Red Schoendienst 1795
5. Curt Flood 1738
6. Ken Boyer 1667
7. Rogers Hornsby 1580
8. Julian Javier 1578
9. Ted Simmons 1564
10. Marty Marion 1502

CARDINALS' ALL-TIME TOP TEN IN BATTING DEPARTMENTS

(Continued)

At-Bats

1. Stan Musial 10972
2. Lou Brock 9125
3. Red Schoendienst 6841
4. Enos Slaughter 6775
5. Ken Boyer 6334
6. Curt Flood 6318
7. Rogers Hornsby 5881
8. Ted Simmons 5725
9. Julian Javier 5631
10. Ozzie Smith 5333

Doubles

1. Stan Musial 725
2. Lou Brock 434
3. Joe Medwick 377
4. Rogers Hornsby 367
5. Enos Slaughter 366
6. Red Schoendienst 352
7. Jim Bottomley 344
8. Ted Simmons 332
9. Frankie Frisch 286
10. Curt Flood 271

Runs

1. Stan Musial 1949
2. Lou Brock 1427
3. Rogers Hornsby 1089
4. Enos Slaughter 1071
5. Red Schoendienst 1025
6. Ken Boyer 988
7. Jim Bottomley 921
8. Curt Flood 845
9. Frankie Frisch 831
10. Joe Medwick 811

Triples

1. Stan Musial 177
2. Rogers Hornsby 143
3. Enos Slaughter 135
4. Lou Brock 121
5. Jim Bottomley 119
6. Ed Konetchy 93
7. Joe Medwick 81
8. Willie McGee 76
9. Pepper Martin 75
10. Garry Templeton 69

Hits

1. Stan Musial 3630
2. Lou Brock 2713
3. Rogers Hornsby 2110
4. Enos Slaughter 2064
5. Red Schoendienst 1980
6. Ken Boyer 1855
7. Curt Flood 1853
8. Jim Bottomley 1727
9. Ted Simmons 1704
10. Joe Medwick 1590

Home Runs

1. Stan Musial 475
2. Ken Boyer 255
3. Rogers Hornsby 193
4. Jim Bottomley 181
5. Ted Simmons 172
6. Johnny Mize 158
7. Joe Medwick 152
8. Enos Slaughter 146
9. Bill White 140
10. Lou Brock 129

Total Bases

1. Stan Musial 6134
2. Lou Brock 3776

Runs Batted In

1. Stan Musial 1951
2. Enos Slaughter 1148

3. Rogers Hornsby 3342
4. Enos Slaughter 3138
5. Ken Boyer 3011
6. Jim Bottomley 2852
7. Red Schoendienst 2657
8. Ted Simmons 2626
9. Joe Medwick 2585
10. Curt Flood 2464

3. Jim Bottomley 1105
4. Rogers Hornsby 1072
5. Ken Boyer 1001
6. Ted Simmons 929
7. Joe Medwick 823
8. Lou Brock 814
9. Frankie Frisch 720
10. Johnny Mize 653

Bases on Balls

1. Stan Musial 1599
2. Enos Slaughter 839
3. Ozzie Smith 694
4. Lou Brock 681
5. Rogers Hornsby 660
6. Ken Boyer 631
7. Ted Simmons 624
8. Keith Hernandez 585
9. Miller Huggins 571
10. Jim Bottomley 509

Stolen Bases

1. Lou Brock 888
2. Vince Coleman 549
3. Ozzie Smith 352
4. Willie McGee 274
5. Jack Smith 203
6. Frankie Frisch 195
7. Miller Huggins 174
8. Lonnie Smith 173
9. Tom Herr 152
10. Ed Konetchy 151

Pinch-Hits

1. Steve Braun 60
2. Red Schoendienst 53
3. Dane Iorg 47
   Peanuts Lowrey 47
5. Stan Musial 35
6. George Crowe 33
   Vic Davalillo 33
8. Tito Landrum 32
9. Tim McCarver 31
10. Lou Brock 29

**CARDINALS' ALL-TIME
HOME RUN LEADERS
SEASON—BY POSITION**

Catcher .... Ted Simmons .... 26—1979
First Base .... Johnny Mize .... 43—1940
Second Base .... Rogers Hornsby .... 42—1922
Shortstop .... Solly Hemus .... 15—1952
Third Base .... Ken Boyer .... 32—1960

CARDINALS' ALL-TIME HOME RUN LEADERS
SEASON—BY POSITION

Left Field	Stan Musial	32—1951
Center Field	Stan Musial	21—1952
Right Field	Stan Musial	39—1948
Pitcher	Bob Gibson	5—1965, 1972

CARDINALS' ALL-TIME RUNS-BATTED-IN LEADERS
SEASON—BY POSITION

Catcher*	Ted Simmons	96—1972
First Base	Jim Bottomley	137—1929
	Johnny Mize	137—1940
Second Base	Rogers Hornsby	152—1922
Shortstop	Doc Lavan	82—1921
Third Base	Joe Torre	137—1971
Left Field	Joe Medwick	154—1937
Center Field*	Willie McGee	104—1987
Right Field	Stan Musial	131—1948
Pitcher	Dizzy Dean	21—1935

*Simmons had 103 RBI in 1974, but drove in only 95 while catching.
 Simmons had 100 RBI in 1975, but drove in only 95 while catching.
 McGee had 105 RBI in 1987, but drove in only 104 while in CF.

STOLEN BASES (FROM 1920)
SEASON LEADER BY POSITION

Pitcher	Bob Gibson	5—1969
Catcher	Tim McCarver	9—1966
	Tom Pagnozzi	9—1991
First Base	Jack Fournier	26—1920
Second Base	Frank Frisch	48—1927
Shortstop	Ozzie Smith	57—1988
Third Base	Pepper Martin	26—1933
Left Field	Lou Brock	118—1974
Center Field	Willie McGee	56—1985
Right Field	Andy Van Slyke	32—1985

*Van Slyke had 34 SB in 1985, but stole only 32 while playing RF.

CARDINAL PLAYERS—HIT FOR CYCLE

Ray Lankford	September 15, 1991		Stan Musial	July 24, 1949
Willie McGee	June 23, 1984		Johnny Mize	July 13, 1940
Lou Brock	May 27, 1975			1st game

Joe Torre	June 27, 1973	Joe Medwick	June 29, 1935
Ken Boyer	June 16, 1964	Pepper Martin	May 25, 1933
Ken Boyer	September 14, 1961,	Chick Hafey	August 21, 1930
	2nd game	Jim Bottomley	July 15, 1927
Bill White	August 14, 1960	Cliff Heathcote	July 13, 1918
	1st game		

PLAYERS WITH MOST SEASONS WITH CARDINALS

Seasons	Players	Years
22	Stan Musial	1941-44, 46-63
18	Jesse Haines	1920-37
17	Bob Gibson	1959-75
16	Lou Brock	1964-79
15	Bob Forsch	1974-1988
15	Red Schoendienst	1945-56, 61-63
14	Bill Sherdel	1918-30, 32

CARDINALS SELECTED ON
SPORTING NEWS' ALL-LEAGUE TEAMS

(Team selected at the conclusion of the season in a poll of NL Players)

1925	Jim Bottomley, 1b	1943	Stan Musial, of
	Rogers Hornsby, 2b		Walker Cooper, c
1926	Rogers Hornsby, 2b		Mort Cooper, p
	Bob O'Farrell, c	1944	Stan Musial, of
	Grover Alexander, p		Ray Sanders, 1b
1930	Frank Frisch, 2b		Marty Marion, ss
1931	Frank Frisch, 2b		Walker Cooper, c
1934	Dizzy Dean, p		Mort Cooper, p
1935	Joe Medwick, of	1945	Marty Marion, ss
	Peper Martin, 3b		Whitey Kurowski, 3b
	Dizzy Dean, p	1946	Enos Slaughter, of
1936	Joe Medwick, of		Stan Musial, 1b
	Dizzy Dean, p	1948	Stan Musial, of
1937	Joe Medwick, of		Harry Brecheen, p
1938	Joe Medwick, of	1949	Stan Musial, of
1939	Joe Medwick, of	1950	Stan Musial, of
1942	Enos Slaughter, of	1951	Stan Musial, of
	Mort Cooper, p	1952	Stan Musial, of

CARDINALS SELECTED ON
SPORTING NEWS' ALL-LEAGUE TEAMS

(Team selected at the conclusion of the season in a poll of NL Players)

1953 .... Stan Musial, of	1974 .... Lou Brock, of
Red Schoendienst, 2b	1977 .... Garry Templeton, ss
1954 .... Stan Musial, of	Ted Simmons, c
1956 .... Ken Boyer, 3b	1978 .... Ted Simmons, c
1957 .... Stan Musial, 1b	1979 .... Keith Hernandez, of
1958 .... Stan Musial, 1b	Ted Simmons, c
1960 .... Ernie Broglio, p	Garry Templeton, ss
1961 .... Ken Boyer, 3b	1980 .... George Hendrick, of
1962 .... Ken Boyer, 3b	Keith Hernandez, 1b
1963 .... Bill White, 1b	Garry Templeton, ss
Ken Boyer, 3b	1982 .... Ozzie Smith, ss
Dick Groat, ss	Lonnie Smith, of
1964 .... Bill White, 1b	1983 .... George Hendrick, 1b
Ken Boyer, 3b	1984 .... Ozzie Smith, ss
Dick Groat, ss	1985 .... Tom Herr, 2b
1967 .... Orlando Cepeda, 1b	Willie McGee, of
Tim McCarver, c	Ozzie Smith, ss
1968 .... Curt Flood, of	John Tudor, p
Bob Gibson, p	1986 .... Ozzie Smith, ss
1969 .... Steve Carlton, p	1987 .... Jack Clark, 1b
1970 .... Bob Gibson, p	Ozzie Smith,ss
1971 .... Steve Carlton, p	1991 .... Lee Smith, p
Joe Torre, 3b	

CARDINALS' INDIVIDUAL RECORDS

Pitching Season

Most Games (Right-Handed)
1987 Todd Worrell 75

Most Complete Games (Right-Handed)
1904 Jack Taylor 39

Most Games (Left-Handed)
1991 Juan Agosto 72

Most Complete Games (Left-Handed)
1900 Cowboy Jones 29

Most Games Started (Right-Handed)
1911 Bob Harmon 41

Most Games Finished (Right-Handed)
1984 Bruce Sutter 63

Most Games Started (Left-Handed)
1920 Ferdie Schupp 37

Most Games Finished (Left-Handed)
1976 Al Hrabosky 45

Most Innings (Right-Handed)
1907 Grant McGlynn 352⅓

Most Innings (Left-Handed)
1907 Ed Karger 310

Most Games Won (Right-Handed)
1934 Dizzy Dean 30

Most Games Won (Left-Handed)
1928 Bill Sherdel 21
1946 Howie Pollet 21
1985 John Tudor 21

Most Games Lost (Right-Handed)
1907 Grant McGlynn 25
1908 Art Raymond 25

Most Games Lost (Left-Handed)
1900 Cowboy Jones 19
1908 Johnny Lush 19
1970 Steve Carlton 19

Lowest Earned Run Average (Right-Handed)
1968 Bob Gibson 1.12

Lowest Earned Run Average (Left-Handed)
1943 Howie Pollet 1.75

Highest Winning Percentage (Right-Handed)
1934 Dizzy Dean (30-7) .... .811

Highest Winning Percentage (Left-Handed)
1987 John Tudor (10-2) .... .833

Most Saves (Right-Handed)
1991 Lee Smith 47

Most Saves (Left-Handed)
1975 Al Hrabosky 22

Most Consecutive Games Won (Right-Handed)
1968 Bob Gibson 15

Most Consecutive Games Won (Left-Handed)
1985 John Tudor 11

Most Consecutive Games Lost
1938 Bill McGee 9
1951 Tom Poholsky 9
1978 Bob Forsch 9

Most Shutouts (Right-Handed)
1968 Bob Gibson 13

Most Shutouts (Left-Handed)
1985 John Tudor 10

Most 1-0 Shutouts, Won
1968 Bob Gibson 4

Most Hits Allowed (Right-Handed)
1901 Jack Powell 351

Most Hits Allowed (Left-Handed)
1900 Cowboy Jones 334

Most Runs Allowed (Right-Handed)
1900 Jack Powell 194

Most Runs Allowed (Left-Handed)
1900 Cowboy Jones 185

Most Earned Runs (Right-Handed)
1900 Jack Powell 142

Most Earned Runs (Left-Handed)
1929 Bill Sherdel 129

Most Walks (Right-Handed)
1911 Bob Harmon 181

Most Walks (Left-Handed)
1920 Ferdie Schupp 127

Most Strikeouts (Right-Handed)
1970 Bob Gibson 274

Most Strikeouts (Left-Handed)
1969 Steve Carlton 219

Most Hit Batsman (Right-Handed)
1953 Gerry Staley 17

CARDINALS' INDIVIDUAL RECORDS

Pitching Season

Most Hit Batsman (Left-Handed)
1919   Jakie May 14

Most Wild Pitches (Right-Handed)
1907, 1909   Fred Beebe 15

Most Wild Pitches (Left-Handed)
1984   Dave LaPoint 15

Most Home Runs Allowed
1948   Murry Dickson 39

CARDINALS' INDIVIDUAL RECORDS

Batting—Season

Most Games
1989   Jose Oquendo 163

Most At-Bats (Left-Handed)
1967   Lou Brock 689

Most At-Bats (Right-Handed)
1964   Curt Flood 679

Most At-Bats (Switch-Hitter)
1979   Garry Templeton 672

Most Runs (Left-Handed)
1901   Jesse Burkett 139

Most Runs (Right-Handed)
1922   Rogers Hornsby 141

Most Hits (Left-Handed)
1948   Stan Musial 230

Most Hits (Right-Handed)
1922   Rogers Hornsby 250

Most Hits (Switch-Hitter)
1985   Willie McGee 216

Most Singles (Left-Handed)
1901   Jesse Burkett 180

Most Singles (Right-Handed)
1964   Curt Flood 178

Most Doubles (Left-Handed)
1953   Stan Musial 53

Most Doubles (Right-Handed)
1936   Joe Medwick 64

Most Triples (Left-Handed)
1894   Roger Connor 25

Most Triples (Right-Handed)
1893   Perry Werden 33

Most Triples, Since 1900 (Right-Handed)
1915   Tom Long 25

Most Hit By Pitch
1910   Lou Evans 31

Most Runs Batted In (Left-Handed)
1929   Jim Bottomley 137
1940   Johnny Mize 137

Most Runs Batted In (Right-Handed)
1937   Joe Medwick 154

Most Consecutive Games With RBI
1961   Bill White 10

Highest Batting Average (Left-Handed)
1899   Jesse Burkett .... .402

Highest Batting Average (Right-Handed)
1924   Rogers Hornsby .... .424

Highest Batting Average (Switch-Hitter)
1985   Willie McGee .... .353

Most Total Bases (Left-Handed)
1948   Stan Musial 429

Most Total Bases (Right-Handed)
1922   Rogers Hornsby 450

Most Long Hits (Left-Handed)
1948 Stan Musial 103

Most Long Hits (Right-Handed)
1922 Rogers Hornsby 102

Most Sacrifice Hits
1943 Harry Walker 36

Most Sacrifice Flies
1982 George Hendrick 14

Most Stolen Bases (Left-Handed)
1974 Lou Brock 118

Most Stolen Bases (Right-Handed)
1982 Lonnie Smith 68

Most Stolen Bases (Switch-Hitter)
1985 Vince Coleman 110

Most Caught Stealing
1914 Miller Huggins 36

Highest Slugging Average (Left-Handed)
1948 Stan Musial .... .702

Highest Slugging Average (Right-Handed)
1922 Rogers Hornsby .... .756

Most Home Runs (Left-Handed)
1940 Johnny Mize 43

Most Home Runs (Right-Handed)
1922 Rogers Hornsby 42

Most Home Runs (Switch-Hitter)
1934 Ripper Collins 35

Most Home Runs At Home
1940 Johnny Mize 25

Most Home Runs - Busch Stadium
1970 Dick Allen 17
1979 Ted Simmons 17
1987 Jack Clark 17

Most Home Runs - Road
1948 Stan Musial 23

Most Home Runs, Rookie (Left-Handed)
1936 Johnny Mize 19

Most Home Runs, Rookie (Right-Handed)
1953 Ray Jablonski 21

Most Home Runs, One Month
1947 Whitey Kurowski (August) 12

Most Grand Slam Home Runs
1925 Jim Bottomley 3
1977 Keith Hernandez 3

Most Bases On Balls (Left-Handed)
1949 Stan Musial 107

Most Bases On Balls (Right-Handed)
1987 Jack Clark 136

Most Bases On Balls (Switch-Hitter)
1910 Miller Huggins 116

Most Intentional Bases On Balls
1958 Stan Musial 26

Most Strikeouts (Left-Handed)
1966 Lou Brock 134

Most Strikeouts (Right-Handed)
1987 Jack Clark 139

Fewest Strikeouts
1927 Frank Frisch (153 Games) 10

Most Consecutive Games Hit Safely (Left-Handed)
1950 Stan Musial 30

Most Consecutive Games Hit Safely (Right-Handed)
1922 Rogers Hornsby 33

Most Grounded Into Double Play
1973 Ted Simmons 29

Fewest Grounded Into Double Plays
1965, 1969 Lou Brock 2

Most Game Winning RBI (Left-Handed)
1982 Keith Hernandez 21

Most Game Winning RBI (Right-Handed)
1984 George Hendrick 16

Most Game-Winning RBI (Switch-Hitter)
1985 Willie McGee 17

CARDINALS' INDIVIDUAL RECORDS

Batting—Season

Most Pinch-Hits (Left-Handed)
1970   Vic Davalillo 24

Most Pinch-Hits (Right-Handed)
1953   Peanuts Lowrey 22

Most Pinch-Hits (Switch-Hitter)
1962   Red Schoendienst 22

Most Hits By Pitcher
1902   Mike O'Neill 43

Most Home Runs By Pitcher
1965, 1972   Bob Gibson 5

Most Runs Batted In By Pitcher
1935   Dizzy Dean 21

CLUB RECORDS

Most Players .... 49 in 1959
Fewest Players .... 25 in 1904
Most Games .... 164 in 1989
Most At-Bats .... 5,734 in 1979 (163 games)
Most Runs .... 1,004 in 1930 (154 games)
Most Opponents' Runs .... 806 in 1929 (154 games)
Fewest Runs .... 372 in 1908 (154 games)
Most Hits .... 1,732 in 1930 (154 games)
Fewest Hits .... 1,105 in 1908 (154 games)
Most Singles .... 1,223 in 1920 (155 games)
Most Doubles .... 373 in 1939 (154 games)
Most Triples .... 96 in 1920 (155 games)
Most Homers .... 143 in 1955 (154 games)
Fewest Homers (154 or 162-game schedule) .... 10 in 1906
Most Homers at Sportsman's Park—Home & Opponent .... 176 in 1955
Most Homers at Busch Stadium—Home & Opponent .... 113 in 1979
Most Grand Slams .... 7 in 1961
Most Pinch Home Runs .... 7 in 1946, 1960
Most Total Bases .... 2,595 in 1930 (154 games)
Most Long Hits .... 566 in 1930 (154 games)
Most Extra Bases on Long Hits .... 863 in 1930 (154 games)
Most Sacrifices (S.H. and S.F.) .... 212 in 1926 (156 games)
Most Sacrifice Hits .... 172 in 1943 (147 games)
Most Sacrifice Flies .... 66 in 1954 (154 games)
Most Stolen Bases .... 314 in 1985 (162 games)
Most Caught Stealing .... 112 in 1977 (162 games)
Most Bases on Balls .... 655 in 1910 (153 games)
Most Strikeouts .... 977 in 1966 (162 games)

Fewest Strikeouts .... 414 in 1925 (153 games)
Most Hit By Pitch .... 78 in 1910 (153 games)
Fewest Hit By Pitch .... 15 in 1925 (153 games)
Most Runs Batted In .... 942 in 1930 (154 games)
Most Game-Winning RBIs .... 94 in 1985 (162 games)
Highest Batting Average .... .314 in 1930 (154 games)
Lowest Batting Average .... .223 in 1908 (154 games)
Highest Slugging Average .... .471 in 1930 (154 games)
Lowest Slugging Average .... .288 in 1908 (154 games)
Most Grounded Into Double Play .... 166 in 1958 (154 games)
Fewest Grounded Into Double Play .... 75 in 1945 (155 games)
Most Left On Bases .... 1,251 in 1939 (155 games)
Fewest Left On Bases .... 968 in 1924 (154 games)
Most .300 Hitters .... 11 in 1930
Most Putouts .... 4,460 in 1979 (163 games)
Fewest Putouts .... 3,952 in 1906 (154 games)
Most Assists .... 2,293 in 1917 (154 games)
Fewest Assists .... 1,595 in 1935 (154 games)
Most Chances Accepted .... 6,459 in 1917 (154 games)
Fewest Chances Accepted .... 5,752 in 1935 (154 games)
Most Errors .... 348 in 1908 (154 games).
Fewest Errors .... 107 in 1991 (162 games)
Most Errorless Games .... 86 in 1989 (164 games)
Most Consecutive Errorless Games .... 15 in 1991
Most Double Plays .... 192 in 1974 (161 games)
Fewest Double Plays .... 114 in 1990 (162 games)
Most Passed Balls .... 38 in 1906 (154 games)
Fewest Passed Balls .... 4 in 1925 (153 games)
Highest Fielding Average .... .983 in 1985 (162 games)
Lowest Fielding Average .... .946 in 1908 (154 games)
Highest Home Attendance .... 3,080,980 in 1989
Highest Road Attendance .... 2,321,960 in 1987
Most Games Won .... 106 in 1942
Most Games Lost .... 111 in 1898
Most Games Lost Since 1900 .... 105 in 1908
Most Games Won—Month .... 26, July 1944
Most Games Lost—Month .... 27, September 1908
Highest Percentage Games Won .... .703 in 1876 (Won 45, Lost 19)
Highest Percentage Games Won—Since 1900 .... .688 in 1942 (Won 106, Lost 48)
Lowest Percentage Games Won .... .221 in 1897 (Won 29, Lost 102)
Lowest Percentage Games Won—Since 1900 .... .314 in 1903 (Won 43, Lost 94)
Games Won—League .... 7,722 in 100 years
Games Lost—League .... 7,580 in 100 years
Most Shutouts Won .... 30 in 1968
Most Shutouts Lost .... 33 in 1908

CLUB RECORDS

(Continued)

Most 1-0 Games Won .... 8 in 1907 and 1968
Most 1-0 Games Lost .... 8 in 1918
Most Consecutive Games Won .... 14 in 1935
Most Consecutive Games Lost .... 15 in 1909
Most Times League Champions 15
Most Last Place Finishes .... 11 (Tied in 1916)
Most Runs—Game .... 28 vs. Philadelphia, July 6, 1929, Second Game
Most Runs—Game—By Opponent .... 28 by Boston, September 3, 1896, First Game
Most Runs—Game—By Opponent—Since 1900 .... 24 by Pittsburgh, June 22, 1925
Most Runs—Inning ....
.... 12 vs. Philadelphia, September 16, 1926, First Game, Third Inning
Most Runs—Shutout Game .... 18 vs. Cincinnati, June 10, 1944
Most Runs—Shutout Game—By Opponent .... 19 by Pittsburgh, August 3, 1961
Most Runs—Doubleheader Shutout .... 16 vs. Brooklyn, September 21, 1934
Most Hits—Game .... 30 vs. New York, June 1, 1895
Longest 1-0 Game Won .... 14 Innings vs. Boston, June 15, 1939
Longest 1-0 Game Lost .... 18 Innings vs. New York, July 2, 1933, First Game
Most Hits—Game—Since 1900 .... 28 vs. Philadelphia, July 6, 1929, Second Game
Most Home Runs—Game .... 7 vs. Brooklyn, May 7, 1940
Most Consecutive Games—One or More Homers .... 12 (18 homers), 1955
Most Total Bases—Game .... 49 vs. Brooklyn, May 7, 1940
Largest Crowd—Day Game .... 50,548 vs. New York, September 14, 1975
Largest Crowd—Doubleheader .... 49,743 vs. Atlanta, June 23, 1968
Largest Crowd—Night Game .... 51,647 vs. Pittsburgh, April 18, 1988
Largest Crowd—Home Opener .... 51,647 vs. Pittsburgh, April 18, 1988

CARDINALS' ALL-TIME FIELDING TEAM

Pos.	Player	Year	G	TC	E	PCT
1B	Keith Hernandez	1981	98	1143	3	.997
2B	Jose Oquendo	1990	150	681	3	.996
SS	Ozzie Smith	1991	150	639	8	.987
3B	Ken Reitz	1977	157	450	9	.980
OF	Curt Flood	1966	159	396	0	1.000
OF	Tony Scott	1980	134	330	1	.997
OF	Johnny Hopp	1944	131	310	1	.997
C	Tony Pena	1989	134	749	2	.997

CAREER GAMES BY POSITION

First Base	*Years*	*Games*
1. Jim Bottomley	1922-32	1,340
2. Keith Hernandez	1974-83	1,118
3. Stan Musial	1941-44; 46-63	1,016
4. Ed Konetchy	1907-13	979
5. Bill White	1959-65; 69	972

Second Base		
1. Julian Javier	1960-71	1,547
2. Red Schoendienst	1945-56; 61-63	1,429
3. Frankie Frisch	1927-37	1,153
4. Rogers Hornsby	1915-26; 33	997
5. Tom Herr	1979-1988	987

Shortstop		
1. Marty Marion	1940-50	1,492
2. Ozzie Smith	1982-	1,474
3. Dal Maxvill	1962-72	1,054
4. Garry Templeton	1976-81	700
5. Leo Durocher	1933-37	681

Third Base		
1. Ken Boyer	1955-65	1,539
2. Ken Reitz	1972-75; 77-80	1,081
3. Terry Pendleton	1984-90	908
4. Whitey Kurowski	1941-49	868
5. Milt Stock	1919-23	661

Outfield		
1. Lou Brock	1964-79	2,206
2. Stan Musial	1941-44; 46-63	1,896
3. Enos Slaughter	1938-42; 46-53	1,751
4. Curt Flood	1958-69	1,687
5. Terry Moore	1935-42; 46-48	1,189

Catcher		
1. Ted Simmons	1968-80	1,440
2. Del Rice	1945-55; 60	1,018
3. Tim McCarver	1959-61; 63-69; 73-74	960
4. Jimmie Wilson	1928-33	638
5. Frank Snyder	1912-19; 27	563

ST. LOUIS CARDINALS' FIRST ROUND
FREE AGENT DRAFT SELECTIONS

JUNE DRAFT

Year	Player	Pos.	Order In Draft
1965	Joe DiFabio	RHP	20
1966	Leron Lee	INF/OF	7
1967	Ted Simmons	C/OF	10
1968	James Hairston	OF	19
1969	Charles Minnott	LHP	20
1970	Jim Browning	RHP/SS	11
1971	Ed Kurpiel	1B/OF	8
1972	Dan Larson	P	21
1973	Joe Edelen	3B	12
1974	Garry Templeton	SS	13
1975	David Johnson	P	16
1976	Leon Durham	1B	15
1977	Terry Kennedy	C	6
1978	Robert Hicks	1B	15
1979	Andy Van Slyke	OF	6
1980	Don Collins	RHP	15
1981	Bobby Meacham	SS	8
1982	Todd Worrell	RHP	21
1983	Jim Lindeman	3B	24
1984	Mike Dunne	RHP	7
1985	Joe Magrane	LHP	18
1986	Luis Alicea	2B	23
1987	Cris Carpenter	RHP	14
1988	John Ericks	RHP	22
	Brad DuVall	RHP	23
1989	Paul Coleman	OF	6
1990	Donovan Osborne	LHP	13
	Aaron Holbert	SS	18
1991	Dmitri Young	3B	4
	Allen Watson	LHP	21
	Brian Barber	RHP	22

JANUARY DRAFT

Year	Player	Post.	Order In Draft
1966	Henry Urbanowica	1B	8
1967	Fred Grooms	RHP	9
1968	Mike Maselbas	RHP	20
1969	Al Hrabosky	LHP	19
1970	Don Reed	RHP	12
1972	Randal Rasmussen	SS	6
1971	Robert Gerdes	P	22
1973	Larry Storti	2B	11
1974	John Urrea	RHP	14
1975	Terry Gray	P	15
1976	Fulvio Bertolotti	C	16
1977	Curtis Reade	RHP	5
1978	Mike Gentry	RHP	16
1979	Bob Ferris	1B	5
1980	Ken Spears	OF	16
1981	Brad Luther	SS	7
1982	Tom Mauch	OF	22
1983	Jeff Perry	RHP	23
1984	Jeff Blauser	SS	8
1985	Chris Lee	RHP	17
1986	Charles Barrs	SS	24

Note: Beginning in 1987, the January draft was discontinued.

CARDINALS' CLUB PRESIDENTS

Chris Von der Ahe	1892-97
Benjamin S. Muckenfuss	1898
Frank De Hass Robison	1899-1906
M. Stanley Robison	1906-10
E.A. Steininger	1911-12
James C. Jones	1912
Schuyler P. Britton	1913-16
Mrs. Schuyler P. Britton	1916
W. Branch Rickey	1917-19
Samuel Breadon	1920-47
Robert E. Hannegan	1947-49
Fred M. Saigh, Jr.	1949-53
August A. Busch, Jr.	1953-73
Richard A. Meyer	1974
August A. Busch, Jr.	1974-89
Fred L. Kuhlmann	1989-present

Index

◆